LEGAL ASPECTS OF COMBATING TERRORISM

NATO Science for Peace and Security Series

This Series presents the results of scientific meetings supported under the NATO Programme: Science for Peace and Security (SPS).

The NATO SPS Programme supports meetings in the following Key Priority areas: (1) Defence Against Terrorism; (2) Countering other Threats to Security and (3) NATO, Partner and Mediterranean Dialogue Country Priorities. The types of meeting supported are generally "Advanced Study Institutes" and "Advanced Research Workshops". The NATO SPS Series collects together the results of these meetings. The meetings are co-organized by scientists from NATO countries and scientists from NATO's "Partner" or "Mediterranean Dialogue" countries. The observations and recommendations made at the meetings, as well as the contents of the volumes in the Series, reflect those of participants and contributors only; they should not necessarily be regarded as reflecting NATO views or policy.

Advanced Study Institutes (ASI) are high-level tutorial courses to convey the latest developments in a subject to an advanced-level audience.

Advanced Research Workshops (ARW) are expert meetings where an intense but informal exchange of views at the frontiers of a subject aims at identifying directions for future action.

Following a transformation of the programme in 2006 the Series has been re-named and re-organised. Recent volumes on topics not related to security, which result from meetings supported under the programme earlier, may be found in the NATO Science Series.

The Series is published by IOS Press, Amsterdam, and Springer Science and Business Media, Dordrecht, in conjunction with the NATO Public Diplomacy Division.

Sub-Series

A.	Chemistry and Biology	Springer Science and Business Media
B.	Physics and Biophysics	Springer Science and Business Media
C.	Environmental Security	Springer Science and Business Media
D.	Information and Communication Security	IOS Press
E.	Human and Societal Dynamics	IOS Press

http://www.nato.int/science
http://www.springer.com
http://www.iospress.nl

Sub-Series E: Human and Societal Dynamics – Vol. 47 ISSN 1874-6276

Legal Aspects of Combating Terrorism

Edited by

Centre of Excellence Defence Against Terrorism,
Ankara, Turkey

IOS Press

Amsterdam • Berlin • Oxford • Tokyo • Washington, DC

Published in cooperation with NATO Public Diplomacy Division

Proceedings on NATO Advanced Training Course on the Legal Aspects of Combating Terrorism
Sarajevo, Bosnia Herzegovina
4–8 February 2008

ISBN 978-1-58603-930-1
Library of Congress Control Number: 2008938949

Publisher
IOS Press
Nieuwe Hemweg 6B
1013 BG Amsterdam
Netherlands
fax: +31 20 687 0019
e-mail: order@iospress.nl

Distributor in the UK and Ireland
Gazelle Books Services Ltd.
White Cross Mills
Hightown
Lancaster LA1 4XS
United Kingdom
fax: +44 1524 63232
e-mail: sales@gazellebooks.co.uk

Distributor in the USA and Canada
IOS Press, Inc.
4502 Rachael Manor Drive
Fairfax, VA 22032
USA
fax: +1 703 323 3668
e-mail: iosbooks@iospress.com

PRINTED IN THE NETHERLANDS

CENTRE OF EXCELLENCE - DEFENCE AGAINST TERRORISM

2004

TURKEY

Preface

The Advanced Training Course (ATC) 'Legal Aspects of Combating Terrorism', the papers of which are published in this volume, took place in Sarajevo 04–08 February 2008. The event was jointly hosted by the government of Bosnia Herzegovina and the Centre of Excellence – Defence Against Terrorism (COE–DAT), which was opened in Ankara in 2005 with the purpose of supporting NATO on defence issues related to terrorism. Turkey is the framework nation, and at present six other nations also contribute with staff and funds, namely the United States, the United Kingdom, Bulgaria, Romania, the Netherlands and Germany. Each year, COE–DAT organizes numerous workshops and courses, bringing academic rigour and institutional expertise in terrorism to interested parties in NATO, Partnership for Peace (PfP), and Mediterranean Dialogue countries, as well as Non-Triple nations and others.

The course had a practical emphasis. It united experts from various disciplines to give participants an understanding of how the various dimensions of the laws and their application fit together. In addition to the lectures which are found in this volume, the course was divided into three modules: (1) The legal response to terrorism in general terms; (2) Combating terrorism using lawful means; (3) harmonizing the Law of Armed Conflict, national laws and NATO in the fight against terrorism.

All participants were invited to participate in Working Groups. In each Group they discussed 'Legal Aspects of Terrorism', after which experts and participants presented their observations and recommendations in the plenary sessions.

One Working Group, for example, was asked to consider how drastic were the changes occasioned by the 9/11 attacks to international law. In fact, much of the discussion at the Sarajevo course, as well as many of the lectures, focused on this issue of the different responses to 9/11. Above all, the question was asked whether, in the face of the new threat, terrorism should still be countered through the ordinary means of criminal law, or whether their should be a significant shift in enforcement methods, including a less multilateral approach to decision-making and an increased use of military force.

The Working Group in question agreed that 'the provisions of the UN legal system previous to the 9/11 attacks was not able to deal effectively with the new threat'. The Group felt, however, that a framework had emerged from Security Council Resolutions 1267 and 1373, and the Counter-Terrorism Committee (CTC). Although they acknowledged that all states have the right to self-defence, many members of the Working Group identified a risk that some countries attacked by terrorists disregard Chapter One of the UN Charter, Art. 2 (4), which urges states to 'refrain in their international relations from the threat or use of force against the territorial integrity or political independence of any state'.

On a related point, a separate Working Group was asked whether the current international legal regime is adequate for anti-terrorism. In particular they addressed the question: Is the Geneva Convention's definition of 'combatant' sufficient to deal with the threat posed by members of terrorist organizations today? Here the Working Group was of the view that the current legal regime is now adequate and robust enough. The Group members noted that the system is a web of interconnecting agreements, with no overarching structure, indeed they listed thirteen international conventions and seven interregional conventions that specifically address different aspects of terrorism. The system would also include Rules of Engagement (ROE) which respected Human Rights Law and the National Law of the host nation. In a reference which drew on experience of the conflicts which followed the break-up of Yugoslavia, the Group highlighted the geographical considerations regarding areas of historical or religious significance. Answering the question of the definition of 'combatants', the Group agreed that the Geneva Conventions were sufficient. Multinational operations must define the combatants and their legal status at the outset.

Two of the Working Groups were asked to identify the advantages, if any, of using domestic criminal law to combat terrorism, as opposed to seeing the struggle in terms of an armed conflict. The criminal law route was generally preferred as more economical, transparent, and adaptable to circumstances. It provides better protection of human rights, and helps to give the public the appropriate perception that justice is being fairly served. Military involvement should be within the framework of a law enforcement operation, after a judgement following the arguments of the Public Prosecutor and defence lawyers. The intervention should respect UN Human Rights Conventions, and where relevant the European Convention on Human Rights.

The approach that sees the struggle against terrorism primarily in terms of an armed conflict carries great risks. Above all, it threatens to destroy the very democratic rights and processes which underlie the society it seeks to defend. The armed conflict model rapidly leads to practices such as extra-judicial assassinations and collective punishment.

On the other hand, other Working Groups addressing these issues identified disadvantages in the criminal law and law enforcement route. There is the well-known problem that the legal process can compromise a government's counter-terrorism efforts, for example by exposing intelligence sources. Another drawback is that criminal justice is slow and reactive rather than pro-active, it usually comes after the terrorists have struck. There are gaps in international law related to the financing of terrorism, where many transactions by-pass the banking system, and where it is difficult to establish the nexus between terrorist activities and legitimate transactions. A final drawback that was identified was that multilateral military interventions are often characterized by legal and organizational problems.

However, the benefits of the criminal law route were felt to outweigh its difficulties. It was also pointed out that, in an acknowledged emergency, a government can derogate from listed rights, so long as the modification is proportionate and necessary. The International Covenant on Civil and Political Rights, the European Convention on Human Rights, and the American Convention, speak openly of possible emergencies, asserting that in such a situation a state may be bound to take measures that would be inappropriate in peacetime. Another way complementary with the legal response is the enhancement of defence, where targets are made harder to attack (target hardening).

The course was opened with speeches by COE–DAT Director Col. Ahmet Tuncer and the Minister of Defence of the Republic of Bosnia Herzegovina, Selmo Çikotiç. Mr Çikotiç, outlining 'Bosnia Herzegovina's Stand against Terrorism', began by recommending that international efforts be renewed to find a accepted definition of terrorism. He went on to note that the measures required for the new threats may take us beyond the conventional legal norms. His speech also described the steps taken by the Ministry of Defence and government in Bosnia Herzegovina to combat terrorism.

Mr Ercan Çitlioğlu was the next speaker, with a lecture on 'Terrorism and Its Globalization' (see Chapter Two). This lecture states that the rise of individualism, the end of the Cold War, and the increasing role of non-state actors have caused a greater complexity in international relations. Many communities feel themselves to be victims, in some circumstances retreating into 'learned despair', and only communicating through violence. Regional conflicts have spread, and this has in turn been exploited by the hegemonic powers as they seek to consolidate their positions. Many more conflicts are likely to result from the growth in world population, climate change, energy and water shortages. This paper also analyzes the term 'global terrorism', and finds that what is called 'global terrorism' does not differ from earlier terrorism in its main features.

Prof. Robert Cryer's lecture, 'An Overview of the Law on Terrorism' (see Chapter Three), also introduces us to the subject of this volume with a broad survey of issues. He notes the fact that became rather a theme of the course, that there have been different ways in which international law has sought to combat the terrorism highlighted by the 9/11 attacks. UN negotiations on a comprehensive terrorism treaty are ongoing, but have so far met with limited success. Professor Cryer asks whether the more appropriate route to take would be to encourage ratifications of the existing treatises rather than to expend diplomatic energy on what might be impossible. Where terrorism is subsumed under other international crimes, international criminal law applies equally to terrorist offences falling under that rubric.

'The United Nations and the Challenge of Combating International Terrorism' is also the theme of Chapter Four, by Assist.-Prof. Isaac Kfir. His lecture opens by defining the term post-modern terrorism and then moves on to look at the role of the Security Council, the General Assembly and the Secretary-General in devising a programme that deals with the threat. Assist-Prof. Kfir's aim is to emphasise that the United Nations operates in three different areas in the war against terrorism: force, morality and economic and social assistance. The UN has made a start, but much more needs to be done.

Assist.-Prof. Isaac Kfir also provides the next lecture (see Chapter Five), this time on national law. 'Islamic Radicalism: the UK Case' explores some of the reasons behind the apparent rise in Islamic radicalism in the United Kingdom over the last few years. Using Fukuyama's and Huntington's theories, it is argued that a spiritual void, coupled with a desire to belong to something 'greater', has led young British Muslims towards Islamism. The author then outlines some of the measures undertaken by British authorities, and concludes with recommendations for improving relations between mainstream British society and the Muslim community.

'Human Rights and Terrorism' (see Chapter Six) of Capt. Derya Yaman identifies the commitment of states to human rights as among the most powerful weapons against terrorism. Counter-terrorism efforts must be carried out in keeping with international human rights obligations. Sacrificing our core values in the process, says Capt. Yaman, would be self-defeating and self-destructive. The lecture concludes, therefore, by arguing that the security needs of a state must be kept in balance with its counter-terrorism efforts.

In Chapter Seven, the central premise of Dr. Nicolas Ridley's 'Combating Terrorist Financing: The Dichotomy between Formulating the Legal Bases and Effective Operational Intelligence' is that anti-terrorist legal measures have actually been compounding the problem of the strategic intelligence time lag involved in acting against terrorist financing in the half decade since 9/11. Dr. Ridley offers some recommendations for preventing legal loopholes and providing a comprehensive approach.

The following paper, 'Weapons to Non-State Armed Groups – Back to Westphalia?' by Dr. Robbie Sabel, is not published in this book. It can be ordered online from the United Nations Institute for Disarmament Research (UNIDIR), in their periodical *Disarmament Forum: Engaging non-state armed groups* (2008). In his paper Dr. Sabel argues that international law can be relevant to some non-state groups, and is clearly so as regards a state's behaviour. This paper examines which, if any, rules of international law apply to non-state armed groups in regard to the supply of weapons and, more pertinently, it asks the question of which rules apply to states supplying weapons to these groups. Dr. Sabel analyses the different types of non-state armed groups, and examines the issue of state responsibility for these group's acts in international law. He contends that the legal situation is that there could be state responsibility where a state transfers weapons knowingly or recklessly by virtue of simply transferring those weapons.

Dr. Phillip Brunst addresses the 'Legal Aspects of Cyberterrorism' (see Chapter Eight). He notes that the internet offers a wide range of possibilities for terrorists and terrorist organizations, including attacks that can be digitally launched and which can affect data, property or human lives. Other important aspects of this threat regard the spreading of terrorist-related contents and the conventional use of the internet, e.g. for communication between terrorists. Dr. Brunst concludes that the legal framework that is available to the international community must address new possibilities for terrorists and at the same time respect the liberties of legitimate users.

Col. Osman Aytaç's 'Laws and Rules for Soldiers in Armed Conflicts, Crises and Counter-Terrorism' (see Chapter Nine) gives an overview of the Law of Armed Conflict (LOAC), referring to such important instruments of international law as the Hague and Geneva Conventions, the Hague Cultural Property Convention, and the protocols added to the Geneva Conventions. The second part of the paper concentrates on Rules of Engagement (ROE), which are defined as guidelines specifying under what conditions or circumstances force may be used to satisfy political and/or military demands. The lecture explains the principles of how ROE should be drawn up, and notes that tension always exits in a system that subordinates armed forces under civilian control. Managing this tension is a major role of ROE.

Inspector Ömer Yılmaz lectures on the controversial topic of 'The Use of Force in Law Enforcement Practices in the Light of ECHR Case-Law' (see Chapter Ten). He argues that, although national laws have developed the necessary controls for the proper use of force, the growing importance of human rights has given rise to some additional international control systems. In particular the European Convention for the Protection of Human Rights and Fundamental Freedoms and its organs provide important protections. Inspector Yılmaz shows that the case law of the European Court of Human Rights on the proper use of force is a valuable source for law enforcers in fulfilling their daily duties, as well as for the counter-terrorism strategies of democratic countries.

In 'A Study of UK Anti-Terror Law' (see Chapter Eleven), Maj. Julian Charvat discusses the development of the UK's terrorism law, from the emergency powers of the Northern Ireland Troubles to the recent developments in the face of contemporary terrorist threats. Maj. Charvat also looks in detail at the London attacks of July 2005 and other events, and at how the laws have been applied.

The expert on EU law, Davide Casale, notes in 'Institutional and Legal Aspects of EU Counter-Terrorism' (see Chapter Twelve) that the EU has since 9/11 been trying to react with a comprehensive strategy grounded on four core objectives: prevent, protect, pursue and respond. The Union has also reshaped its institutional and legal counter-terrorist framework, with the role of some EU bodies being strengthened, and new institutional actors being established. The most important EU institutions in the fight against terrorism have proved to be the European Commission, Europol and Eurojust. Despite some good results achieved, lack of co-ordination and difficulties in information sharing are weaknesses that still hamper the realization of effective intelligence and judicial co-operation. A new common European definition of terrorist offences, the introduction of the European Arrest Warrant and the use of biometrics have enhanced the efficacy of the EU action in preventing and suppressing terrorism. On the other hand, they have raised concerns with fundamental rights and civil liberties.

"Military Response to Terrorism and International Law on the Use of Force" is the theme of Dominika Svarc's paper (see Chapter Thirteen). Ms Svarc points out that in the post-Cold War security environment there have been factual developments and ambiguities that pose important challenges to the basic concepts, principles and rules of international law, especially concerning the use of force. The first part of this paper considers the option of multilateral employment of military force to prevent or to respond to acts of terrorism, and looks particularly at the Security Council's gradual enlargement of the notion of threat to international peace and security with respect to (international) terrorism. The second, and central, part of the paper then to examines the complex issue of a unilateral military response to terrorism, focusing on some its most murky features, such as: (a) the appropriate interpretation of the concept of 'armed attack' in the context of terrorist activities; (b) the requirement of attributability to States of terrorist attacks; and (c) the doctrines of anticipatory and preventive self-defence.

Prof. Robert Cryer's second lecture looks into 'The Future of Legal Aspects of Combating Terrorism' (see Chapter Fourteen). While the professor does not speculate directly about exactly what will happen to the law in the future, he identifies trends that are likely to have an impact on the law. The first part of the lecture argues that the rhetoric adopted by many after the 11 September attacks was of a 'war on terrorism' as a legal paradigm. However, the concept of a separate, non-territorial armed conflict on terrorism has begun to fall from favour internationally. There is a move towards improving the existing law on the basis of the conviction that the relevant law is criminal law. This is the approach that has been taken by various organs of the United Nations. This second part of this paper outlines the development of the law on terrorism: the UN Global Counter-Terrorism Strategy, and developments regarding human rights and terrorism. While not compromising with the terrorists, there is an increased recognition of the social conditions which have facilitated the spread of terrorism.

Col. Mete TAHMİSOĞLU
ATC Director
COE–DAT, Ankara

Contents

Legal Aspects of Combating Terrorism
Centre of Excellence Defence Against Terrorism, Ankara, Turkey (Ed.)
IOS Press, 2008

doi:10.3233/978-1-58603-930-1-1

Opening Speech: Bosnia Herzegovina's Stand against Terrorism

Selmo ÇIKOTIÇ
Minister of Defence, Republic of Bosnia Herzegovina

Abstract. International efforts should be renewed to find a definition of terrorism and take effective measures against it. The measures required for the new threats may take us beyond the conventional legal norms. This paper also describes the steps taken by the Ministry of Defence and government in Bosnia Herzegovina in combating terrorism.

Keywords. Terrorism, international law, counter-terrorism in Bosnia Herzegovina.

Welcome and Introductory Remarks

It is my honour and pleasure to welcome our speakers, experts in 'The Legal Aspects of Terrorism', and our participants to this Advanced Training Course (ATC). I am delighted to see participants from the South-East Europe region. Those from this area, as well as those from further afield, can benefit from the topics we are to discuss concerning international law and national law.

Terrorism has been identified as 'the greatest threat to transatlantic defence for the foreseeable future'. The Centre of Excellence – Defence Against Terrorism (COE–DAT) is one of the new COEs that provide NATO with expert opinion as it responds to a changing security situation. The centre arranges courses and workshops for NATO countries, PfP countries like Bosnia Herzegovina, and others.

I wish to thank the organizers for offering us a wonderful opportunity to discuss such an important issue.

Legal Definition

A couple of observations stand out concerning 'The Legal Aspects of Terrorism'. As is well known, no common and internationally adopted definition of terrorism exists. Unfortunately, the UN's failure to agree has left a lot of room for misleading excuses and misinterpretations. But, given catastrophic effects terrorist attacks have on the population and infrastructure, they cannot stay unaddressed. I want to add my voice to those calling for renewed efforts.

In particular, it is important to note the difference between the 'rightful cause', which we call the ideology, by which terrorists may seek to justify their existence, and the way they perpetrate their terrorist actions. While nations argue at length over the merits of the former, they could certainly find legal ways to prevent, deter, fight and deal with the consequences of the latter. All terrorist attacks should be incriminated and treated as crimes.

A New Threat Requires New Measures

A second point is that the conventional approach of justice to terrorism seems to be not enough, because the threat we face is not a conventional one. Laws need to be adapted to meet the changing nature of the threat. This has been expressed in the phrase 'an asymmetric threat needs an asymmetric response'.

The lead has been taken by the UN's anti-terrorism conventions, and no doubt revised agreements will need to be adopted in years to come. BiH is also a member of the Council of Europe and OSCE. Like many other countries it has been strengthening its laws against terrorism, much of the work being done within the framework of anti-terrorism assistance, which brings national and international experts together on subjects of common concern. We seek a comprehensive and inter-agency approach to fighting terrorism.

However, it is clear that the struggle should not be allowed to disturb the happiness and well-being of citizens. There should be a balance in terms of deprivation of some human rights and fundamental freedoms set against a need for effective measures.

The Ministry of Defence of BiH

In the Ministry of Defence we have developed an 'Action Plan for Fighting Terrorism'. Much of our activity at the moment is concentrated on providing military assistance to the civil authorities, which comes within the Armed Forces' Mission.

In addition, there are Special Forces to be engaged, working for the Military Intelligence Branch and the Military Police. On the international front, BiH is a member of the 'Antiterrorist Coalition' led by the USA.

BiH Achievements

As a nation, BiH is currently implementing a comprehensive 'Strategy for Fighting Terrorism 2006-2009'. The Strategy addresses each of the three main areas: legislation, institutions and activities. Institutions such as the Ministry of Security, the Ministry of Defence, the Intelligence and Security Agency, the State Protection and Investigation Agency, the Border Police, the State Court, and numerous other bodies are dealing with terrorism. Together these institutions are seeking to improve co-operation and information exchange.

The legislation involved is in the framework of international conventions and agreements, as well as the state's and entities' prosecution laws, the Law Forbidding Money Laundering, the Law on Protection of Secret Data, the Law on Foreigners, the Law on Witness Protection, the Law on Export/Import of Weapons and Military Equipment, etc..

These activities come within the framework of the State Action Plan, which aims to legacy of the war in the 1990s. The main objective is to join the prosperous family of Euro-Atlantic countries, recognizing that economic and environmental issue are often among the root causes of violence. Part of this objective is to gain membership of the EU and NATO.

Concluding Remarks

In conclusion I return to my main points, above all the importance of a balanced approach to fighting terrorism if we are to preserve democracy and the other values attached to it. I have also stressed the need for an inter-governmental, inter-agency, comprehensive approach that builds capacity in our countries. This will have a direct consequence in efficient fighting of terrorism and other types of threat, such as organized crime, especially WMD proliferation, money laundering, human trafficking, drug smuggling and illegal immigration.

I wish you luck in this week-long endeavour, while hoping you are able to create a network of experts, one of the most important objectives such an activity can achieve.

Legal Aspects of Combating Terrorism
Centre of Excellence Defence Against Terrorism, Ankara, Turkey (Ed.)
IOS Press, 2008

doi:10.3233/978-1-58603-930-1-5

Terrorism and Its 'Globalization'

Ercan ÇİTLİOĞLU
President, Bahçeşehir Üniversity Strategic Research Center, Turkey

Abstract. The rise of individualism, the end of the Cold War, and the increasing role of non-state actors have caused international relations to transform into a much more complex system. This new system has created many communities which feel themselves to be victims. Such populations may abandon rational debate and retreat into 'learned despair', only communicating through violence. Regional conflicts have spread, and this has in turn been exploited by the hegemonic powers as they seek to consolidate their positions. Many more conflicts are likely to result from the growth in world population, climate change, energy and water shortages. In this context, terrorist groups are likely to base their ideologies on the two most enduring elements of popular identity: religion and ethnicity. This paper also analyzes the term 'global terrorism', and finds that what is called 'global terrorism' is no different from earlier terrorism.

Keywords. Terrorism, future threats to stability, environmental threats to security, terrorist ideologies, 'global terrorism'.

The continuing rise of individualism, a universal problem in this age of information and communication technologies and increasing expectations, has eroded the fundamental values of societies, including solidarity and cooperation. Also, with regard to finding solutions to today's social problems, there is the fact that when people raise their voices against unfair treatment it is often recognized too late.

As the Cold War ended with the collapse of the USSR in 1991, the international scene changed from the common forms which had dominated international relations. Increasingly we witnessed the participation of non-state actors, including single-issue campaigners and militant groups, and this contributed to the creation of a new environment. At this time, it was realized—very late—that the conventional cause/reason analyses had lost their bearings.

Through NATO and the Warsaw Pact, dominated respectively by USA and the USSR, international relations had been compressed between two blocks. The comforts of interpretation in this plane of deconstruction ended, the participation of new civilian and non-states actors in the system led to greater complexity, and the implications of these changes were only recognized very late.

After the bi-polar Cold War era the blocks dissolved, and many of the familiar state-level conflicts ended, while other conflicts emerged. In a new, unstable and unaccustomed process, new structures were constantly developing, and these forced countries to alter their known positions, recognized attitudes, stereotyped behavior and reactions. As a result, it has gradually become harder to estimate what elements will be drawn into the states' and non-state actors' efforts to reach their political and economic targets. If perceptions are locked onto permanent alliances and their unchangeability, it will be difficult to find out the nature of the new threats. The reductive analyses which draw their references from the sovereignty conflicts caused by the Western/Eastern composition are very deficient for interpreting the roots of today's political developments, with the new formations, changing interests, and the conflicts they cause.

From the socio-economic and socio-cultural point of view, the masses of people who feel themselves excluded, denigrated, exploited, and subjected to unfair treatment have gradually increased in number, and these 'grapes of wrath' have transformed into violence, with violence becoming an ever more widespread means of expression.

With an abandonment of rationalism, whether through 'Learned Despair',[1] or 'Passive Obedient Society',[2] or an unjust treatment psychology manifested in chosen traumas, certain societies follow these models and adopt an 'us and them' world view, which readily turns to violence based on radical religious sects and/or ethnic nationalist movements. The dialogue has turned into a monologue, settled situations have turned into conflicts, uniting has turned into disunity.

What we find is often a clear negligence of studying the root causes. In this process, where reductive analyses have lost their validity, our perceptions of terrorism must undergo a transformation and adapt to new interpretations. This is because, with terrorism having turned into an instrument applied and used by some states to obtain and carry forward their political and economic purposes and interests, the weak states, being subject to such operations, have caught an opportunity to fight the hegemonic powers.

This new era brought a transition from symmetry to asymmetry, from conventional, total and multilateral wars to low intensity fighting, from global and regional wars to local and internal conflicts, and to new traumatic war methods targeting the psychological destruction of people.

At this point, some state sponsors, and religious and ethnic groups within states, whose economic and military power is not sufficient to confront the hostile or rival superior powers, have discovered terrorism as a new system of warfare to be used for reaching their aims and obtaining results.

Parallel to this, some powerful states have seen terrorism as the means to wage a 'covert war' to increase their power, to broaden their areas of dominance, to

---

[1] Learned Despair: American psychologist Martin Seligman carried out a series of experiments on the behavior forms of trapped people and animals. He used dogs in these experiments and applied low voltage electricity shocks on dogs kept in a cage. He applied higher voltages to the ones who go to the gate to escape. 65% of the dogs, having tried to escape for a long time, gave up trying even though the gate of the cage was opened and no voltage was applied. Seligman defines this as 'learned despair', and proves that similar processes stimulate the same behavior also in humans. The most deterministic and devastating part of this finding, similar to the conditioned reflex theory of Pavlov, is that this inability occurs in people who always fail to overcome problems, leading them into a form of inertia (Int. Ter. and the Drug Connection, Ank. Ün., Ank. 1984, p. 148-151).

[2] Passive Obedient Society: This concept is based on a theory of which foundations were laid by Russian scientist Pavlov. Individuals and society, by means of scaring, misleading, almost hypnotized by their own fears, are forced to confuse what is true and what it not. With the loss of value judgments and an anarchy of concepts, constantly changing enemies and slogans confuse the masses and, in the end, a passive and indifferent population is formed. The societies formed by such individuals begin to accept all things that they refused in the past, even if they are harmful, with a passive obedience. Unable to distinguish the harmful from beneficial, such societies fail to analyze relations between cause and effect, any assume what is imposed on them as if it were their own thoughts (Int. Ter. and the Drug Connection, Ank. Ün., Ank. 1984, p. 153-155).

consolidate their positions, and exercise control, in spite of the fact that international law and established rules do not allow them to use such methods.

As a result, the terrorism of today has evolved away from the accustomed definitions, well-known clichés, and methods against which countermeasures have been developed, into 'a half-military strategy' using technologies which are simple but effective.

Parallel to all these developments, since terrorism has been carried to the level which questions the hegemonic relationships of the globalized world, and since people have started to raise their voices more against the injustices of the status quo, we find that violence has grown into an anonymous style of expression and communication. Terrorism, going beyond its classical meaning, has turned into a kind of communication phenomenon based on modern technologies.

The world of today has become a much smaller place in terms of information exchange, communication, decision-making and supervision mechanisms, and this is the effect of globalization. This has made the terrorists' target selection easier, as people are far more conscious of the power centers of our smaller world. People are more aware of each other, and more aware of their perceived enemies.

By contrast, the principal powers have tried to consolidate their positions by spreading their military activities, sovereignty, interests and conflicts into neighboring areas. This is designed to prevent the conflict reaching inwards, to the centers of their political culture, and it can be seen as a prevention tactic to block conflicts which would otherwise be carried to those centers by a kind of centripetal force.

As a result of all these developments, the powers who want to increase and preserve their political and economic superiority and the terrorist groups who want to reach their targets have accordingly formed a supply/demand equilibrium, that is open to cooperation.

This assessment, related to formation of terrorism today, is not only aimed at perceiving the current process, but also at making projections as to terrorism's extent and effect as a threat after mutating in its own dynamic structure. Just as no prediction could have been formulated with regard to the current sources of threat on the basis of the 1970-1990-2000 periods alone, it is also impossible to make futuristic assessments based on the present sources of threat. Because the threats in the past lost their validity, as their root causes altered, the threat sources and perceptions will lose their validity by undergoing subjective and objective transformations.

Since the strong and oppressive socio-economic model that accompanies globalization is intervening in the 'nation-state', and the information technologies age is fuelling a hunger for information, the expectations of the masses are increasing throughout the world. This combination is worth scrutinizing as it creates a fertile ground for widespread terrorism in the form of religious and ethnic organizations.

It is above all the feeling of belonging among individuals that plays a principal role in the development of identities, and in the shaping of social structures. As these may emerge as religious and/or ethnic identities in time, the terrorist actions and groups based on the radical religious and ethnic nationalism constitute the two main movements. These protect their continued existence by the promotion of ideological justifications.

These can be seen as times in which many ideologies have lost their effectiveness and importance, rejected, and as a result externalized, and replaced by individual conjectures. Against this background, religious faith and ethnic identity are two fundamental factors which are the key elements constituting social dynamics.

Throughout history, when separatist actions based on racism are examined neutrally, it can be observed that once these movements have emerged they never disappear, no matter how conditions change on the basis of the 'time–place–opportunity and ability' triangle.

After making their cause and aims heard by violence-based actions, the separatist terrorist organizations work together with other illegal organizations (as these are equally against the system), and they all continue their struggles with tactics that aim to support each other in 'political and operational areas'.

The terrorists may retreat underground, or live a long period as sleepers and in silence, when there are conditions which do not suit them, or when their ideology is questioned. However, in spite of this tactic of withdrawal and postponing, they never depart from the aims that they decided to make their reason of being.

Separatist terrorist organizations, religious radicals, and ethnic nationalists, are all naturally supported, politically and economically, by some circles which are seeking to reach certain aims. Eventually this required categorical support enables these types of terrorist organizations to maintain the identities they have created, as well as their continued existence.

Once their continued existence as separatist terrorist organizations and their ability to preserve their identities are ensured, these characteristics transform the terror groups so that they become centers of attraction. The characteristics make them entities that should be supported, from the 'political and economic' points of view, both by some states and non state powers in their efforts to realize their aims and purposes.

Radical religious and ethnic separatist terrorist organizations need to preserve their existence for a long term in an effort to realize their purposes, and this is essential to their nature. In time they become hungry for political and economic support and open themselves to cooperation, based on transmitted parameters and changes. No terrorist organization would survive without the support of one or more states, or non-state actors, in the form of political or economic backing, or physical, covert or explicit support.

It is a proven fact that at the time of their foundation and emergence all terrorist organizations define themselves as idealist, and they believe in such idealism, but after some time, for financial reasons, they form relations and cooperate with criminal organizations.

In order to meet their logistical needs, for accommodation, arms, explosives, communication assets, fake passports, identity cards, propaganda means, and intelligence activities, terrorist organizations need funds.

Once they grow numerous, and transfer their activities from the local perspective to the international arena, their financial requirements increase. Accordingly, they begin marketing their malicious activities, and they associate more with powerful circles who could support them, rather than with organized crime organizations.

At this juncture some states and/or non-state actors intervene in terrorist activities to realize their objectives. Frequently, terrorist organizations move their activities beyond their own objectives in order to provide armed and political services to others.

Since the activities of organized crime organizations are especially focused on the smuggling of humans, arms, drugs and nuclear materials, a parallel system starts to work. The two types of organization feed off each other, and create structures utilizing human resources, communication, transportation, and protection networks, and aiming to meet the logistical requirements of the terrorist organizations.

Looking into the future, one can only estimate that there will be increasing local and regional conflicts, with limited conflicts transforming into a new war and pay-back method. When making predictions about the world in the years 2015-2025-2050, one can only perceive increasingly widespread terrorism.

The reasons for the prediction of growing conflict are found in the fact that each threat has its own sources and roots as to time, space and conditions. In 2000, the world sustains a population of 6.1 billion, which will grow to 7.2 billion by 2015, and 9.1 billion by 2050. The resources necessary for preserving our life and welfare will be shared by a further 1.1 billion new people 8 years from now, and 3 billion new people 43 years from now. This should be a satisfactory evidence of increasing threat perceptions.[3]

Dwindling primary energy resources (petrol, natural gas, coal, etc.), which are necessary to maintain our well-being, and decreasing water resources, which are essential for life, and the resultant depletion of agricultural land, make future conflict more unavoidable.

It is wise to consider that 80% of the increase in the world's population will take place in under-developed and developing countries, so that, by 2015, 45% of the global population will be in four countries (China, India, Pakistan, and Indonesia), by 2025, 60% of the global population will reside in 6 countries (China, India, Pakistan, Indonesia, Iran, and Bangladesh), and, by 2050, 80% of the world's population will be concentrated in Asia and the Middle East. It can be foreseen that the sources and root causes of the threats caused by these changing equilibriums will undergo a considerable alteration.

Asia and the Middle East will see increases in population density. These are areas where energy reserves are concentrated (67.8% of the oil reserves are in Middle East, 80% of natural gas reserves are in the Middle East and Asia). In view of the demographic variations mentioned, the conflicts due to the displacement of the centers of gravity will become much more severe.

30% of the world's population, expected to reach 7.1 billion in 2015, will be endangered by a lack of water, while over 30 countries, particularly those in the Middle East, Northern Africa and Central Asia, will provide for their water requirements from cross-border running waters. The water shortages will increase due to global warming and the growth in population. These facts all show that sharing water will become an issue of primary importance in the foreseeable future.

Today, developed countries hold 11% of energy resources while their share of total consumption is 80%. On the other hand, under-developed and developing countries hold 89% of the resources, but use only 20% of total consumption. These are very significant concerns for threat perceptions of the future.

Countries holding most of the energy resources in their soil, either due to their increasing population or their increasing prosperity, are forced to increase their consumption accordingly. The disadvantages this brings for industrialized countries, which do not have such energy resources, could turn into new conflicts.

Climatic zone displacements, unpredictable rainfall, and draughts due to global warming will turn some areas of settlement into places where human life is not possible, causing migrations of up to 2 billion people by 2050. This new 'migration of the

---

[3] Climate Change 2007, The Physical Basis, http:/www.ipcc.ch.

nations' will cause cultural conflicts, which are even now evident as new threat perceptions of the future.[4]

The predictions of UN Global Warming Reports state that in the next century 30% of the world's current land mass could lie under water. In consideration of this, the conflicts of the future will be for survival rather than increasing and preserving prosperity, and in turn, the level of violence could be beyond our imagination.

Leaving for a moment the threat perceptions of future, and returning to the history of terrorism, most of the ideologically based terrorist organizations have been forced to leave the arena since the subjective and objective parameters supporting their very existence have been eliminated. However, violent movements which based themselves on one or both of two factors have survived, although somehow transformed, and it seems that their survival will go on for much longer, perhaps even to eternity. These two factors, the roots of which have not undergone an alteration, although there have been formal changes, are 'religion' and 'ethnic (racist) nationalism'.

Today, although the primary reason for terrorist movements and conflicts may differ, the part of their thinking reflected to the surface is generally based on religion and ethnicity, and it is globalized under such identities. The reasoning for and timing of the inclusion of 'global terror' as a phrase in the literature should be studied in more detail. Terrorism, which has existed throughout the history of humanity, and which it appears will throughout the future of humanity, goes beyond the local, country specific, regional levels and becomes global. The existence of this global status should be investigated.

The milestone for terror's being mentioned with the adjective 'global' is generally thought to be the 9/11 airplane attacks on World Trade Center in New York and the Pentagon in Washington (USA). In spite of the overseas operations of the USA in retaliation for these imaginative and startling attacks, the globalizing of terrorism was not mentioned as a claim or as a reality, and not turned into a theory. If, based on this terrorist attack suffered by the USA, terrorism is considered to gain a global identity with global targets, then the attacks of ASALA (Armenian Secret Army for Liberation of Armenia) and JCAG (Justice Commandos for Armenian Genocide) between 1975 and 1986, which took place over five continents, in twenty-two countries, including 699 operations, and killing seventy-two people, thirty-nine of whom were Turkish diplomats and their families, could well be the first examples of the global terror.[5] Or the terrorist operation of Al-Fateh and PFLP (Popular Front for Liberation of Palestine) against Israeli athletes at the Munich Olympics, or the hijacking of Lufthansa planes to Entebbe, should be acknowledged as having a global identity in terms of their targets and geographical location.

In the 1970s, where the said overseas terrorist acts took place, 'global terrorism' and the threat of it were not even named. This necessitates making a more credible identification for this concept.

The heterogeneous character of a terrorist organization's membership, in contrast to organizations where the terrorists belong the same nation, race or religion, could be considered as a basis for the 'global terrorism', taking the 9/11 attacks as a milestone. Yet this is unacceptable.

The geographical spread, the variety of the targets of the operations, and the different religious and racial ties of the members of the organization, do not constitute

---

[4] Climate Change 2007, The Physical Basis, http:/www.ipcc.ch.
[5] Strategic Analysis, ASAM Publications, Ömer Engin Lütem, issue 89, p. 44.

the emergence of a new concept, nor require us to coin a new term which puts the words 'terror' and 'global' together. So the question 'what are we to understand as global terrorism's definition?' still remains unsolved.

Since the terrorist attacks in the USA called '9/11' provide the birth date for this term, and as we know the organization behind these attacks is referred to as Al-Qaeda, is it possible to define 'global terrorism' in categories provided in this single, narrow box? With an operating capacity in a vast geography (global from the geographical point of view), with its militants belonging to various nations (Saudi Arabia, Jordan, Iraq, Algeria, UK, Turkey, Malaysia, Indonesia, Somalia, etc.), is it scientifically possible to define Al-Qaeda as a global terrorist organization, forgetting its Sunni-Wahhabi roots? Al-Qaeda's being turned into a manifesto, with various organizations sharing the same views and hatred carrying out their operations using the title Al-Qaeda in some form of 'franchising' system, with a horizontal structure rather than a vertical one, could be given as an example of global terrorism. At this point, what gains a global identity is not the operation under the franchise of Al-Qaeda, but the ideological standing of those organizations.

There is an internal contradiction in the arguments aimed at a definition of global terrorism (from the point of geography and homogeneity). One point of reference of far-reaching significance remains, and it focuses on the fact that the socio-political order imposed by globalization is what in fact globalizes the terrorism. In summary we can say that 'globalization has turned terror into a global phenomenon'.

Nevertheless, in spite of this interconnection between the globalized order and global terrorism, this theory is just hollow rhetoric from the scientific point of view. This is because globalization faces a dynamic process within itself, with unique parameters. As such, terrorism updates itself and adapts to new conditions, it changes and acquires a different dynamic structure and identity. So the theory that one of these independent and distinct dynamic processes is the result of another, in other words, that global terrorism is the result of globalization, contradicts scientific reality.

At this point we can support the claim that interference in nation-states results from the pressurizing and self-imposing socio-economic model of globalization, accompanied by the widespread information opportunities of the communication era, and the claim that this causes a more severe terrorism, turning it into a way of expression, the basis of which is violence. We cannot, however, agree from a deterministic point of view, that it has 'created' terror.

In comparison with the recent past, when communication means were not at today's level, and when one-sided information sources or means of communication were available, today it is not easy to exercise control on the news sources. People have much higher expectations of the authorities, and raise their voices against unfair treatment, and the age of information has created a global human society with an unlimited hunger for information.

Accordingly, one of the primary reasons for the delusion of identifying the words 'terrorism' and 'global' derives from the unrestricted access of people to information in whatever part of the world. As a consequence of the speed of the information network and its wide-reaching availability, which have converted societies from a closed model into an open one, we can be led to delusory results. For example, about attacks which existed before, but which we neglected through lack of information. Merely because their number has increased we are prone to accept global terrorism as a new concept.

In fact, terrorism always existed, from the Roman Empire of Tiberius and Caligula, to Hasan Sabbah's Hashashis, the Sicari of the Israelis, the first and second reigns of terror of the French Revolution, with the law applied by the Paris Revolutionary Court presided over by Robespierre,[6] the Narodnaya Volya and Narodnicks in the Russia of the Czars,[7] the separatists of Corsica, the Tamil guerillas, the Contras of Guatemala, ETA and the IRA.

The emergence of terrorist violence as products of the West's contradiction with its own values caused meant the imprisonment of terrorism within the boundaries of a state ended, although there had been no need to turn it into a global threat. Only after terror's transformation into a new kind of war in societies which are insulted, externalized, exploited or imposed, and 'others', have people come to realize that it formed a common threat to the entire humanity.

This new kind of terror or covert war has become a source of power for the neighboring countries and the radical religious and ethnic communities therein. They do not require improved and superior technology, a strong and healthy economy, large armies, a sophisticated armament system, but only require limited but dedicated human resources, which are very cheap, but very effective and traumatic with regard to their outcome.

Some dominant powers transferred power and interest conflicts to the surrounding countries, rather than see the conflicts reach inwards to their centers. They imposed it on the 'others' for the purpose of reinforcing and making permanent their own existence, and in order to control and direct the communities, and the surrounding countries. They started transferring such wars to these areas, making use of terror as an instrument, and creating a new dilemma. This era of new and global terrorism can be defined as a reversal of a centrifugal force and a transformation of the attracting power of the centers into repulsion.

It is possible that when one addresses directly the cause-result relations of today's global terrorism, which are left to a confusion of concepts and definitions, one finds that the fact causing this mental confusion and global terrorism is in fact a very plain one. Either the mental confusion caused by the variability of global dynamics, or the incredible disinformation campaign which is the natural result of the information age, has forced people into a mental laziness, and instead of reaching their own 'fact' through research, investigation and questioning, they absorb and accept the 'facts' of others as if their own. So the term 'global terrorism' does not have a scientific basis.

The sources which define the 'global terrorism' concept as a common threat to humanity should objectively answer the question of why they failed to define terrorism as 'global' or 'a common threat against humanity' when it was aimed Latin America, Europe, the Middle East or the Far East.

The conclusions of this paper do not of course mean that terror is not a strong and anonymous threat. Terrorism is an undeniable threat, because, in addition to its damage, it targets normative values and perceptions of humanity. Our behaviors are based on normative value systems, as a set of unwritten rules forming our lives and our perceptions, but these are totally strange to the members of terrorist organizations. According to terrorists, the set of rules which are valid for our personal and social lives are obsessions, artificialities, and deviations. This is because all the values forming terrorist behaviors and their thought structures are normative ones within their own subjective worlds. A terrorist organization's identity is either ideological, religious or

[6] Larousse Encyclopedia, 1985, Istanbul, volume 11.
[7] Ibid., volume, 11, p. 341.

ethnic-nationalist, and their judgments will not change at any time or under any conditions.

The primary aspect that differentiates terrorists in ideological organizations is their sense of belonging and identity. People's sense belonging forms a reverse pyramid, beginning with the immediate surroundings. At the base of the pyramid is belonging to the nuclear family (parents and siblings), then the close environment (relatives, friends, school, professional colleagues, etc.), belonging to one's own society (large family), belonging to the locality (neighborhood, village, city, country), and in the end, belonging to the nation as a large society, and this turns a geography into a motherland with the spread of national ideas.

Isolating people from their sense of belonging means cutting the roots which are the arteries connecting them to life. The sense of belonging of terrorists have been formed, however, on a very different basis. The individuality of terrorists has been destroyed. They have gained a collective identity, so their only sense of belonging is to their organization. They are isolated from their past and deliberately taken away from their former affiliations, which are defined as harmful to their normative values. So terrorists see their organization as a source of life, and define their belonging to the organization as a reincarnation.

Since the strongest sense of belonging people can has been shown over time to be to religion and ethnic identity, these two factors in the development and forming of terrorists' identities play a dominant role. As a matter of fact, terrorist movements and groups based on radical religion and ethnic nationalism are the most threatening ones. Because of this, terrorist organizations formed through racist nationalism and radical religious components have a high level of dedication, leading to a much greater severity of violence in comparison to other types.

We should also emphasize that Islam's relation and even identification with violence and terror after 9/11 is a totally subjective approach, if not a deliberate tactic. It is impossible to say that Serbian nationalism/racism in Bosnia Herzegovina and Kosovo, dominated by orthodoxies, is different to, or less than, that of the Taliban with its Wahhabi origins in Afghanistan.

Societies which lack hope transform themselves and prioritize religion, forming narrow and closed spiritual societies (congregations) with a closed circuit of relations. Ethnic groups consider themselves to be unjustly treated and become racist-nationalist ones. The founding sensations for these two are identical at one point. Another common element of radical religious terrorist organizations and racist separatist terrorist organizations is the effort to preserve their identities, although they have been transformed objectively with the passage of time.

Racist and separatist terrorist organizations, forming illegal structures to challenge the system, publicize their causes through violent operations. After that they transform themselves into political movements and continue their struggle with tactical practices, and the political and military fields support each other. The terrorists may go to underground when conditions are unfavorable, or have a long dormant periods, but they never renounce their cause in spite of these temporary tactical retreats or displacements.

Today, when one the radical religious and ethnic-nationalist types of terror, which allegedly provide terrorism with a 'global' identity, in spite of artificialness and partisan character of this definition, it is clear that terrorist operations will become an integral part of global life for a very long time to come. In fact, this is an undeniable reality. Although this conclusion is not very hopeful, we can state that terrorism will continue its existence, exploiting any technological means, in varying and ever more devastating forms.

References

[1] Avrich, Paul, *Anarşist Portreler* (Anarchist Portraits), Ankara, 2003.
[2] Avrasya Dosyası (Euorasian Dossier) ASAM Publications, Terör, Asam, Ankara, 2006, p. 168-172.
[3] E. H. Carr, Michael Bakunin, New York, 1961, see especially p. 18.
[4] Climate Change 2007, The Physical Basis, http:/www.ipcc.ch.
[5] *Dünyada ve Türkiye'de Terör*, (Terror in the World and in Turkey), Central Bank of Turkey Publication, Ankara, 2002, see especially p. 268.
[6] *International Terrorism and the Drug Connection*, Ankara University Publications, Ankara, 1984, see especially p. 148-151.
[7] Historical Overview of Climate Change Science.
[8] Larousse Encyclopedia, 1985, Istanbul.
[9] *A Military Guide to Terrorism in the Twenty-First Century*, US Army Training and Doctrine Command, Kansas, USA, 2005, see especially p. 3-8.

Legal Aspects of Combating Terrorism
Centre of Excellence Defence Against Terrorism, Ankara, Turkey (Ed.)
IOS Press, 2008

doi:10.3233/978-1-58603-930-1-15

An Overview of the Law on Terrorism

Prof. Robert CRYER
Professor of International and Criminal Law, University of Birmingham, UK

Abstract. The purpose of this piece is limited to an overview of the various different ways in which international law seeks to combat terrorism. The UN Security Council, the General Assembly, and the Secretary-General have engaged extensively with the issue of terrorism. Although negotiations on a comprehensive terrorism treaty are ongoing, it is admittedly with limited success. One might ask whether the more appropriate route to take would be to encourage ratifications of the existing treatises rather than to expend diplomatic energy on what might be impossible. Where terrorism is subsumed under other international crimes, the considerations that apply to international crimes apply equally to any terrorist offences that fall under that rubric. In opposition to this, some scholars, like Antonio Cassese, believe that terrorism has matured into a fully-fledged international crime in its own right. However, so far, States and international organisations dealing with terrorism have used the mechanisms of transnational, rather than international, criminality.

Keywords. International law on terrorism, United Nations conventions, international crimes, transnational crimes.

Introduction

Terrorism is a subject which has, for obvious reasons, become an academic growth industry. It has gone in something over half a decade from a small specialism to a topic upon which there is a huge, and expanding, literature.[1] A similar thing can be said about international criminal law. There are considerable overlaps between the subjects too, and thus there is a considerable body of literature on international criminal law and terrorism.[2] The purpose of this piece, however, is limited to an overview of the various different ways in which international law seeks to combat terrorism. They are both complex and overlapping, which reflects in many ways the decentralised nature of the

---

[1] For a recent monograph see Ben Saul, *Defining Terrorism in International Law* (Oxford: OUP, 2006); See also Vaughan Lowe, 'Clear and Present Danger: Responses to Terrorism' (2005) 54 *International and Comparative Law Quarterly* 185; Anne-Marie Slaughter and William Burke-White, 'An International Constitutional Moment' (2002) 43 *Harvard International Law Journal* 1; Louise Arbour, 'In Our Name and On Our Behalf' (2006) 55 *International and Comparative Law Quarterly* 511; Sean Murphy, 'Terrorism and the Concept of Armed Attack in Article 51 of the UN Charter' (2002) 43 *Harvard International Law Journal* 41; Tal Becker, *Terrorism and the State: Rethinking the Rules of State Responsibility* (Oxford: Hart, 2006).

[2] See, e.g. Andrea Bianchi, *Enforcing International Law Norms Against Terrorism* (Oxford: Hart, 2004); Roberta Arnold, *The International Criminal Court as a New Instrument for Repressing Terrorism* (New York: Transnational, 2004).

international legal order, and the level of agreement between States on what ought to be criminalised at the international level.

International Crimes and Transnational Crimes

To investigate the law on point, it is necessary to differentiate two different bodies of criminal law, international crimes in the narrow sense, and what are often called 'transnational crimes'.[3] Despite the fact that the two are different, they are sometimes dealt with together, under the general rubric of 'international crimes'. It is true that the two are 'fuzzy sets'; the boundaries between the two sets of crimes are not impermeable, and there are disagreements about whether certain crimes fall within one category or the other. However, the distinction remains important, in particular with respect to the question of retrospectivity and jurisdiction.

1. International Crimes

What we often call international crimes are traditionally seen as those which have been tried before international criminal tribunals, i.e. aggression, crimes against humanity, genocide and war crimes. The most important thing about these crimes is covered by the Nuremberg IMT's dictum that:

> Crimes against international law are committed by men, not abstract entities, and only by punishing individuals who commits such crimes can the provisions of international law be enforced … individuals have international duties which transcend the national obligations of obedience imposed by the individual state.[4]

In other words, the fundamental point to understand about these crimes is that the locus of the criminal prohibition is not the domestic legal order, but the international one. States have decided that international law, in exceptional circumstances, ought to bypass the domestic legal order, and criminalise behaviour directly. Although doubt has occasionally been expressed on point, an international crime can be created by customary law,[5] or by treaties.[6]

2. Transnational Crimes

Transnational crimes, which are sometimes also called 'crimes of international concern' cover a broad range of conduct. The notable aspect of these crimes is that they are subject to an international legal requirement that States domestically criminalise the conduct at hand, and extradite or prosecute possible offenders. The fundamental

---

[3] Two useful discussions are Bruce Broomhall, *International Justice and the International Criminal Court: Between Sovereignty and the Rule of Law* (Oxford: OUP, 2003) pp. 10-23, and Neil Boister, 'Transnational Criminal Law' (2003) 14 *European Journal of International Law* 953.

[4] 'Nuremberg IMT: Judgment and Sentence' (1947) 41 *American Journal of International Law* 172, p. 221.

[5] See, e.g. Jean-Marie Henckaerts and Louise Doswald-Beck, *Customary International Humanitarian Law* (Cambridge: CUP, 2005) pp. 569-621. Some are more sceptical, see, e.g. Vladimir-Djuro Degan, 'On the Sources of International Criminal Law' (2005) 4 *Chinese Journal of International Law* 45, pp. 51, 64-73. Such a view is based on a strict, civilian interpretation of the *nullum crimen* principle and is inconsistent with at least half a century of judicial practice.

[6] *Prosecutor v Tadić*, Decision on Interlocutory Appeal on Jurisdiction, IT-94-1-AR72, 2 October 1995, para 94; *Prosecutor* v *Kordić and Čerkez*, Judgment, IT-95-14/2-A, 17 December 2004, paras. 40-46.

difference between these offences is that the relevant legal order that actually provides the criminal prohibition is the domestic, rather than international one. There is no individual liability for violation of the relevant international norm, but a State can be liable if it fails to criminalise the relevant conduct and deal with suspects in the mandated manner. Examples of such crimes include, for example, cutting submarine cables,[7] engaging in the slave trade,[8] hijacking[9] and trafficking in obscene materials.[10] Often the crimes covered under this rubric have little in common, other than the fact that it has been decided, or accepted, at some point that some form of international legal action ought to be taken to ensure States mutually suppress such behaviour.

This sometimes leads the subject to be considered coterminous with the body of law known as the 'suppression conventions'.[11] This is no longer, if it ever was, quite the case. There is the possibility that such treaties could enter the corpus of customary law.[12] There is little evidence of this happening often, but there is a possibility that aspects of the torture convention have done so.[13] More solidly, the Security Council, in its extraordinary Resolution 1373, practically legislated into being a suppression convention.[14] Although, formally, this means that the basis of the obligation is a treaty provision, namely Article 25 of the UN Charter, it shows that the United Nations Treaty Series[15] is not the sole repository of the law here.

Terrorism as a Transnational and/or an International Crime

1. Terrorism as a Transnational Crime[16]

It is well known that, in particular in the UN era, various acts of terrorism have been covered by a series of treaties,[17] such as the Tokyo Convention (which covers various acts against aviation),[18] the Hostages Convention[19] and the Convention on Crimes against Diplomatically Protected Persons.[20] Probably the most comprehensive of these,

---

[7] United Nations Convention on the Law of the Sea, (1999) UKTS 91, Articles 112-115.

[8] E.g. International Convention for the Suppression of the Traffic in Women and Children 9 LNTS 415.

[9] E.g. Hague Convention for the Suppression of Unlawful Acts Against the Safety of Civil Aviation 975 UNTS 177.

[10] E.g. Agreement for the Suppression of the Circulation of Obscene Publications of 4 May 1910, and Amended by the Protocol of 4 May 1949, 47 UNTS 159.

[11] See, e.g. see, Roger Clark, 'Offences of International Concern: Multilateral Treaty Practice in the Forty Years since Nuremberg' (1988) 47 *Nordic Journal of International Law* 49.

[12] Boister, *supra* n. 4 p. 963.

[13] As much might be extracted from *Prosecutor* v *Furundžija*, Judgment, IT-95-17/1-T, 10 December 1998, para 149. See also *A and Others* v *Secretary of State for the Home Department* [2005] UKHL 71, paras 33-34.

[14] See, Matthew Happold, 'Resolution 1373 and the Constitution of the United Nations' (2003) 16 *Leiden Journal of International Law* 593; Paul Szasz, 'The Security Council Starts Legislating' (2002) 96 *American Journal of International Law* 901; Stefan Talmon, 'The Security Council as World Legislator' (2005) 99 *American Journal of International Law* 175.

[15] And its historical analogues, for the older treaties.

[16] For an extremely useful overview see Robert Kolb, 'The Exercise of Extraterritorial Jurisdiction over International Terrorists' in Bianchi, *supra* n.3, 227, pp. 227-46.

[17] Although there are many regional treaties, this lecture concentrates on those open for ratification by all States.

[18] Convention on Offences and Certain Other Acts on Board Aircraft 704 UNTS 219.

[19] International Convention Against the Taking of Hostages, 1316 UNTS 305.

[20] Convention on the Prevention and Punishment of Crimes Against Internationally Protected Persons, Including Diplomatic Agents GA Res. 3166. For a compilation of other documents see M. Cherif Bassiouni (ed), *International Terrorism: A Compilation of UN Documents (1972-2001)* (New York: Transnational,

in terms of what is covered, is the crime contained in the 1997 Convention on Terrorist Bombings, Article 2 of which explains:

> 1. Any person commits an offence within the meaning of this Convention if that person unlawfully and intentionally delivers, places, discharges or detonates an explosive or other lethal device in, into or against a place of public use, a State or government facility, a public transportation system or an infrastructure facility:
>
> (a) With the intent to cause death or serious bodily injury; or
>
> (b) With the intent to cause extensive destruction of such a place, facility or system, where such destruction results in or is likely to result in major economic loss.
>
> 2. Any person also commits an offence if that person attempts to commit an offence as set forth in paragraph 1.
>
> 3. Any person also commits an offence if that person:
>
> (a) Participates as an accomplice in an offence as set forth in paragraph 1 or 2; or
>
> (b) Organizes or directs others to commit an offence as set forth in paragraph 1 or 2; or
>
> (c) In any other way contributes to the commission of one or more offences as set forth in paragraph 1 or 2 by a group of persons acting with a common purpose; such contribution shall be intentional and either be made with the aim of furthering the general criminal activity or purpose of the group or be made in the knowledge of the intention of the group to commit the offence or offences concerned.[21]

It is equally well known that, owing to the disagreements relating to whether or not actions undertaken in self-determination conflicts are to be covered, an omnibus definition of terrorism has yet to be brought into positive international law for the purpose of being incorporated into domestic criminal legislation.

The General Assembly, in 1994,[22] adopted a declaration on terrorism, which defined it as:

> Criminal acts intended or calculated to provoke a state of terror in the general public, a group of persons or particular persons for political purposes are in any circumstances unjustifiable, whatever the considerations of a political, philosophical, ideological, racial, ethnic, religious or other nature which may be invoked to justify them.

2002). There are also regionally based treaties, such as the 1977 European Convention on the Suppression of Terrorism 1137 UNTS 93; 1999 OAU Convention on the Prevention and Combating of Terrorism 1438 UNTS191 and the 1998 Arab Convention on the Suppression of Terrorism .

[21] It is true that Article 3 excludes the cases "where the offence is committed within a single State, the alleged offender and the victims are nationals of that State, the alleged offender is found in the territory of that State and no other State has a basis under article 6, paragraph 1, or article 6, paragraph 2, of this Convention to exercise jurisdiction". However, in such cases there will undoubtedly be domestic crimes which do not need additional interaction from the international legal order.

[22] Declaration on Measures to Eliminate International Terrorism (1994), GA Res. 49/60 (Annex).

However, as in basic international law, the General Assembly does not in itself create international law,[23] and there was no intention manifested in the Resolution that it was to set out a legal definition of terrorism. Indeed, had it sought to do so, it would probably not have achieved consensus. Still, it does give voice to two of the general aspects of the treaties to date that actually require States to criminalise certain terroristic acts. The first is that they tend to be acts that are already criminal under most domestic penal codes, and secondly that they are also committed with a specific intent to cause fear.

It is true that the 1999 International Convention for the Suppression of the Financing of Terrorism, in addition to setting out particular acts, drawn from the terrorism treaties, also provides a more generic definition of terrorism, that it is made up by:

> Act[s] intended to cause death or serious bodily injury to a civilian, or to any other person not taking an active part in the hostilities in a situation of armed conflict, when the purpose of such act, by its nature or context, is to intimidate a population, or to compel a government or an international organization to do or to abstain from doing an act.[24]

However, this Treaty does not, in itself, require states to criminalise those acts, but criminalise their funding, hence the definition is only, as yet, for a specialised purpose. Negotiations on a general treaty to criminalise terrorism generically have yet to lead to a result.[25] Therefore, although it cannot be said that there is a transnational 'crime' of terrorism *per se*, a large number of the manifestations of terrorism are subject to State obligations to domestically prosecute and punish. However, unless they can be considered reflective of customary international law (which is a very controversial proposition), the obligations those treaties contain are limited to the parties to those conventions.

In one circumstance, the Security Council has attempted to overcome this problem. Consistent with its increasing concern with terrorism, which began in relation to the Lockerbie Bombing, the Security Council condemned the attacks on the United States on 11 September 2001 in Resolution 1368.[26] Very soon after (on the 28th September), the Security Council issued Resolution 1373, which, in all but name, legislated into being a regime for the suppression of financing of terrorism that paralleled that of 1999.[27] This resolution binds all UN member States, and imposes mandatory obligations on them to suppress the financing of terrorism and co-operate in preventing it. Although few doubt the advisability of such measures being brought into being, concerns have been expressed both about the extent to which such measures can be implemented consistently with States' human rights obligations,[28] and the ability of the Security Council to legislate in this manner (although this latter matter is

---

[23] *Advisory Opinion on the Legality of the Threat or Use of Nuclear Weapons* [1996] ICJ Rep. 4, pp. 254-5, para 70.

[24] International Convention for the Suppression of the Financing of Terrorism, General Assembly Resolution 54/109, Article 2(a). See Antonio Cassese, 'Terrorism as an International Crime' in Bianchi *supra* n. 2, 213, p. 215.

[25] Helen Duffy, *The 'War on Terror' and the Framework of International Law* (Cambridge: CUP, 2005) pp. 20-23. See also Becker, *supra* n.2 chapter 4.

[26] UN Doc. S/RES/1368 (12 September 2001).

[27] UN Doc. S/RES/1373 (28 September 2001).

[28] See e.g. Robert Cryer, Hakan Friman, Darryl Robinson and Elizabeth Wilmshurst, *An Introduction to International Criminal Law and Procedure* (Cambridge: CUP, 2007) pp. 291-2.

controversial).[29] Even so, this is far from implementing a comprehensive and universal system for suppressing terrorism.

2. Terrorism by Another Name

From the point of view of international crimes, there are a number of different terroristic acts which, committed with the relevant *mens rea* and against the background of the relevant contextual circumstance may be international crimes. To begin, there are war crimes of taking hostages, and acts of terror committed in international and non-international armed conflicts are specifically criminalised directly by international law.[30] In particular, Article 51 of Additional Protocol I and Article 13(2) of Additional Protocol II both proscribe 'Acts or threats of violence the primary purpose of which is to spread terror among the civilian population.'[31] On the basis of Article 51 and an (unnecessary) evaluation of whether there was a separate rule criminalising serious violations of that rule, the ICTY in the *Galić* case averred that there was a separate war crime of terror attacks with the following elements:

1. Acts of violence directed against the civilian population or individual civilians not taking direct part in hostilities causing death or serious injury to body or health within the civilian population.
2. The offender wilfully made the civilian population or individual civilians not taking direct part in hostilities the object of those acts of violence.
3. The above offence was committed with the primary purpose of spreading terror among the civilian population'.[32]

A perfectly reasonable case can be made that the war crime concerned does not require that death or serious injury be caused, and that proof of a serious violation of the particular article is sufficient.[33] Whether or not this is the case need not cause delay here, the point is not which definition is accurate, but that there is such a war crime. Similarly, a number of terroristic acts can amount to crimes against humanity so long as they come under one of the relevant proscribed acts and are committed with the relevant nexus to a widespread or systematic attack on the civilian population.[34] Although the specific intent for genocide is difficult to establish, and if the view is taken that some form of plan or collective action is required for genocide this raises the threshold for the crime,[35] there is no reason in principle why an act intended to terrorise

---

[29] See Mathew Happold, 'Resolution 1373 and the Constitution of the United Nations' (2003) 16 *Leiden Journal of International Law* 593 *contra* Paul Szasz, 'The Security Council Starts Legislating' (2002) 96 *American Journal of International Law* 901.

[30] Hans-Peter Gasser, 'Prohibition of Terrorist Acts in International Humanitarian Law' (1986) 253 *International Review of the Red Cross* 200.

[31] Measures of intimidation and terrorism against civilians protected by Geneva Convention IV are contrary to Article 33 of that Convention.

[32] *Prosecutor* v *Galić*, Judgment and Opinion, IT-98-29-T, 5 December 2003, para 136. This was upheld on Appeal, see *Prosecutor* v *Galić*, Judgment, IT-98-29-A, 30 November 2006, paras 79-104.

[33] Cassese, *supra* n. 25, pp. 221-22.

[34] See, e.g. Mark Drumbl, 'Judging the 11 September Terrorist Attack' (2002) 24 *Human Rights Quarterly* 232; although see W.A. Schabas, 'Is Terrorism a Crime Against Humanity?' (2002) 8 *International Peacekeeping: The Yearbook of International Peace Operations* 255.

[35] See, e.g. J. R. W. D. Jones 'Whose Intent Is It Anyway? Genocide and the Intent to Destroy a Group' in Lal Chang Vohrah *et al.* (eds.), *Man's Inhumanity to Man: Essays in Honour of Antonio Cassese* (The Hague: Kluwer, 2003) 467; Valerie Oosterveld, 'The Context of Genocide' in Roy S. Lee (ed.), *The International Criminal Court: Elements of Crimes and Rules of Procedure and Evidence* (New York: Transnational, 2001) 44.

the civilian population could not also fulfil the definition of genocide. The intent to terrorise which characterises terrorism does not exclude a genocidal intent, and that intent may co-exist with other intentions and motivations.[36]

However, this is not the end of the matter for some scholars, who believe that, in addition to this, terrorism has also matured into a fully fledged international crime in its own right, rather than being the description of activity which can be brought under the rubric of other international crimes. Primary amongst these scholars is sometime President of the ICTY and the Darfur Commission, Antonio Cassese.[37] Cassese takes the view that there is a discrete international crime:

> When (i) they are not limited in their effects to one State solely, but *transcend national boundaries* as far as the persons implicated, the means employed and the violence involved are concerned and (ii) are carried out with the support, the toleration or acquiescence of the State where the terrorist organization is located or of a foreign State … [are] … (iii) a phenomenon of concern for the *whole international community* and a threat to the peace … (iv) are *very serious or large scale*.[38]

Mindful of the principle of legality, Cassese also provides a definition of this offence. It is that the acts:

> Constitute a criminal offence under most national legal systems (for example assault, murder, kidnapping, hostage-taking, extortion, bombing, torture, arson, etc.); (ii) … aimed at spreading terror…by means of the threat or use of violent action among the public or particular groups of persons and (iii) … be politically, ideologically or religiously motivated, that is not motivated by private ends … As for the *mens rea* … In addition to the subjective element required for the underlying offence…there must be a *special intent*, that is, to spread terror among the population.[39]

This is an interesting and controversial proposal. It also deals with one of the most difficult aspects of international criminal law, how an international crime originally comes into being. In spite of its merits, the suggestion that there is a separate international crime of terrorism does not reflect the *lex lata*. There is no treaty that makes this clear, and State practice and *opinio juris* is, as yet, insufficient to ground such a direct liability crime in international criminal law. This is not to say that it may not in the future, but as things stand, it has yet to crystallise into existing law.

Conclusions

Terrorism is unquestionably a matter upon which States need to cooperate if they are to suppress it. That necessity has long been accepted. The necessity of doing so has only increased since the September 11 attacks. International law has, through a succession of treaties dealing with manifestations of terrorism, placed a complex web of obligations on States with respect to terrorist offences. However, although ratification of those

---

[36] *Proseuctor* v *Niyetegeka* Judgment, ICTR-96-14-A, 9 July 2004 para 53.

[37] Cassese, *supra* n. 25. A similar suggestion is made in Jordan Paust, 'Terrorism as an International Crime' in Guiseppe Nesi, *International Cooperation in Counter-Terrorism* (Aldershot: Ashgate, 2005) 25.

[38] *Ibid.*, p. 223.

[39] *Ibid.*, p. 224.

treaties is quite high, not all States are parties to all, or enough, of them, and those that have ratified them are not always solicitous of their obligations. Furthermore, although negotiations on a comprehensive terrorism treaty are ongoing, this is admittedly with limited success, although it might be questioned whether the more appropriate route to take would be to encourage ratifications of the existing treaties rather than to expend the relevant diplomatic energy on chasing what may turn out to be a will-o-the-wisp. The Security Council, the General Assembly and the Secretary-General have all engaged themselves considerably with issues related to terrorism. However, all this together does not in itself make terrorism an international crime giving rise to individual liability in international law. Where terrorism is subsumed under other international crimes, the considerations that apply to international crimes apply equally to any terrorist offences that fall under that rubric. However, so far, States and international organisations dealing with terrorism have done so through the mechanisms of transnational, rather than international, criminality, with all the consequences that entails. Whether they are right to do so or not is a different question.[40]

[40] At least one strong argument in favour of some form of international oversight of terrorism prosecutions (other than such supervision as is undertaken by the international human rights bodies) is that a body entitled to appraise the substantive law applied would be able to highlight unfortunate or inappropriate uses of the law, even if it adopts a deferential attitude to governmental action. See Eyal Benvenisti, 'National Courts and the 'War on Terrorism'' in Bianchi (ed), *supra* n. 3, 309.

Legal Aspects of Combating Terrorism
Centre of Excellence Defence Against Terrorism, Ankara, Turkey (Ed.)
IOS Press, 2008

doi:10.3233/978-1-58603-930-1-23

The United Nations and the Challenge of Combating International Terrorism

Assist.-Prof. Isaac KFIR
Lauder School of Government, Diplomacy and Strategy, Interdisciplinary Centre; Senior Researcher, International Institute for Counter-Terrorism, Herzliya, Israel

Abstract. The article discusses the United Nation's approach to international terrorism in the post-9/11 world. It opens by defining the term post-modern terrorism and then moves on to look at the role of the Security Council, the General Assembly and the Secretary-General in devising a programme that deals with the threat posed by Islamic terrorism. The aim of the article is to emphasise that the United Nations operates in three different areas in the war against terrorism: force, morality and economic and social assistance. The paper concludes by arguing that the UN has made a start but much more needs to be done.

Keywords. Combating international terrorism, United Nations, al-Qa'ida.

Introduction

The al-Qa'ida sponsored terrorist attacks on September 11, 2001 made it clear that international terrorism poses a real and serious threat to the maintenance of international peace and security.[1] Thus, what had been considered a regional or state problem was suddenly propelled to become a central issue in international politics demanding not only substantial and purposeful discussion but more importantly action. Central to this new need for action has been the role of the United Nations, which arguably embraced the challenge posed by international terrorism by calling for new ideas and demanding action. Conversely, international terrorism has also shown the shortcomings of the United Nations in dealing with such a complex issue.[2]

Prior to 9/11, the United Nations largely treated terrorism as a national or regional problem enabling it to focus on specific terror acts such as the Lockerbie Bombing,[3] the attempted assassination of President Mubarak,[4] or the bombing of the American embassies in East Africa.[5] To express its outrage and deal with the aforementioned terror incidents, the Security Council used sanctions against those supporting or

---

[1] See for example the wording of Security Council Resolution 1368 (2001) adopted hours after the attack.

[2] The major problem has been in the realm of defining the concept of terrorism; something that the UN's Legal (Sixth) Committee has sought to do since the mid-1970s.

[3] Security Council Resolution 748, adopted on March 31, 1992.

[4] Security Council Resolution 1054, adopted on April 26, 1996.

[5] Jane Boulden and Thomas G. Weiss. "Whither Terrorism and the United Nations?" Jane Boulden and Thomas G. Weiss. (ed.) *Terrorism and the UN: Before and After September 11.* (Bloomington: Indiana University Press, 2004), pp. 3-26.

assisting terrorists.[6] However, 9/11 demanded a new approach, as seen with Security Council Resolution 1368 (2001),[7] which largely closed the door on the use of Chapter VI to deal with terrorist threats to international peace and security.[8]

The aim of this article is to examine how the United Nations has sought to deal with the scourge of the twenty-first century: international terrorism of the al-Qa'ida model, as al-Qa'ida has increasingly posed a threat to the maintenance of international peace and security. One cannot think of another terror entity that has undermined global security to the magnitude of al-Qa'ida, which explains why the Security Council began taking action against the organisation prior to 9/11.[9] The paper is composed of three key sections: first, it examines what is international terrorism, exploring the key concepts and its aims. In the second part, the author looks at how the United Nations has sought to combat international terrorism by looking at: the Security Council and its role in demanding action through resolution 1373; the role of the Secretary-General; and finally, the role of UN conventions in combating terrorism. The author concludes by arguing that the United Nations has made some progress in the realm of combating international terrorism, however, due to the nature of the organisation, unless member states embrace a new agenda of greater cooperation, the UN will increasingly lose its influence in the campaign against international terrorism.

Defining International Terrorism

The concept of terrorism has existed in one way or another for over millennia. It is a highly divisive and illusive concept, with scholars, politicians and laypersons repeatedly stating the age-old mantra: 'one man's terrorist is another man's freedom fighter'. Consequently, there have been various attempts to define the concept of terrorism with the premise being that once a definition exists, one would be able to counter the phenomenon.

---

[6] See for example David Cortright and George A. Lopez. *The Sanctions Decade: Assessing UN Strategies in the 1990s*. (London: Lynne Rienner Publishers, 2000). The authors argue that imposition of sanctions on Libya encouraged Qaddafi to abandon terrorism.

[7] The importance of Resolution 1368 comes from its vagueness, allowing countries a wider scope vis-à-vis terrorist threats. Professor Oudraat has noted that President Putin has used Resolution 1368 to justify possible Russian action against Georgia. Chantal de Jonge Oudraat. "The Role of the Security Council." Jane Boulden and Thomas G. Weiss. (ed.) *Terrorism and the UN: Before and After September 11*. (Bloomington: Indiana University Press, 2004), p. 165. China somewhat surprisingly voted in favour of the resolution, as the Chinese traditionally oppose (or at least abstain) when it comes to the dispatch of international forces. Rosemary Foot. *Human Rights and Counter-Terrorism in America's Asia Policy. Adelphi Paper 363* (Oxford: Oxford University Press, 2004), p. 10.

[8] The resolution while calling for collaboration also enabled the United States to use the defence of self-defence to initiate military action against the Taliban and al-Qa'ida in Afghanistan. In the words of one commentator, "Resolution 1368 legitimizes the unilateral use of force against terrorist attacks. The U.S. appears to think of this resolution as a blank check. In its letter to the Security Council informing it of its action against al-Qa'ida and the Taliban – as it was required to do by Article 51 of the UN Charter – the U.S. hinted that action might be taken against other targets." Chantal de Jonge Oudraat. "The Role of the Security Council." Jane Boulden and Thomas G. Weiss. (ed.) *Terrorism and the UN: Before and After September 11*. (Bloomington: Indiana University Press, 2004), p. 164; Security Council Resolution 1368, S/Res/1368 (2001). A day after 9/11, Jean-Marie Colombani declared in *Le Monde* "Nous sommes tous Américains" ("We are all Americans").

[9] The Security Council in 1999 adopted Security Council Resolution 1267, designed to deal with the threat posed by al-Qa'ida.

Defining international terrorism is determined by two key issues, the theoretical and the practical. Put simply, it is relatively easy to formulate a definition, but it is more difficult to apply it and enforce it without any exception. Yet, one must also distinguish between pre-9/11 terrorist and post-9/11 terrorists. The former focused either on attaining a political (ideological) agenda such as the Italian Red Brigade or the American Symbionese Liberation Army. In the pre-9/11 period there were also ethno-nationalist movements, such as the Free Aceh Movement (GLA) or the Moro National Liberation Front.[10] The al-Qa'ida terrorists have an unwavering agenda as they strive to establish *shar'ia* across the world and to that end, they are willing to engage in acts of violence unparallel in human history. Their commitment and devotion to their cause is total and they are willing to spend years preparing for a single operation, as seen with the 9/11 terrorists. They operate in small cells, sometimes with no direct or even indirect link to the leaders of the movement, as what motivates them is the ideology expounded by clerics, quasi-clerics and ideologues.[11] A subsidiary theme is that definitions of terrorism exist, however they exist on either a national (domestic) level or a regional level.[12] This raises the issue of a lack of consistent definition which hampers the campaign against international terrorism. As things stand, it appears that the search for a universal definition of terrorism is a bridge too far, and the international community must come to terms with this serious deficiency.

An Overview of the UN and Terrorism Prior to 9/11

The 1267 Committee and the Monitoring Group / Team

On October 15, 1999, the United Nations Security Council adopted Resolution 1267, emphasising the increasing concern of the international community over the continuous violations of human rights, gender discrimination, opium production, and the murder of Iranian diplomats and a journalist in Mazar-e-Sharif in Afghanistan by the Taliban. Resolution 1267 also held that the failure of the Taliban movement to surrender Osama bin Laden to the United States following America's extradition request breached international peace and security. Consequently, the Council justified the imposition of selective sanctions on the Taliban movement.[13] For geopolitical considerations or merely *Realpolitik* the Security Council chose not to take action against those who supported and facilitated the rise of the Taliban, mainly the Pakistani Inter-Service Intelligence (ISI).[14] In 1999, the members of the Security Council and the UN largely

---

[10] See for example Walter Laqueur. *The New Terrorism: Fanaticism and the Arms of Mass Destruction*. (London: Phoenix Press, 2001); Bruce Hoffman. *Inside Terrorism*. (New York: Columbia University Press, 2006); Walter Laqueur. *The History of Terrorism*. (London: Transaction Publishers, 2002).

[11] See for example Marc Sageman. *Understanding Terror Networks*. (Philadelphia: University of Pennsylvania Press, 2004).

[12] The African Union, the Organisation of Islamic Conference, and the European Union have all adopted their own definitions of what is terrorism.

[13] The aviation sanctions excluded humanitarian aid or religious obligations such as Islamic pilgrimage. Security Council Resolution 1267 (1999). It is noteworthy that in 1999 the Taliban did not control the whole of Afghanistan, which raises the issue of whether they were the government of the country.

[14] On the ISI's role in creating the Taliban, see for example, Michael Rubin. "Who is Responsible for the Taliban?." *Middle East Review of International Affairs*. Vol. 6, No. 1 (March 2002), pp. 1-16; Ahmed Rashid. *Taliban: The Story of the Afghan Warlords*. (London: Pan Books, 2001); Martin Ewans. *Afghanistan: A Short History of its People and Politics*. (London: Perennial Press, 2002).

failed to recognise the Taliban and their ideology as an international problem, but rather saw them as a national (Afghanistan) or regional (South Asian) problem.[15]

Experience with sanctions had taught the Security Council that imposing them is insufficient, as they also require a monitoring regime,[16] and thus the Council ensured the formation of a sanctions committee.[17] The Committee of Experts led to the formation of the Monitoring Group based in New York, composed of five experts, including a Chairman and a 15-member Sanctions Enforcement Support Team, with the support team located in Afghanistan's neighbouring states and composed of experts in border security, counter-terrorism and customs.[18]

The Group monitored the implementation of all the measures imposed by resolutions 1267 (1999) and 1333 (2000), including arms embargoes, counter-terrorism related legislation and, in view of the link to the purchase of arms and financing of terrorism, money laundering, financial transactions and drug trafficking.[19] Security Council Resolution 1333 emphasised the Council's determination to use non-military means (Chapter VI) to persuade the Taliban to accept some international norms, without really castigating the religious aspects of the Taliban movement, which abhors many of the values of Western liberal society. Moreover, it required all states to report within 30 days of the resolution coming into force on how they have dealt with its various demands (sanctions).

9/11 changed some of the focus of the 1267 Committee and of the Monitoring Group as the international community realised that its previous efforts to counter the spread of al-Qa'ida had been insufficient. Security Council Resolution 1390 expanded the remit of the Monitoring Group beyond Afghanistan to cover individuals and entities belonging to or associated with al-Qa'ida, Bin Laden or the Taliban.[20] By January 2003, the Council determined that it needed to improve the implementation measures imposed by Resolutions 1267 (1999), 1333 (2000) and 1392 (2002), and it adopted Resolution 1455 (2003), which incorporated new measures against Bin Laden, al-Qa'ida and the Taliban.[21]

The 1267 Committee, the Monitoring Group and the Monitoring Team highlight the determination of the Security Council to engage al-Qa'ida and its associates in a process that involves sanctions and a 'naming and shaming' campaign against countries that harbour al-Qa'idaists. The reports initially submitted by the Monitoring Group and later on by the Monitoring Team are highly informative and offer a review of the international campaign against al-Qa'ida and the Taliban. Furthermore, using the Consolidated List assists in emphasising the global threat that al-Qa'ida poses, as entities and individuals that make the List come from various countries and backgrounds. In other words, the List does not focus on a particular state, region, race,

---

[15] Afghanistan was largely left to international non-governmental organisations and inter-governmental organisations, as the international community concentrated on other issues, such as the collapse of the Soviet Union, the democratisation process in Eastern Europe and the deteriorating situation in the Gulf region.

[16] David Cortright and George A. Lopez. *The Sanctions Decade: Assessing UN Strategies in the 1990s.* (London: Lynne Rienner Publishers, 2000).

[17] Security Council Resolution S/Res/1267 (1999) October 15, 1999. See paragraph 6 of the resolution.

[18] Security Council Resolution S/Res/1363 (2001) July 30, 2001.

[19] Security Council Resolution S/Res/1363 (2001) July 30, 2001.

[20] Security Council Resolution S/Res/1390 (2002) January 16, 2002.

[21] Security Council Resolution 1455 covered the freezing of financial and economic assets, travel bans, and arms embargo and demanded that all member states apply the measures against individuals and entities that the Sanctions Committee designated Al-Qa'ida or Taliban. Security Council Resolution S/Res/1455 (2003) January 17, 2003.

religion or culture, as anyone can make the List. The List and reports are useful 'open source' facilities, providing pertinent information on terrorist organisations/affiliations and counter-terrorism measures. The problem however is that the List is not composed of criminals but rather of individuals and entities that have engaged or supported al-Qa'ida or the Taliban.[22] Secondly, because the focus is on al-Qa'ida and the Taliban it allows such terrorist organisations as *Jemaah Islamiyah*, *Hizbollah* and others to continue their violent campaigns.

The Security Council's Role: The Counter-Terrorism Committee and Counter-Terrorism Executive Directorate

On September 28, 2001, Security Council Resolution 1373 (2001) marked a watershed in the global campaign against terrorism. The Council, through the resolution, placed a responsibility on its member-states to impose measures against acts of terrorism and against the perpetrators, sponsors and facilitators. Resolution 1373 called on member states to cease providing any financial assistance or physical support to terrorists. It further obligated countries to assist one another through information sharing, prosecution of terrorists and ratification of international conventions.[23] 1373 began a process that led to further Security Council Resolutions to counter international terrorism, as seen for example with 1456 (2003) and 1526 (2004).

A key feature of Resolution 1373 is the creation of the Counter-Terrorism Committee (CTC) which is tasked with the duty of monitoring the member-states' implementation of 1373 and, where necessary, to provide them with relevant technical assistance. The approach vis-à-vis 1373 is a piecemeal one, centring on three key stages: Stage A examines whether a state has the necessary legislation needed to combat terrorism, with emphasis on terrorist financing. The next stage, (Stage B), explores the entire anti-terrorist programme of the state, examining mainly what the executive machinery is doing to prevent terrorist recruitment, movement, safe-havens and whatever else may assist terrorists or their organisations. The final stage, (Stage C), focuses on monitoring the compliance and implementation of Resolution 1373, which includes ratifying international conventions and protocols relating to terrorism, enhancing information sharing, etc.[24]

Within the realm of technical assistance, the CTC established two programmes: the CTC Assistance Matrix and the Directory. The Matrix acts as a centralised, comprehensive indicator of states' needs and it provides information on programmes that countries have to combat terrorism. The Directory is a compilation of information on standards, best practices and sources of assistance in the area of counter-terrorism. These two facilities assist the implementation of 1373 by providing states with a pool of information.[25]

On March 26, 2004, the Security Council adopted Resolution 1535, establishing the Counter-Terrorism Executive Directorate (CTED). The objective behind the

---

[22] "Third report of the Analytical Support and Sanctions Monitoring Team appointed pursuant to resolution 1526 (2004) concerning Al-Qa'ida and the Taliban and associated individuals and entities." UN Security Council S/2005/572. September 9, 2005. (05-40794 (E) 150905), p. 15.

[23] "Note by the Chairman." of the CTC, October 16, 2001. (S/AC.40/2001/CRP.1).

[24] Security Council Resolution 1373 (2001) September 28, 2001.

[25] CTC Directory of Counter-Terrorism Information and Sources of Assistance. Available on line at: http://www.un.org/Docs/sc/committees/1373/ctc_da/index.html

creation of another UN body was to strengthen the CTC's efforts. The CTED aids with coordinating the capacity and efforts of international, regional and sub-regional organisations and brokering assistance to those states that need help to meet their 1373 obligations.[26] The work of the CTC and the CTED resulted in:[27]

- Every member state has submitted at least one report (some countries have issued as many as four reports following queries by the CTC) on their efforts to comply with Resolution 1373.[28]
- International, regional and sub-regional institutions have provided the Committee with information on compliance with Resolution 1373.[29]
- Since 9/11, there has been a substantial increase (between 20-40 per cent) in the ratification of counter-terrorism conventions, as seen for example with the Convention for the Suppression of Terrorist Bombing (1997), in which membership rose from 28 countries to 115; the Convention for the Suppression of the Financing of Terrorism (1999), saw ratification increase twenty-fold from five to 117 countries.
- As of March 31, 2004, approximately 100 countries had expressed an interest in technical assistance to fight terrorism.

The CTC and the CTED face many challenges, however progress to date has been (by UN standards) impressive. Countries and international, regional and sub-regional organisations have all submitted reports on their progress, or lack of it, vis-à-vis the implementation of 1373. Furthermore, countries and organisations have ratified international conventions relating to terrorism, which assist in the development and formulation of a concrete global campaign against international terrorism. The CTC has sponsored regional conferences and engaged countries in reviewing their counter-terrorism programmes and legislations. The ability of the CTC to ask countries to explain their legislations and elaborate on their programmes assists in receiving a proper understanding of how states approach counter-terrorism. From the reports, it is abundantly clear that most countries have adopted some measures to deal with terrorist funding and money laundering. For example, the CTC has provided the Asia Pacific Economic Cooperation (APEC), with guidance and assistance in relation to 1373.[30] 1373 also led to a change in Africa with the African Union (AU) reporting that since the 1990s, and even more so since 9/11, African countries "...have adjusted their national legislation with provisions in their penal codes and in some cases, specific anti-terrorism bills have been articulated to criminalize, punish and suppress crimes of terrorism including the financing, dissemination of information, establishment of

---

[26] See for example, "Report by the Chair of the Counter-Terrorism Committee on the Problems encountered in the implementation of Security Council resolution 1373 (2001)." – Security Council CTC, January 26, 2004, S/2004/70. See also, "Proposal for the revitalisation of the Counter-Terrorism Committee." UN Security Council CTC, February 19, 2004, (S/2004/124).

[27] CTED "Countering Terrorism: Progress and Challenge." UN Department of Public Information, January 2005 (DPI/2375B).
Available on line at: http://www.un.org/News/dh/infocus/terrorism/CTED_progress_and_challenges.pdf

[28] On the state's reports see the website:
http://www.un.org/Docs/sc/committees/1373/submitted_reports.html

[29] "Index of International, Regional and Subregional Organizations." United Nations Security Council, (S/AC 40/2003/SM.1/2).

[30] See for example the statement "United Nations Counter-Terrorism Committee Technical Assistance Programme" by Helene Seligman, Technical Assistance Team, UNCTC to APEC Counter Terrorism Task Force, Phuket, August 20, 2003; "Counter Terrorism Action Plan Combined Report from APEC Fora." Senior Official's Meeting, Bangkok Thailand, October 14-15, 2003. (2003/CSOM/025)

associations or groups that support or harbour and encourage participation in terrorist-related activities."[31]

The CTC and the CTED have been criticised for many things, but it starts with CTC itself expressing unhappiness with the 'Stage' Process being artificial and hindering its monitoring duties. The CTC holds that the 'stages' are interconnected and that a better way to determine implementation of 1373 is to examine the states' legislative and operational programmes, rather than taking one step at a time.[32] Interestingly, the Committee has failed to challenge countries known to harbour and support terrorist organisations. Taking Syria as an example, in the four reports submitted by Syria since December 2001, the Committee has failed to ask Syria to explain the presence of such organisations as the *Hamas*, *Hizbollah* and *Islamic Jihad* in Damascus.

Moreover, the CTC depends on cooperation, transparency and even-handedness as it is an intergovernmental entity, with no enforcement powers beyond the written word.[33] The international community may chastise a country that refuses to abide by the CTC ruling, but, it is unlikely that the international community will take more stringent actions against the country's failure to do as the CTC directs. Finally, the reports themselves vary in their usefulness, as some simply say very little about the state's counter-terrorism programmes.[34] The African Union claimed that implementing 1373 has "...been constrained by certain prevailing factors in the continent, such as conflict and political instability, diversity in African legal traditions, poverty and poor standard of technology, and budgetary constraints in many member States."[35]

The Secretary-General: Policy Working Group on the United Nations and Terrorism

In October 2001, Secretary-General Kofi Annan established the Policy Working Group on the United Nations and Terrorism (PWG) to identify the implications of terrorism and provide broad policy dimensions to enable the United Nations to prioritise its activities in combating terrorism.[36] The PWG called on the organisation to adopt a tripartite strategy of dissuasion, denial and cooperation.

---

[31] "Index of International, Regional and Subregional Organizations." UN Security Council, (S/AC. 40/2003/SM.1/2).

[32] "Report by the Chair of the Counter-Terrorism Committee on the Problems encountered in the implementation of Security Council resolution 1373 (2001)." UN Security Council, January 26, 2004, S/2004/70. The report provides other criticism.

[33] "Note by the Chairman." of the CTC, October 16, 2001 (S/AC. 40/2001/CRP.1),

[34] Some commentators have viewed the reports as a way for states to highlight what they want from the international community. Karin von Hippel. "Improving the International Response to Transnational Terrorist Threat." Jane Boulden and Thomas G. Weiss. (ed.) *Terrorism and the UN: Before and After September 11*. (Bloomington: Indiana University Press, 2004), pp. 102-119.

[35] "Index of International, Regional and Subregional Organizations." UN Security Council. (S/ACHANTAL 40/2003/SM.1/2).

[36] "Report of the Policy Working Group on the United Nations and Terrorism." UN Security Council (A/57/273-S/2002/875)

Dissuasion

The dissuasion process emphasises the use of international legal instruments such as the protection of human rights[37] and the twelve UN conventions on counter-terrorism. States and aggrieved persons must know that there are international norms to aid them in times of injustice, thus discouraging people from turning to violence to settle their grievances.[38] The PWG's view is that ratification of UN conventions aides the counter-terrorism campaign by uniting states in publicly rejecting terrorism. Dissuasion relies on the wealthier and stronger members supporting the weaker ones, as resolutions, ideas and programmes amount to nothing without money and political will. The programme of 'Strengthening the Legal Regime against Terrorism' that began in January 2003 and ended in December 2006 is a good example of dissuasion as it actively encourages and assists states to ratify international conventions that deal with terrorism and basic rights.[39]

Denial

The PWG stressed the importance of the 'Programme of Action' adopted in July 2001 by the United Nations Conference on the Illicit Trade in Small Arms and Light Weapons. The Convention aims to combat the illicit trade in small arms and light weapons, which appeal to terrorists, as they are inexpensive, durable and easy to carry and conceal.[40] This issue is linked to the PWG's belief that terrorism is the result of an armed conflict. The PWG holds that by dealing effectively with an immediate crisis, the international community forestalls the possibility of terrorists using the crisis for recruitment or creating a base of operation.[41] Afghanistan is a prime example of the importance of structural prevention. The international community chose not to take progressive action in Afghanistan following the Soviet withdrawal. Anarchy soon ensued, which created favourable conditions for the Taliban to rise, as the Taliban fought lawlessness and warlordism.[42] More recently, the continued presence of coalition forces in Iraq and the failure to stem the violence has created an 'Afghanistan effect'—men (some of European extraction) are heading to Iraq to fight against the coalition forces.[43] Yet, despite mounting casualties and financial costs, the United

---

[37] Terrorism is a violation of human rights (Article 6), International Covenant on Civil and Political Rights, (1966).

[38] "Report of the Policy Working Group on the United Nations and Terrorism." UN Security Council (A/57/273-S/2002/875).

[39] The work of the UN and its specialised agencies led to a rise in ratification of UN conventions, which emphasise UN commitment to ideals of the Policy Working Group. "Strengthening the Legal Regime against Terrorism." UN Office on Drugs and Crime, (FS/GLO/02/R35). "Report of the Policy Working Group on the United Nations and Terrorism." UN Security Council (A/57/273-S/2002/875); Karin von Hippel. "Improving the International Response to Transnational Terrorist Threat." Jane Boulden and Thomas G. Weiss. (ed.) *Terrorism and the UN: Before and After September 11*. (Bloomington: Indiana University Press, 2004), pp. 102-119.

[40] "Report of the United Nations Conference on the Illicit Trade in Small Arms and Light Weapons in All Its Aspects." July 9-20, 2001. (A/CONF.192/15).

[41] "Report of the Policy Working Group on the United Nations and Terrorism." UN Security Council (A/57/273-S/2002/875); "Prevention of Armed Conflict" Report of the Secretary General, 2001." (A/55/985-S/2001/574).

[42] Ahmed Rashid. *Taliban: The Story of the Afghan Warlords*. (London: Pan Books, 2001); Martin Ewans. *Afghanistan: A Short History of its People and Politics*. (London: Perennial Press, 2002).

[43] Peter Beaumont. "Insurgents Trawl Europe for Recruits." *The Observer* June 19, 2005; Nick Fielding. "European Terror Network Sends 'Martyrs' to Iraq." *The Times*. June 19, 2005.

States and its allies have remained steadfast in their commitment to rebuilding Afghanistan and Iraq, repeatedly emphasising that democracy and freedom will defeat al-Qa'ida terrorism.

Cooperation

The third leg in the strategy calls for enhanced cooperation, which resulted in multilateral and regional organisations launching a host of counter-terrorism initiatives to compliment existing international conventions on terrorism.[44] The PWG looked at the cooperation that existed in the European Union (EU) between the police and the judiciary, which led to such measures as the common arrest warrant,[45] the common list of terrorist organisations, routine exchange of information, joint investigative teams, etc.[46] The PWG argued that the greater the cooperation, the greater the reward.

The General Assembly Contribution

In 2004, the High-Level Panel on Threats, Challenges and Change chaired by the former Thai Prime Minister, Anand Panyarachum, was a General Assembly initiative that explored the challenges faced by the world following the end of the Cold War, the tumultuous 1990s and 9/11. The Report issued by the Panel declared that, "Sixty years later, we know all too well that the biggest security threats we face now, and in the decades ahead, go far beyond States waging aggressive war. They extend to poverty, infectious disease and environmental degradation; war and violence within States; the spread and possible use of nuclear, radiological, chemical and biological weapons; terrorism; and transnational organized crime. The threats are from non-State actors as well as States, and to human security as well as State security."[47]

The Report focused on such matters as collective security, conflict prevention, terrorism, the United Nations and the issue of reform of the organisation. Overall, the Panel contributed to the long-running debate on what is the best way to deal with terrorists; a debate that has divided Europe and the United States. Europeans hold that terrorism thrives in environments where there is despair, humiliation, poverty, political oppression, extensive human rights abuses, foreign occupation and weak state control, all of which hinder the state's ability to control law and order and provide basic services. Europeans therefore want to address the root causes of terrorism. Americans on the other hand emphasise the military option in defeating terrorism, which means focusing on the physical destruction of terrorist cells, as seen in Iraq and Afghanistan. American policymakers stress the need for establishing a stable economic, social and

---

[44] Osman Yavuzalp. "Working with Partners to Fight Terrorism." *NATO Review*. (Spring 2003); *Partnership Action Plan against Terrorism*. (Prague: NATO Basic Text: November 22, 2002).

[45] The decision of the German Constitutional Court to block the extradition of Mamoun Darkazanli to Spain on charges that he helped raise money for al-Qa'ida led to serious doubts as to the effectiveness of the European common arrest warrant. The Court held that under Article 16 of the German Constitution a German citizen could only face extradition in exceptional circumstances. *The Guardian*. July 19, 2005.

[46] "Report of the Policy Working Group on the United Nations and Terrorism." UN Security Council (A/57/273-S/2002/875).

[47] "A More Secure World." Report of the High-level Panel on Threats, Challenges and Change, United Nations, 2004.

political infrastructure, as part of the overall strategy against insurgents, as the Bush administration holds that democracies do not support terrorism.[48]

In seeking a solution, the Report built on the recommendations and views expressed by the PWG, the CTC, CTED, and the al-Qa'ida and Taliban Sanctions Committee.[49] These UN organs focused on improving the legal mechanism through ratification of international conventions, better mechanisms to deal with terrorist financing, money laundering, and greater usage of Security Council sanctions against Sudan over its involvement in the attempted assassination of Mubarak and the Taliban.[50] The Panel maintained that since the 'war on terror' began, there has been an erosion of the values which terrorists seek to target: human rights and the rule of law. The Panel called on states affected by terrorism not only to focus on military means but also adopt a comprehensive programme that promotes human rights and the rule of law. The Panel referred to the *Arab Human Development Report* of the United Nations Development Fund (UNDP), which it claims offers a positive innovation as it promotes debate in the Middle East on the need for gender empowerment, political freedom, rule of law and civil liberties.[51] The Panel at the same time recognised that the campaign against international terrorism requires action against the funding of terrorist organisations. It therefore called for increased vigilance whilst underlining the importance of transparency to ensure that only groups affiliated with terrorism are sanctioned.[52]

The significance of the High Panel Report is its call for a comprehensive and collaborative effort by the international community to promote global security matters. The Report declared that terrorism offends the very nature of the UN Charter because it disregards human rights, the rule of law, and the rules of legal warfare, all of which protect civilians in times of war and peace. The Panel found that terrorist methods – indiscriminate attacks against military and civilian targets, violent rhetoric and usage of illegal means to secure funds and materials – mean that terrorist organisations exist outside of normative society because their methods of operation reject the very essence of modern liberal society.[53] Consequently, the Panel maintained that there is an urgent need for an internationally accepted definition of terrorism, but more important is tackling the root causes of terrorism, which for the Panel include grave human rights abuses, little or no civil and political freedom, poor economic and social facilities, and so on. Thus, the Panel concluded that, "Terrorism flourishes in environments of despair, humiliation, poverty, political oppression, extremism and human rights abuse;

---

[48] The United States is spending around $4.5 billion a month to support its operation in Iraq. James Dobbins et al. *The UN's Role in Nation's Building: from the Congo to Iraq*. (Santa Monica: The Rand Corporation, 2005), p. 248; John F. Burns and Dexter Filkins. "US Generals See Way to Win War against Iraqi Rebels." *The New York Times*. December 1, 2005.

[49] "A More Secure World." Report of the High-level Panel on Threats, Challenges and Change, United Nations, 2004.

[50] For a good critique of economic sanctions, Chantal de Jonge Oudraat. "Making Economic Sanctions Work." *Survival*. Vol. 42, No. 3 (Autumn 2000), pp. 1-22.

[51] "A More Secure World." Report of the High-level Panel on Threats, Challenges and Change, United Nations, 2004.

[52] Americans have been quicker at shutting down charities suspected of providing – directly or indirectly – funds to terrorists, an approach that brought some criticism from Europe. Anne C. Richard. "The Money Trail: Europe Can Do More to Shut Down Terrorist Funds." *International Herald Tribune*. March 19, 2004.

[53] "A More Secure World." Report of the High-level Panel on Threats, Challenges and Change, United Nations, 2004.

it also flourishes in contexts of regional conflict and foreign occupation; and it profits from weak State capacity to maintain law and order."[54]

The shortcoming of the Report is that it largely failed to address the issue of the post-9/11 al-Qa'ida type terrorism, which rejects western secularism and materialism. Al-Qa'ida holds that western-defined human rights, gender equality and modernity are examples of societal corruption that undermines Islam. In the words of one commentator, "Al-Qaeda wants the United States, indeed the West more generally, out of the Persian Gulf and the Middle East. In bin Laden's view, the United States helps to keep Muslim peoples in poverty and imposes upon them a Western culture deeply offensive to traditional Islam. He blames the United States for the continued suffering of the people of Iraq and for the Israeli occupation of the West Bank and the Gaza Strip."[55] Moreover, the al-Qa'ida type of terrorist organisation exists outside the community. It has neither offices or headquarters nor recognised delegates. In this, it differs from such terrorist organisations as *Islamic Jihad*, *Hamas* or *Hizbollah* who have offices and recognised leadership and structure.[56]

The Ad Hoc Committee on International Terrorism

In 1972, the General Assembly adopted Resolution 3034 (XXVII) establishing the Ad Hoc Committee on International Terrorism, which consists of 35 members. In 1996, the Ad Hoc Committee centred its attention to provide an international convention for the suppression of terrorist bombing and an international convention for the suppression of acts of nuclear terrorism, which also included a convention on suppressing terrorist financing.[57] At the same time, historical, cultural and national differences prevent the Committee from adopting a comprehensive international convention on what is terrorism. In the words of the coordinator, "Some other delegations noted the need for distinguishing acts of terrorism from the legitimate struggle of peoples for self-determination. In addition, a suggestion was made to include the concept of State terrorism in the definition of terrorism."[58] However, the Committee attempted to resolve the impasse by establishing a Working Group, which began meeting in October 2002. The aim of the Group is to devise an international solution to the problem of defining terrorism. The Group is open to all member states (including such countries as Syria, Iran, North Korea and Sudan), members of the UN Specialised Agencies and members of the International Atomic Energy Agency (IAEA). The problem is that the aforementioned countries regularly violate the principles and purposes of the UN Charter as they sponsor terrorism (and in the case of Sudan arguably practice 'acts of genocide'[59]).

---

[54] "A More Secure World." Report of the High-level Panel on Threats, Challenges and Change, United Nations, 2004.

[55] Barry R. Rosen. "The Struggle against Terrorism: Grand Strategy, Strategy and Tactics." *International Security*. Vol. 26, No. 3 (Winter 2001/2002), pp. 39-40.

[56] For example, the US has managed to hold talks with some insurgent groups in Iraq, but not with al-Qa'ida. Hala Jabar. "UN 'In Talks with Iraq Rebels'." *The Times*. June 26, 2005.

[57] General Assembly Resolution 51/210, December 6, 1996. (A/Res/51/210); General Assembly Resolution 52/164, January 9, 1998 (A/Res/52/164); General Assembly Resolution 54/109 February 25, 2000 (A/Res/54/109); General Assembly in resolution 59/290, April 15, 2005 (A/Res/59/290).

[58] "Report of the coordinator on the results of the informal consultations on a draft comprehensive convention on international terrorism, held from 25 to 29 July 2005." *United Nations General Assembly* August 12, 2005. (A/59/894)

[59] See for example: CBS News. Available on line at:
http://www.cbsnews.com/stories/2004/10/08/60minutes/main648277.shtml

United Nations Office on Drugs and Crime

The United Nations Office on Drugs and Crime (ODC) heads many of the UN efforts against terrorism. The ODC focuses mainly on technical assistance and advisory services to countries, based on mandates recommended by the UN Commission on Crime Prevention and Criminal Justice (a subsidiary body of the UN Economic and Social Council) and approved by the General Assembly. In other words, the involvement of the ODC ensures the participation of the other principal organs of the United Nations in the war against terrorism. Responsibility for the mandates falls on the ODC Terrorism Prevention Branch (TPB), created in 1999, which operates within the Division of Treaty Affairs (DTA).[60] The TPB up until 9/11 focused mainly on research and analysis. After 9/11, the TPB took more of a lead in the campaign against terrorism, getting involved in such projects as 'Strengthening the Legal Regime Against Terrorism', which focused on the provision of direct legal advisory services to assist states in incorporating the relevant provisions, contained in the twelve universal anti-terrorism conventions, and protocols into national legislation. Of the 61 states that have received bilateral assistance from the TPB since the launch of the project in October 2002, 40 have become parties to one or more of the conventions.[61]

Secondly, the ODC through the Centre for International Crime Prevention provides states with measures that enhance cooperation and exchange of information.[62] Thus, for example, following a request by the Afghan Government, the ODC sent technical advisors to Kabul on June 5 to June 12, 2004, to advise the authorities on legislation needed to combat terrorism and transnational crime. The Afghani authorities in their letter to the CTC stated that their country had no laws or administrative measures dealing with terrorism. ODC experts reviewed the legislation and following requests by the ministries of justice and education, drafted new counter-terrorism legislation. They also assisted in the drafting of laws and relevant amendments to the penal code.[63]

The ODC's final involvement is in the Global Programme campaign. The Programme focuses on advocacy and prevention and covers such things as public awareness and civil society mobilisation; public service announcements on prevention;

---

[60] The objectives of the DTA are: (a) Fulfil the treaty obligations of the UN Secretariat regarding the international treaties and conventions on drug control and crime prevention. (b) Provide advice and assistance to Governments in formulating, implementing and monitoring treaties, conventions and other internationally binding instruments on drug control, crime prevention and criminal justice, especially in strengthening related legal frameworks, institutional capacity building and international cooperation. (c) Provide advice and assistance to Governments in ratifying and implementing the international legal instruments relating to terrorism, especially in strengthening related legal frameworks, institutional capacity building and international cooperation; (d) Provide necessary services to the member countries and the intergovernmental bodies of the United Nations for dialogue, standard setting and policy formulation on drug and crime issues.

[61] "Strengthening international cooperation and technical assistance in promoting the implementation of the universal conventions and protocols related to terrorism within the framework of the activities of the United Nations Office on Drugs and Crime." Report by the Secretary-General, Commission on Crime Prevention and Criminal Justice, Vienna, May23-27, 2005. E/CN.15/2005/13.

[62] Alex P. Schmid. "Terrorism and Human Rights: A Perspective from the United Nations." *Terrorism and Political Violence*. Vol. 17, No. 1-2 (Winter 2005), pp. 25-35.

[63] "Note from the Permanent Mission of Afghanistan to the CTC." UN Security Council, March 10, 2003, S/2003/353. "Strengthening international cooperation and technical assistance in promoting the implementation of the universal conventions and protocols related to terrorism within the framework of the activities of the United Nations Office on Drugs and Crime." Report by the Secretary-General, Commission on Crime Prevention and Criminal Justice, Vienna, May23-27, 2005. E/CN.15/2005/13. The report also notes the support given to Paraguay to ratify all UN conventions relating to terrorism.

contribution to the ODC's National Profiles; contribution to National Country Strategies; creation of a 'best practices' kit.[64]

Conclusion

The United Nations has sought to adapt to the post-9/11 world by developing mechanisms to combat the new scourge of international terrorism, even though there is not yet an internationally accepted definition of what international terrorism constitutes. Each entity of the United Nations that is involved in combating terrorism plays a different function. The Security Council, through the CTC and the CTED, and even the more recently formed 1544 Committee (the WMD committee), emphasises the need for imposing certain demands on member states in combating terrorism, as seen with Resolution 1373, which placed obligations on all member states. The Secretary General, as the "world's first diplomat", provides a dual role: on the one hand he (and his office) offer a moral barometer as to what needs to be done, whilst also initiating reports and studies as to what needs to be done. The General Assembly, prior to 9/11 certainly led the campaign against terrorism, and significantly this was through legal mechanisms, specifically legal conventions.

Ultimately, the United Nations has a valuable role to play in combating international terrorism. However, increasingly it is becoming apparent that the international coalition against terrorism that emerged after 9/11 is slowly coming apart due to national and regional interests. It is imperative that the international community ensures that it remains united against international terrorism and continues to work towards its eradication, as terrorists such as bin Laden know no national boundaries, and have shown complete disregard towards all those who disagree with them.

---

[64] Alex P. Schmid. "Terrorism and Human Rights: A Perspective from the United Nations." *Terrorism and Political Violence*. Vol. 17, No. 1-2 (Winter 2005), pp. 25-35.

Legal Aspects of Combating Terrorism
Centre of Excellence Defence Against Terrorism, Ankara, Turkey (Ed.)
IOS Press, 2008

doi:10.3233/978-1-58603-930-1-37

Islamic Radicalism: The UK Case

Assist.-Prof. Isaac KFIR
Lauder School of Government, Diplomacy and Strategy, Interdisciplinary Centre; Senior Researcher, International Institute for Counter-Terrorism, Herzliya, Israel

Abstract. The paper explores some of the reasons behind the apparent rise in Islamic radicalism in the United Kingdom over the last few years. By using Fukuyama's and Huntington's theories, the author argues that a spiritual void coupled with a desire to belong to something 'greater', has led young British Muslims towards Islamism. In the second part, the author explores some of the measures undertaken by British authorities to combat Islamic militancy. The paper concludes with recommendations as to what could improve relations between mainstream British society and the Muslim community in the hope of reducing Islamic militancy.

Keywords. Counter-terrorism, Islamic radicalism in Britain, root causes of radicalism, British policy for combating terrorism.

Introduction

On July 7, 2005, Londoners came face to face with Islamic terrorism, when four British Muslims committed the first suicide attack on British soil, which left 54 people dead and hundreds injured. The ensuing investigation revealed that the bombers were British nationals who harboured deep-seated hatred towards the United Kingdom. The bombings further galvanised the debate about multiculturalism, integration, immigration as well as British foreign policy. Increasingly at the heart of the debate is whether liberalism and democracy breed terrorism and radicalism.[1]

The July 7 bombings arguably have direct links to the collapse of the Soviet Union, as the end of the Soviet Empire was meant to usher in a 'new world order' and a new sense of optimism. However, within a decade the world found itself facing a global menace, in the shape of radical Islam.[2] Adherents of radical Islam call for a 'holy jihad' against those who reject their interpretation of Islam and those who do not embrace Islam.[3] There is growing evidence to suggest that Britain is becoming a hotbed of

---

[1] Paul Wilkinson. *Terrorism versus Democracy: the Liberal State Response*. (London: Frank Cass, 2006); Rosemary Foot. *Human Rights and Counter-Terrorism in America's Asia Policy*. (Oxford: Oxford University Press, 2004).

[2] Arguably, radical Islam of the al-Qa'ida mode began within a few years of the end of the Cold War, with the 1996 Khobar Tower bombings in Saudi Arabia followed by the East Africa bombings in 1998.

[3] Danna Harman. "Radical Islam Finds Unlikely Haven in Liberal Britain." *Christian Science Monitor*. August 5, 2002; Henry Porter. "Tolerating intolerance is still this country's besetting sin." *The Observer* February 4, 2007. The British Security Service and Police use the phrase Islamism when describing Muslims that use religion to justify their terrorist activities. The larger British counter-terrorism community prefer the

Islamic radicalism and that unless immediate action is taken more events such as July 7 and July 21 will occur.[4] Sir Ian Blair, the Metropolitan Police Commissioner, expressed the aforementioned concern following the transatlantic airline bomb plot, when he said "...the apparent speed with which young, reasonably affluent, some reasonably well educated British-born people became not only radicalised but also willing to commit mass murders through suicide attacks is worrying."[5] Consequently, there have been calls for toughening up the UK's anti-terrorism laws.

The purpose of the paper is to examine the roots of Islamic radicalism in Britain by looking at four main issues: socio-economic factors (materialism), culturalism (seen as a form of civilisation), alienation and British foreign policy. In the second part, the author turns to how Britain has sought to deal with the threat posed by Islamists. The subsidiary aim of the paper is to ascertain why young British Muslim youths join the rank-and-file of the global jihadi movement to assist the development of a counter-radicalism programme. The question faced by scholars and practitioners is whether there is something fundamentally wrong with either British society or with the perception of British society by British Muslims that encourages them enlist in the global jihad. Once that is ascertained, one could begin formulating a solution that is either based on social-economic policies (if the root causes are based on poverty and inequality), legal remedies (if the problem lies with criminal activity such as incitement or cultism) and so on.[6]

The Roots of Disenchantment

In the hope of understanding the allure of radicalism and Islamic martyrdom for British youths, one must examine two somewhat flawed theses: Francis Fukuyama's 'The End of History' and Samuel P. Huntington's 'Clash of Civilizations.' Both scholars have come under tremendous amount of criticism for their respective theses. A third issue, linked to the Fukuyama and Huntington theses, is the generational clash.[7] However,

---

terms 'international terrorism and "AQ-related" terrorism". "Report into the London Terrorist Attacks on 7 July 2005." *House of Commons, Intelligence and Security Committee*. (May 2006).

[4] In a speech in 2006, Dame Eliza Manningham-Buller, as the MI5 Director-General, claimed that since July 2005, GCHQ thwarted a further five major conspiracies in the UK. She further stated that the security services must contend with around 200 groupings or networks, "...who are actively engaged in plotting, or facilitating, terrorist acts here and overseas." "Terrorist threat to UK - MI5 chief's full speech." *The Times*. [UK] November 10, 2006.

[5] Abdul Taher and Dipesh Gadher. "Islamists infiltrate four universities." *The Sunday Times*. [UK] November 12, 2006. About a week after the July 7 bombings, a leaked Whitehall document stated that a network of "extremist recruiters" are circulating around British universities targeting individuals with technical and professional qualifications" focusing especially on those taking engineering and IT degrees. Robert Winnett and David Leppard. "Leaked No. 10 dossier reveals Al-Qaeda's British recruits." *The Times*. [UK] July 10, 2005.

[6] It has been suggested that radical Islam is a cult or similar to a cult and therefore it should be treated as such. See for example, Charles Allen. *God's Terrorists: The Wahhabi Cult and the Hidden Roots of Modern Jihad*. (London: Abacus, 2006).

[7] This idea is developed from Michael Roskin. "From Pearl Harbor to Vietnam: Shifting Generational Paradigms and Foreign Policy." *Political Science Quarterly*. Vol. 89, No. 3 (Autumn, 1974), pp. 563-588; Arthur M. Schlesinger, Jr. *The Cycles of American History*. (Boston, Houghton Mifflin, 1986).

despite their shortcomings each approach assists scholars to understand why young British Muslims have embraced radicalism, militancy and even jihad.[8]

In 1989, Francis Fukuyama argued that the collapse of the Berlin Wall meant the 'end of history' in that neo-liberalism defeated socialism. At the core of Fukuyama's argument is the belief that wars are the result of conflicting ideas and dogmas (ideologies), which people wish to impose on each other. Secondly, for Fukuyama it is these ideas that drive history.[9] Fukuyama argued that two conflicting ideologies - neo-liberalism, epitomised by the United States and socialism, which the Soviet Union promoted - divided the world for over four decades. However, the collapse of the USSR, coupled with Deng Xiaoping's economic reforms in the 1980s as well as Rajiv Gandhi's economic reform indicated in 1989 that the dominate ideology for the foreseeable future was neo-liberalism.

In 1993, Samuel P. Huntington in a controversial essay argued 'civilizations' will dominate the post-Cold War period. Huntington simplified the concept of a 'civilisation' to that of a "cultural entity" (villages, regions, ethnic groups, nationalities and religious groups). This means that according to the Huntington formula, a 'civilisation' may transcend borders (physical, metaphysical, spiritual, social, economic, and so on) as it could exist on different levels: language, religion history or customs. Consequently, for him Europe and the United States could become a single civilisation because of language (English dominance), religion (Christianity) and institutions (liberal democracy). On that basis, there are common grounds between Japan and the United States, as Japan embraced a liberal democracy, market economics and sport (baseball). The most interesting element in Huntington's theory is the assertion that people may determine their own civilisational affiliation, as a civilisation is a subjective self-identification process.[10]

> "A civilization is thus the highest cultural grouping of people and the broadest level of cultural identity people have short of that which distinguishes humans from other species. It is defined both by common objective elements, such as language, history, religion, customs, institutions, and by the subjective self-identification of people. People have levels of identity: a resident of Rome may define himself with varying degrees of intensity as a Roman, an Italian, a Catholic, a Christian, a European, a Westerner."[11]

The third issue in the process is a generational clash, which arises from a clash between first generation immigrants and their children. In relation to the United Kingdom, Muslim immigrants that came over to the UK preserved their cultural, ethnic, tribal and religious affiliations. They behaved and worshipped as they had in their home countries, married within their own communities and retained caste and tribal separatism. The

---

[8] The process is a piecemeal: first, one joins a radical movement; second is adopting militancy, which involves some level of political activity, with martyrdom being the ultimate stage from which there is no return.

[9] Fukuyama in his essay declared, "What we may be witnessing in not just the end of the Cold War, or the passing of a particular period of post-war history, but the end of history as such: that is, the end point of mankind's ideological evolution and the universalization of Western liberal democracy as the final form of human government." Francis Fukuyama. "The End of History?." *The National Interest.* (Summer 1989).

[10] Samuel P. Huntington. "The Clash of Civilization." *Foreign Affairs.* Vol. 72, No. 3 (Summer 1993), p. 23-49; Samuel P. Huntington. *The Clash of Civilizations and the Remaking of World Order.* (New York: Touchstone, 1997).

[11] Samuel P. Huntington. "The Clash of Civilization." *Foreign Affairs.* Vol. 72, No. 3 (Summer 1993), p. 24.

children however, faced the problem of cultural identity: at home, they are surrounded by their parents' culture and history.[12] However, they may not speak the language of their parents (Urdu, Hindi, Pushtan); they do not understand tribal, ethnic or cultural affiliations nor the love or longings of their parents towards the homeland. This creates an internal clash of civilisation (a clash between the cultural existence of their parents and the plural culture of Britain). Shiv Malik has noted that "Although poverty and exclusion are themes that wound their way through the lives of the Beeston bombers, it is the internal frictions within a traditional Pakistani community in Britain that best explain the radicalisation that led to the deaths of 56 people."[13]

Applying the Theory

Islamists reject neo-liberalism as a force of evil as it encourages a form of *jahiliyah* (ignorance – a time in which humanity shunned God and religion)[14] in that it creates a fixation with material acquisition that leads to decadence, sexual immorality, drugs, and spiritual emptiness. This stems from the notion of allowing the market to dictate human norms and thus if the market wants pornography this is what the people will receive. Mohammad Sidique Khan, the leader of the July 7 cell, captured this Islamist contempt towards neo-liberalism and the West when he stated, "I and thousands like me are forsaking everything for what we believe... Our driving motivation doesn't come from tangible commodities that this world has to offer..."[15] This builds on the views of Mawlana Mawdudi, a leading Islamist ideologue and the founder of *Jamaat-i-Islami* (Islamic Association), who saw everything to do with Western civilisation as "...wrong and harmful because it is not God-given but elaborated by political leaders on the basis of false beliefs. To him and his followers, the West denied the sovereignty of God. Therefore all things its people have constructed are unacceptable."[16] On the civilisation issue, Islamists somewhat ironically embrace Huntington's 'Clash of Civilization' in that they believe that the Western civilisation seeks to subvert the Muslim world and they point to all the corrupting influences with which the West bombards the Muslim world (such as the sale of *Playboy* in Indonesia). For British Muslims, the view is that British society attacks Islam and portrays it as a religion of intolerance, violence and death,[17] whilst neo-liberalism and its political offshoots of multiculturalism are exalted.[18] British Muslims also feel that the forces of modernity

---

[12] This is seen clearly in the movie *Bend It Like Beckham* where the actress Parminder Nagra portrays the difficulties of a British born daughter of an orthodox Sikh who wishes to play football.

[13] Shiv Malik. "My brother the Bomber." *Prospect Magazine*. Issue 135, (June 2007). See also Aatish Taseer. "A British Jihadist." *Prospect Magazine*. Issue 113, (August 2005).

[14] For the concept of *jahiliyah* see Sayyid Qutb. *Milestones*. (New Delhi: Islamic Book Service, 2007).

[15] Text taken from "London bomber: Text in full." *BBC News On-Line*. September 1, 2006. [http://news.bbc.co.uk/2/hi/uk_news/4206800.stm]

[16] Krishna Kumar. "Religious Fundamentalism in India and Beyond." *Parameters*. Vol. 32. No. 3 (Autumn 2002), p. 22.

[17] The Muslim Council of Britain has declared, "Recent years have seen the characterisation of British Muslims as a 'problem community' in much of the media and through statements made by Government and police officials. These have contributed to a growing anti-Muslim climate in the UK." "Electing to Deliver: Working for Representation in Britain." *The Muslim Council of Britain*. (2005), p. 11. [http://www.mcb.org.uk/vote2005/ELECTINGTODELIVER.pdf]

[18] This was clearly seen with the reaction against Jack Straw's controversial statement on the *niqab* (full veil). "Fallout over Straw veil call spread." *The Daily Telegraph*. [UK] October 9, 2006. [http://www.news.com.au/dailytelegraph/story/0,22049,20548012-5001028,00.html]

undermine Islam (material clash) in that a person's position and standing in society is determined by their material possessions.[19] On the generational issue, British Muslim youths find solace and support only within their own small community ('civilisation'), as they are drawn together by their appearance (dark skin and facial features), religion (Islam), language (English) and most importantly a sense that mainstream British society hates them and that their parents' do not understand them. Aatish Taseer, a half-Indian half-Pakistani journalist, captured this sense of unity when he wrote, "For young British Muslims, if Pakistan was not the place to look for an identity, being second-generation British was still less inspiring. While their parents were pioneers, leaving Pakistan in search of economic opportunities, enduring the initial challenges of a strange land, the second generation's experience has been one of drudgery and confusion."[20]

The Types of Islamic Radical Recruits

Experience has shown that two types of groups of young men have embraced the teaching of radical Islam in the United Kingdom: the educated British-born Muslims and the less-educated and foreign-born Muslims or new converts, attracted to Islam due to some sort of void in their lives.

Ahmed Omar Saeed Sheikh, a British-born Muslim of Pakistani origin, currently facing a death sentence in Pakistan for his involvement in the killing of the American journalist Daniel Pearl, is another good example of a British-born Muslim that came to reject his British identity. Sheikh, a former student of a private school in Snaresbrook England, abandoned his studies at the London School of Economics and went to work as an aid worker in Bosnia. Reportedly, Sheikh became a close associate of Maulana Azhar Masood – founder of *Jaish-e-Mohammad* (JEM). In 1994, Indian police arrested Sheikh for alleged involvement in the kidnapping of three Britons and an American in India, but after five years in prison, a hostage exchange led to his release.[21] It is unclear where Sheikh's radicalisation began, but what is clear is that he too came to reject his Britishness and adopted an Islamic global outlook. Omar Khyam is another example of a radicalised British-born Muslim who found Islamic terrorism. Khyam, whose grandfather served in the British Army, became interested in religion at college following meetings of *al-Muhajiroun,* where videos depicting the conflicts in Chechnya, Kashmir and Bosnia were shown. His commitment to militant Islam intensified following 9/11 after which he reportedly said, "I was happy. America was, and still is, the greatest enemy of Islam. They put up puppet regimes in Muslim countries like Saudi Arabia, Jordan and Egypt…".[22] Commentators believe that Khyam, convicted of the fertiliser bomb plot conspiracy, embraced Islamic radicalism following

---

[19] Ed Hussein clearly shows this. Ed Husain. *The Islamist*. (London: Penguin Books, 2007).

[20] Aatish Taseer. "A British Jihadist." *Prospect Magazine*. Issue 113 (August 2005); see also Ed Husain. *The Islamist*. (London: Penguin Books, 2007). Raza Jaffrey, the chairman of the *Muslim Youth Hotline* stated, "…for the past two or three years we have seen a situation where people have become very frustrated because the government is not listening to what they have been saying – and that's why some young Muslims feel alienated." Dominic Casciani. "What do young Muslims think?." *BBC News On-line*. August 1, 2005. [http://news.bbc.co.uk/2/hi/uk_news/4735127.stm]

[21] "Profile: Omar Saeed Sheikh." *BBC News On-Line*. July 16, 2002. [http://news.bbc.co.uk/2/hi/uk_news/1804710.stm]

[22] David Pallister. "British defendant in terror plot trial tells of gradual conversion to militant jihadist." *The Guardian*. [UK] September 15, 2006.

a visit to a Pakistani militant training camp in late 1990 where he met other British-born Islamists. Significantly, Khyam's move towards Islamism arose out of his interest in Kashmir, where he also attended a training camp run by *Al-Badr Mujahideen*. In his trial, Khyam testified that at the camp in Muzaffarabad he was taught "…everything I needed for guerrilla warfare in Kashmir, AK47s, pistols, sniper rifles, reconnaissance". He also spent time in the North West Frontier Province, surrounded by men holding the view that the West is engaged in a war against Islam.[23]

The other group of Muslim radicals in the UK are Muslim converts or asylum seekers, generally less educated and less integrated. These individual's involvement in terror operations is less intricate, which may explain why, to date, they have all failed, as seen with the July 21 plot. In other words, Islamist ideology appears to inspire them but they lack the means (they generally cannot afford to travel to Pakistan), sophistication (they rarely have university education) and connection to al-Qa'ida and such Islamic organisations in Pakistan, which in turn allows the security services to foil their operations. The presence of Muslim converts in terror plots has become a worrying development, as seen with Richard Reid (shoe-bomber) Germaine Lindsay (one of the July 7 bombers) and Don Stewart-Whyte and Brian Young (aircraft liquid terror plot). All these young men converted to Islam and became Islamists.[24] On the asylum seekers front, there is evidence of radicalisation within prisons with at least one of the July 21 suspected terrorists (Muktar Said-Ibrahim) having adopted militant Islam while in prison,[25] as was the case with the shoe-bomber, Richard Reid.

When looking at these young men, certain trends and issues appear, as each terrorist came from a relatively comfortable background and yet once they reached their teens or university age, they began to embrace Islamic radicalisation. They attended lectures, talks, and seminars run by militant Islamists who persuaded them that their affinity should not be to their adopted (birth) country – Britain – but rather with Muslims across the world. One of the first questions that arise when looking at these individuals is: what does someone like Ahmed Omar Saeed Sheikh, who comes from a privileged background, have in common with a poor Muslim in Kashmir? The answer is religion. Sheikh was able to identify with the poor Muslims in Kashmir, Chechnya, Bosnia and so on, by his and their commitment to Islam. In other words, by embracing this type of Islam, all barriers fell and they were accepted almost without question, as all that they had to prove was a devotion of a rigid interpretation of Islam. The next question that follows is: did Sheikh look for some sort of spiritual fulfilment or a sense of belonging, which he found through the adoption of militant Islam, as it connected him to a greater community, a proud tradition and a civilisation? Ed Husain, a British-born Muslim who embraced militant Islam for a period in his life, provides some insight into these questions. What is clear in Husain's biography is that militant Islam gave him – for a time at least – spiritual answers and made him feel like he was part of something greater; something that transcended national boundaries and time.[26] Looking at the British-born Islamists, similar things appear; these young men seem to

---

[23] Richard Smith. "Bomb plot's roots in Pakistan." *BBC News On-Line*. April 30, 2007. [http://news.bbc.co.uk/2/hi/uk_news/6172742.stm]

[24] Adam Fresco, Elsa McLaren, Lewis Smith, Lucy Bannerman and Nicola Woolcock. "Who are the 'bomb plot' suspects?." *The Times*. [UK] August 11, 2006.

[25] Muktar Said Ibrahim after various criminal activities ended up at the Feltham Young Offenders institution, where he converted to Islam and abandoned his errant ways. Paul Tumelty. "Reassessing the July 21 London Bombing." *Terrorism Monitor*. Vol. 3, Issue 17 (September 8, 2005), pp. 1-4.

[26] Ed Husain. *The Islamist*. (London: Penguin Books, 2007).

be searching for something to believe in because: neo-liberalism does not speak to them, either because they are discriminated against by mainstream British society (they cannot get the high-paying jobs) or because they lack the education to get the high-paying jobs. From a civilisational perspective, 'Western' civilisation adherence to neo-liberalism leaves them with a spiritual void, which only militant Islam appears to fulfil.[27] From a generational gap view, these men feel disconnected from their elders as they do not know their ancestral homeland, if not a romantic notion of the 'old country'.

Is British Foreign Policy Aiding Recruitment?

British foreign policy lies at the centre of the debate about the rise of Islamic radicalism in the United Kingdom, with an increasing number of politicians, decision-makers, bureaucrats and military personnel holding that the British presence, particularly in Iraq, is encouraging anti-British sentiments.[28] This is part of a global movement, which asserts that the American-led invasion of Iraq was a colossal mistake fuelled by misinformation, if not downright lies. However, Islamists always find a new cause to promote and use in their recruitment campaigns. It is also a truism that there are many places which radical Muslims can use to exemplify their claim that the West is either attacking Islam or not doing enough to protect Muslims.

Osama Saeed of the Muslim Association of Britain has argued that British Muslims engage in terror campaigns not because of what happens in the mosques in England but because of a sense of injustice against Muslims throughout the world.[29] In other words, British Muslims only identify with their co-religions when Muslims are treated badly. A 2005 report by the Federation of Student Islamic Societies found that "The problem of loyalty arises when students feel that injustices are being committed by Britain against people around the world, especially to Muslims. This makes them feel let-down at how Britain – their home country – could perpetrate such crimes in their name. Many could not feel any loyalty to the UK knowing it had ignored their pleas to avoid the Iraq war and continued to deny it had acted irresponsibly."[30] In other words, these Muslims see themselves as part of the new *mujahideen*, whose goal is the preservation and protection of Islam and Muslim communities (arguably there is no difference between these new *mujahid* and the young Arabs who travelled to Afghanistan in the 1980s to partake in a war against the Soviet Union). Thus, young Muslims who are already alienated from mainstream British society are able to find

[27] Ed Husain notes that when he worked for HSBC, he felt spiritually empty. Throughout the book, it is clear that Husain is constantly looking for spiritual fulfilment, which arguably explains why he eventually adopts a form of Sufi Islam. Ed Husain. *The Islamist.* (London: Penguin Books, 2007).

[28] A Report by the Federation of Student Islamic Societies in 2005 found that over 80% of Muslim students questioned were unhappy with British foreign policy. 42% of those questioned claimed that British foreign policy was a major factor in the July 7 bombings, and 62% believed that Britain's foreign policy played a major or complete role in the July 7 London bombings. *The Voices of the Muslims Students: Attitudes and perceptions of British Muslim students following the London attacks on July 7th 2005.* Federation of Student Islamic Societies. (August 2005), pp. 47-49. [http://www.fosis.org.uk/sac/FullReport.pdf]

[29] Fareena Alam. "Vision of a new Islam." *The Observer.* [UK] April 4, 2004. [http://observer.guardian.co.uk/comment/story/0,6903,1185265,00.html]

[30] *The Voices of the Muslims Students: Attitudes and perceptions of British Muslim students following the London attacks on July 7th 2005.* Federation of Student Islamic Societies. (August 2005), p. 18. [http://www.fosis.org.uk/sac/FullReport.pdf]

answers as to why they and their communities suffer discrimination and hostility by turning to radical Islamic groups, as *Al-Muhajiroun* claimed:

> "The feeling for Jihad (holy war) at the current time in the light of Iraq and Afghanistan and the continuing intifada in Palestine is very hot within the Muslim community... People are very eager to support their Muslim brothers and sisters in Palestine and in other areas as much as they can... Of course, the ultimate sacrifice for a Muslim is to lay down his life for the sake of Allah in the struggle of Jihad."[31]

In other words, it is the 'silence' if not apparent 'collusion' of mainstream British society that encourages young British Muslims to become active in the 'defence' of their religion and their brethren. This sense of a desire to defend the Muslim *umma* has increased with the British involvement in Iraq and Afghanistan. Islamist websites and preachers portray Iraq and Afghanistan as examples of the West's (especially the United States') attempt to subvert Islam, as part of a new crusade against the Muslim world. In the words of Mohammad Sidique Khan, "We are at war and I am a soldier. Now you too will taste the reality of this situation."[32]

Responding to the Threat

Since 9/11, Britain has attempted to grapple with Islamic radicalism through three tracks: legislation dealing with security issues; second, inter-community and inter-faith dialogue and programmes designed to encourage greater Muslim participation in mainstream British society; and, finally a 'moral' foreign policy.

On the legislative side, the government adopted numerous anti-terrorism measures[33] that included punishing those who incite or glorify terrorism.[34] Under the 2006 Terrorism Act for example, a person commits an offence of glorifying terrorism if they publish a statement that induces another to commit, prepare or instigate the act of terrorism as defined under the Council of Europe Convention on the Prevention of Terrorism offences (section 1(1) and 1(2)). The Act requires that at the time the individual publishes the statement, they intend members of the public to either directly or indirectly, commit, prepare or instigate the act of terrorism.[35] There have also been measures dealing with detention of suspects for 28 days without charge coupled with a stronger willingness to extradite those promoting an Islamist agenda.[36] The government

---

[31] "UK Muslims shocked by 'bombers'." *BBC News On-line*. May 1, 2003. [http://news.bbc.co.uk/2/hi/uk_news/2990841.stm]

[32] Text taken from "London bomber: Text in full." *BBC News On-Line*. September 1, 2006. [http://news.bbc.co.uk/2/hi/uk_news/4206800.stm]

[33] See for example, Terrorism Act (2000), Anti-Terrorism, Crime and Security Act (2001), the Prevention of Terrorism Act (2005) and Terrorism Act (2006).

[34] Mizanur Rahman, a 23-year-old web designer from North London, was convicted of incitement to stir up race hatred during a demonstration against the publication of the Danish cartoon depicting Muhammad. Rahman called for the killings of those who insult Islam and death to British soldiers serving in Iraq. Jenny Percival and Agencies. "Cartoon protester guilty of race hate." *The Times*. [UK] November 9, 2006. [http://www.timesonline.co.uk/article/0,,2-2445654,00.html]

[35] "Explanatory Notes to Terrorism Act 2000." [http://www.opsi.gov.uk/acts/en2006/ukpgaen_20060011_en.pdf]

[36] The 2006 Queen's Speech emphasised that security and the need to be tough on terrorism remains central to the British government, which is why the government is considering extending the period under which the security forces may detain a suspect without charge beyond 28 days. See for example, Alan Travis.

felt compelled to introduce these measures because of individuals such as Abu Hamza who were able to stand in the streets of London for years and call for death and destruction, which inspired men such as Reid, Moussaoui and Omar Sharif. Significantly, Abu Hamza faced charges under the 1861 Offences Against the Person Act 1861 and the 1986 Public Order Act for using threatening or abusive behaviour to stir up racial hatred rather than terrorism. This suggests that there are serious limitations with the post-9/11 terrorism legislations, as seen already in Part IV of the Anti-Terrorism, Crime and Security Act (2001) which the courts rejected, necessitating the passing of a new legislation to facilitate the detention of suspects without breaching international and/or European law.

The British government has attempted to deal with the threat of Islamist preachers by engaging in a limited debate on immigration[37] and the role of imams, coupled with initiatives designed to enhance integration. This has led to a debate on the issue of 'Britishness' as radical Muslim preachers are able to convince British Muslim youths to abandon their British identity and identify with others Muslims (especially the oppressed and downtrodden). In terms of integration, the British government has conducted various studies and commenced a number of initiatives aimed at improving race and community relations between mainstream British society and the Muslim community. The Cantle Commission set the tone in defining the process of improving relations between communities, as it conducted a comprehensive study into community cohesion in the UK following a number of disturbances in various towns in England in the summer of 2001. The Commission produced sixty-seven recommendations on how to improve community cohesion, defined in much broader terms than mere economics, as it also focused on education, employment, poverty, social inequalities, social and cultural diversity and access to communication and information technologies.[38] Under the 'Preventing Extremism Together' study,[39] the government recognises that the only way to counter extremism is through cooperation with the Muslim community and thus the first body that should counter the rising tide of extremism is the Muslim community. This emphasises the need for Muslim scholars, academics and clerics to engage young Muslims in universities in intellectual debates. Muslims must be encouraged to challenge and debate matters that affect their lives and their interests.

When turning to the July 7 bombers, it is difficult to see how community cohesion could have prevented the atrocity. The Official Report into the bombing emphasises that the four were integrated into British society and that they were, as well, open about

---

"Watchdog warns against 'rush to judgment' on extending 28 day detention." *The Guardian*. [UK] November 16, 2006. [http://politics.guardian.co.uk/queensspeech2006/story/0,,1948847,00.html]

[37] New applicants for British citizenship are required to sit an exam entitled "Life in UK" designed to instil a sense of 'Britishness' amongst new citizens. They must also prove that they are able to speak basic English. Simon Freeman and Agencies. "Citizenship test runs into flak for lack of perspective." *The Times*. [UK] October 31, 2006.

It is noteworthy that due to pressure from Muslims, Sikhs and Hindus, the Home Office scrapped a 'Britishness Test' for foreign-born imams despite concerns from government ministers and security officials that foreign-born imams are radicalising young British Muslims. Richard Ford. "'Britishness test' for imams is abandoned." *The Times*. [UK] December 20, 2005.

[38] "Community Cohesion." A report of the Independent Review Team, Chaired by Ted Cantle, *Home Office* (November 2001). Appendix C: Rosalyn Lynch. "An Analysis of the Concept of Community Cohesion." *Home Office Research, Development and Statistics Directorate*. [http://communities.homeoffice.gov.uk/raceandfaith/reports_pubs/publications/race_faith/community-cohesion.pdf?view=Binary]

[39] "Preventing Extremism Together Places of Worship." *UK Home Office* (October 6, 2005). [http://www.homeoffice.gov.uk/documents/cons-prev-extreme/cons-prev-extreme?view=Binary]

their religious views. The Report states, "...there was little outward sign that this had spilled over into potentially violent extremism." Moreover, the Report declares, "...there is little in their backgrounds which mark them out as particularly vulnerable to radicalisation, with the possible exception of Lindsay."[40]

Conclusion: Why Britain?

Overall, there is a tremendous debate over Britain's domestic and foreign polices. Internally, the country is striving to find a balance between the challenges of modernity, multiculturalism and the post-9/11 world of indiscriminate international terrorism. Attempts at dealing with Islamists leads to allegations that mainstream British society is intrinsically anti-Muslim and racist, which fuels the division between mainstream British society and the devout Muslim community. Mainstream British society appears to subscribe to the view that devout Muslims reject the fundamentals that lie at the epicentre of traditional liberal society, which embraces and encourages pluralism.[41]

To foster change, the government must focus on encouraging British Muslims to enter mainstream British society. This requires a joint effort by the authorities and Muslim community leaders to deal with the sense of social and economic injustice which British Muslims feel exists in the United Kingdom. The emphasis here is on the perception that large sections of the community feel discriminated against. This in itself is not necessarily true, as British society feels that it has embraced Muslims and Islam: there are Muslim members of parliament, leading Muslim industrialists, lawyers, sports personalities, and so on.

However, more attention is needed to deal with poverty in the Muslim and immigrant communities: 20 percent of Bangladeshis living in Britain in 2001-2002 were unemployed. This is four times that of White British or White Irish men. The picture is similar for women, with Bangladeshi women having the highest unemployment rate of all (24 percent, six times greater than that for White British or White Irish women). For all ethnic groups, unemployment was highest among young people aged under-25. Over 40 percent of young Bangladeshi men were unemployed, while young Pakistani men and women had unemployment rates above 20 percent. The rate for young white British men and women was 12 percent and 9 percent respectively.[42] The sense of discrimination is not only affecting groups but also areas, Beeston, the suburb in Leeds from where two of the July 7 bombers came from, is a deprived area in that 47 percent of households rely on some form of state benefit, which is more than double the average for Leeds as a whole. Moreover, 93 percent of the homes are in the poorest council tax band.[43] These factors enhance the belief that Muslim communities suffer undue or excessive discrimination and receive a smaller

---

[40] "Report of the Official Account of the Bombings in London on 7th July 2005." (London: The Stationary Office, 2006) HC-1087. [http://www.homeoffice.gov.uk/documents/7-july-report.pdf?view=Binary]

[41] See for example, "Fallout over Straw veil call spread." *The Daily Telegraph.* [UK] October 9, 2006. [http://www.news.com.au/dailytelegraph/story/0,22049,20548012-5001028,00.html]; Nigel Morris and Sarah Cassidy. "Race equality head backs Straw on wearing of veil." *The Independent.* [UK] October 12, 2006.

[42] Figures takes from "Terrorism and Community Relations." Sixth Report of Session 2004-2005 Vol. I *House of Commons Home Affairs Committee.* (London: The Stationary Office Ltd., April 6, 2005): para. 22-23 (Para 69).

[43] Urmee Khan. "Young, British and Muslim: one woman's journey to the home of the 7/7 bombers." *The Observer.* [UK] June 18, 2006. [http://www.guardian.co.uk/attackonlondon/story/0,,1800423,00.html]

portion of the welfare budget fuelling the culture of resentment.[44] Thus, more effort must also come from the Muslim community itself with Muslim entrepreneurs taking the lead in educating and motivating the younger generations to improve their socio-economic conditions. Moreover, the Muslim community must utilise the role of individuals such as Nasser Hussein, England's former cricket captain and boxer Naseem Hamed in promoting tolerance and making it clear that mainstream British society does not discriminate against Muslims.

On the foreign policy front two things must occur. First, the most effective way to defeat Islamic militancy in the United Kingdom is by tackling radicalism overseas. This demands a long-term strategy centring on secular education and economic growth and empowerment, not just in the UK but also in countries such as Pakistan, which is why the decision to provide more development aid in Muslim countries is correct. Secondly, more effort needs to go into explaining the situation in Iraq and Afghanistan, and to show that these are not hopeless causes as there have been some positive developments in those countries with elections, the empowerment of women, and reconstruction programmes. The lay public must appreciate that clandestine Syrian and Iranian involvement fuels the instability in Iraq, with the two encouraging civil unrest in Iraq. Syria and, even more so, Iran have a vested interest in making Iraq as unstable as possible as it undermines the western effort to promote neo-liberal values in the Muslim world. The public must understand that, ultimately, western governments want to end their presence in Iraq and Afghanistan and return their weary soldiers home. However, they cannot do so until Iraq and Afghanistan have secure regimes, as otherwise they will end up as failed states which would create more instability and insecurity to the international system. Therefore, the calls for a reassessment in Britain's foreign policy are worrying as they come after a number of successful anti-Western and anti-British attacks. Drastically changing British foreign policy sends the message that terrorism and anti-Westernism pay dividends.[45] Critics of Britain's foreign policy must understand that in the post-9/11 world, nations must work together to promote the maintenance of international peace and security. Without international cooperation, instability in Iraq, Afghanistan, and Somalia, affects the home front, especially as Islamists always find a reason to blame the West for something. The international community is engaged in a global war to protect its way of life, which embraces pluralism, multiculturalism and democracy, ideals abhorred by Islamists. It is only by promoting these fundamental issues within our own society, as well as encouraging Muslim communities to participate in mainstream society, that our civilisation can stem the flow of moderate Muslims embracing the Islamist mantra.

[44] A Pew Survey noted that 78% of British Muslims worry about unemployment. Jodie T. Allen. "The French-Muslim Connection: Is France Doing a Better Job of Integration than Its Critics?." *Pew Research Centre*. August 17, 2006. [http://pewresearch.org/obdeck/?ObDeckID=50]

[45] Nick Harvey, the Liberal Democrats Defence Spokesperson, said following the incident, "You have to ask whether we are doing more harm than good in Iraq." In a separate comment prior to the attack Alex Salmond, the SNP leader said, "Those who are responsible for this blood-soaked quagmire now have the duty to tell us how they propose to remove our soldiers from this morass." Patrick Wintour and Richard Norton-Taylor. "Four soldiers die in boat bomb as Blair prepares shift on Iraq." *The Guardian*. [UK] November 13, 2006.

Legal Aspects of Combating Terrorism
Centre of Excellence Defence Against Terrorism, Ankara, Turkey (Ed.)
IOS Press, 2008

doi:10.3233/978-1-58603-930-1-49

Human Rights and Terrorism

Capt. Derya YAMAN
Turkish General Staff, Ankara, Turkey

Abstract. Commitment of States to human rights is among the most powerful weapons against terrorism. Although definitions of terrorism are rife with conceptual difficulties, human rights norms help to establish a clear moral threshold that should not be crossed. Terrorist acts that violate the fundamental right of human beings—the right to life—are unjustifiable and inexcusable. Counter-terrorism efforts must be carried out in keeping with international human rights obligations. Sacrificing our core values in the process of combating terrorism will be self-defeating and self-destructive. Security needs of the State must be kept in balance with counter-terrorism efforts. Human rights are a guarantee and a precondition for individual freedom. But they will only be respected in a society where the State upholds the rule of law.

Keywords. Human rights, Universal Declaration of Human Rights, treaties related to terrorism, criminal investigation, questioning for intelligence purposes, prosecution, detention, torture, inhuman or degrading treatment, combatant's privilege.

Human Rights are rights which a person enjoys for just being a human. It has been claimed that we are now living in an "age of rights"; with this claim goes an image of a "global culture of rights". The Universal Declaration of Human Rights of 1948 has been hailed as the first truly international document on human rights; as Vaclav Havel has said: " A number of diverse texts have played fundamental roles in human history. The Universal Declaration of Human Rights differs from all the others primarily in one aspect: its impact has not been meant to remain confined within one culture or one civilization. From the very outset, it has been envisaged as a universal, so to speak planetary, set of principles to govern human coexistence, and it has gradually become the point of departure for countless successive guidelines defining the rules of a worthy life together for the people and nations of this Earth. Texts of such fundamental nature are not easily born."[1]

In this particular case, the text was born out of the Second World War and has become a cornerstone document of human rights law. After bad experiences, human rights are guaranteed today much better than was the case in the past.

Human Rights standards operate in two different ways:

---

[1] Hastrup, Kirsten. Representing the common good. Human Rights in Global Perspective, Edited by Richard Ashby Wilson and Jon P. Mitchell.203, Routledge, London. Page 17.

1. They protect individual citizens from actions by governments. This assumes that there are some individual freedoms that government cannot take away without proper justification.
2. They place an obligation on government to provide certain benefits. This assumes that governments have an affirmative obligation to provide certain services to the individuals, and that the individuals are entitled to claim the provision of these services.

In the context of the war on terrorism much of the human rights discussion is directed toward those who seek to defend against terrorist acts and capture and prosecute terrorists. These discussions are focused on human rights standards designed to protect suspected terrorists who are the subject of criminal investigation, questioning for intelligence purposes, prosecution, and detention. International concern is also focused on the legal limits on the use of military force against terrorists. Consequently, defense against terrorists has raised several important questions concerning the interpretation of basic human rights conventions and international treaties on the law of armed conflict.

Another interesting aspect of the discussion on human rights and terrorism is the motivation of persons who are involved in terrorist acts. Terrorists sometimes attempt to justify their acts by human rights standards. In essence, they claim the authority of the rule of law to legitimize human rights protections or benefits and then argue that terrorist acts are a legitimate means to achieve redress of these claims.[2] The attempt to justify their crimes can by no means be accepted and it must be stressed that international human rights law does not allow the use of violence to achieve human rights goals.

General Assembly Resolution 49/185 (23 December, 1994) is an instrument depicting the legal objection to terrorism as a violation of human rights. It states: "Mindful of the need to protect human rights of and guarantees for the individual in accordance with the relevant international human rights principles and instruments, particularly the right to life, (the UN General Assembly) reiterates its unequivocal condemnation of all acts, methods and practices of terrorism, as activities aimed at the destruction of human rights, fundamental freedoms and democracy, threatening the territorial integrity and security of States, destabilizing legitimately constituted Governments, undermining pluralistic civil society and having adverse consequences on the economic and social development of States."

International human rights treaties provide a common understanding of human rights acceptable to all cultures, they test the legitimacy of the causes that terrorist fight for, and strictly prohibit the methods of terrorism and terrorist acts.

When surveying international human rights instruments, it may be said that the United Nations system and its key documents for the promotion and protection of human rights—the 1945 UN Charter and the 1948 Universal Declaration of Human Rights—formed the basis of the international human rights law. These two documents were subsequently followed by two legally binding instruments, promulgated in 1966 and entered into force in 1976: the International Covenant on Civil and Political Rights and the International Covenant on Economic, Social, and Cultural Rights. Further treaties addressing specific human rights concerns (racial discrimination, discrimination against women, prohibition of torture, and the rights of the child) have

---

[2] Legal Aspects of Combating Terrorism, Defense Institute of International Legal Studies, National Defense University School for National Security Executive Education, November 2004.

entered into force since 1976. The Convention on the Rights of the Child has the largest number of states as parties, while the Second Optional Protocol to the International Covenant on Civil and Political Rights, which prohibits the practice of the death penalty in all member states, has the lowest.

In addition to these legal instruments, there are monitoring bodies attached to each treaty that examine the degree to which states are fulfilling their legal obligations under the terms of each treaty. For example, UN Human Rights Commission, established in 1946 by the UN Economic and Social Commission (ECOSOC); UN Human Rights Committee, established by the International Covenant on Civil and Political Rights; UN Security Council, using its authority under the United Nations Charter, and regional organizations like the European Human Rights Commission and the European Human Rights Court, or the Organization of American States (OAS) Human Rights Commission and the American Court of Human Rights. Taken together, these human rights instruments and the monitoring bodies form an international legal regime that seeks to limit state behavior in order to protect and promote human rights.[3]

Over the last years the international community, acting through the United Nations, regional or specialized organizations, has adopted international treaties in order gradually to build up a body of international law against terrorist activities in their various forms. Resolution 1373 calls for States to ratify them as soon as possible. The Counter-Terrorism Committee is committed to assisting States in this effort. These Conventions are:

1. Convention on Offences and Certain Other Acts committed on Board Aircraft, Tokyo, 14 September 1963, 182 States Parties (as of April 2007).
2. Convention for the Suppression of Unlawful Seizure of Aircraft, The Hague, 16 December 1970, 182 States Parties.
3. Convention for the Suppression of Unlawful Acts Against the Safety of Civil Aviation, Montreal, 23 September 1971, 185 States Parties.
4. Convention on the Prevention and Punishment of Crimes Against Internationally Protected Persons, Including Diplomatic Agents, New York, 14 December 1973, 166 State Parties.
5. International Convention Against the Taking of Hostages, New York, 17 December 1979, 168 State Parties.
6. Convention on the Physical Protection of Nuclear Material, Vienna, 26 October 1979, 122 State Parties.
7. Protocol for the Suppression of Unlawful Acts of Violence at Airports serving International Civil Aviation, Supplementary to the Convention for the Suppression of Unlawful Acts against the Safety of Civil Aviation, done at Montreal on 23 September 1971, Montreal, 24 February 1988, 161 State Parties.
8. Convention for the Suppression of Unlawful Acts Against the Safety of Maritime Navigation, Rome, 10 March 1988, 141 State Parties.
9. Protocol for the Suppression of Unlawful Acts Against the Safety of Fixed Platforms located on the continental shelf, Rome, 10 March 1988, 124 State Parties.
10. Convention on the Marking of Plastic Explosives for the Purpose of Detection, Montreal, 1 March 1991, 130 State Parties.

[3] Landman, Todd. Studying Human Rights, Routledge London and New York, 2006, page 13.

11. International Convention for the Suppression of Terrorist Bombings, New York, 15 December 1997, 149 State Parties.
12. International Convention for the Suppression of the Financing of Terrorism, New York, 9 December 1999, 156 State Parties.
13. International Convention for the Suppression of Acts of Nuclear Terrorism, New York, 13 April 2005, 100 State Parties.

Each of these treaties listed above focuses on a specific type of terrorist activity, specifically describes the prohibited activities, authorizes the expansion of national domestic jurisdiction to prosecute alleged offenders, obligates States to cooperate with each other in the investigation of offenses defined in the treaties and requires States holding offenders to extradite suspects in case that prosecution will not be undertaken locally.[4] They are especially important when a terrorist commits a crime and goes to another country. As a common definition of terrorism could not be reached, the issue is regulated on a sectoral basis by treaties against terrorism.[5]

The UN's commitment to human rights is among its most powerful weapons against terrorism. General Assembly Resolutions A/RES/60/158, A/RES/59/191, A/RES/58/187 and A/RES/57/219 about protection of human rights and fundamental freedoms while countering terrorism and A/RES/59/195, A/RES/58/174, A/RES/56/160, A/RES/54/164, A/RES/52/133, A/RES/50/186, A/RES/49/185, A/RES/48/122 about human rights and terrorism generally, call upon all States to adopt measures in accordance with the Charter of the United Nations and the relevant provisions of international law, including international standards of human rights, to prevent terrorism and to strengthen international cooperation in combating terrorism. Although definitions of terrorism are rife with conceptual difficulties, human rights norms help to establish a clear moral threshold that should not be crossed. Terrorist acts that violate the fundamental right of human beings—the right to life—are unjustifiable and inexcusable. At the same time, counter-terrorism efforts must be carried out in keeping with international human rights obligations. Sacrificing our core values in the process of combating terrorism will be self-defeating and self-destructive. The balance is therefore very important, combating terrorism in the scope of human rights and the security needs of the State should always be in balance.

In a speech in Madrid in March 2005, on the first anniversary of the terrorist railway bombings, Secretary-General Annan sketched out the broad outlines of a global counter-terrorism strategy. The five elements contained in the strategy are:

- to dissuade disaffected groups from choosing terrorism as a tactic to achieve their goals;
- to deny terrorists the means to carry out their attacks;
- to deter states from supporting terrorists;
- to develop state capacity to prevent terrorism; and
- to defend human rights in the struggle against terrorism.

Terrorism is not only a threat to all societies, but also an attack on values that define the international community—the rule of law, respect for human rights, protection of civilians, intercultural faith and tolerance, and the peaceful resolution of

---

[4] Legal Aspects of Combating Terrorism, Defense Institute of International Legal Studies, National Defense University School for National Security Executive Education, November 2004, page 4-2.

[5] Başeren, Sertaç. "Terrorism and International Relations, Presentation at Symposium of Global Terror and Turkey", 29 May 2002, SAREM.

conflicts. Counter-terrorism efforts can best succeed by pursuing them on all fronts and in all countries.[6]

Human rights are a guarantee and a precondition for individual freedom. But they will only be respected in a society where the State upholds the rule of law, even under difficult circumstances. Observance and realization of human rights by States is one of the major achievements of the second half of the twentieth century, although, as we all know, the concept has not yet been realized globally. The annual reports of the UN High Commissioner for Human Rights and the Human Rights Committee, as well as the reporting of non-governmental organizations such as Human Rights Watch and Amnesty International, reveal how much still needs to be done.

Systematic and protracted violations of basic human rights are one of the main sources of contemporary armed conflicts. Respect for human rights by States therefore affects our common security, in particular when they are fighting international terrorism. When States violate human rights for shortsighted advantages, e.g., by allowing torture during the interrogation of suspects, they surrender the moral high ground, as well as the State's underlying constitutional legal foundation. The winner will always be the terrorists, not the State's security organs, because human rights violation can be used by the media to demonstrate the ruthlessness of a government, which in turn increases the number of direct or indirect supporters of terrorist organizations. Human rights must therefore be defended against the temptation to limit their application when derogation is inappropriate.[7]

It is well known that in war, combatants are legally entitled to use lethal force against enemy combatants. They may not be punished for intentionally killing the enemy, nor are they even necessarily subject to reporting or review. This is known as "combatant's privilege". The question as to whether a killing was lawful, therefore, usually centers on whether the person attacked was a combatant or not, and if not, whether the person was killed incidentally to an attack on a legitimate military objective and whether that death was proportionate to the military objective to be gained or preventable through taking feasible precautions. Although the right to life is regarded as non-derogable, armed conflict presents this important and universally recognized qualification.

Outside of war, there is no "combatant's privilege". Police, as well as military personnel acting in a law enforcement capacity, are held to strict standards on the use of lethal force. One may only shoot in self-defense, to defend others against "the imminent threat of death or serious injury", to prevent a "particularly serious crime involving grave threat to life", or to arrest such a perpetrator, and only when less extreme measures will not suffice. One may shoot to kill only "when strictly unavoidable in order to protect life". Every incident of firearm use by officers in performance of their duty must be reported and subject to review, particularly where death, injury, or other grave consequences result.

This divergence is of plain relevance to the practice of targeting individuals for assassination. In armed conflict, it is legal, if not always prudent, to target officials who are in the chain of command, either formally or functionally, up to and including the commander-in chief, even when they are sleeping or undefended (but not when they lay down arms and surrender). Apart from war, the deliberate killing of a public enemy is

---

[6] Gambari, İbrahim A. United Nations Under-Secretary-General for Political Affairs, Commonwealth Ministers Reference Book,2006.

[7] Hostettler, Peter. Human Rights and the "War" Against International Terrorism, presentation at the "Meeting of Independent Experts on Terrorism and International Law", San Remo, 30 May-1 June 2002.

unlawful except under the above exigent circumstances, and in any event, such a killing must be thoroughly investigated.

According to Çaycı, leaders and armed militants of a terrorist organization waging terrorist warfare, as well as their military assets and capability, are legitimate targets. Therefore, any military operation resulting in their death cannot be regarded as summary execution; it is combat, not a law enforcement operation. Similarly, when taking an active/direct part in hostilities, collaborators are also legitimate targets. The wounded and sick leaders, militants, or collaborators (persons out of combat) who have been captured or have surrendered, and innocent civilians in general, on the other hand, are to be respected and protected.[8]

There are likewise gaps between the two regimes with respect to detention. Under human rights law, anyone arrested or detained on a criminal charge must be brought promptly before a judicial officer and is entitled to have a court review the legality of their detention. Indefinite detention, even under an administrative detention regime, is arbitrary and violative of international human rights law.

In time of war, the prohibition of "arbitrary" detention is supplemented and interpreted through reference to the *lex specialis* of International Humanitarian Law, under which captured enemy combatants may be detained, and civilians of an occupied territory may be interned.

It is therefore crucial in the battle against terrorism to distinguish carefully between operations amounting to an armed conflict (e.g. the operations in Afghanistan starting on 7 October 2001) and other forms of struggle where police and security forces clearly operate outside of an armed conflict.[9]

The prohibition of torture, inhuman, or degrading treatment is absolute, there are no exceptions on any grounds whatsoever. It is contained in both universal and regional treaties, and there is a specific convention against torture. It is backed by a similar provision in common Article 3 to the four Geneva Conventions of 1949. As a result, torture and inhuman or degrading treatment are prohibited in all situations.

Conflicts emerge with regard to questioning detainees, particularly in exceptional situations when a detained person allegedly could provide evidence on a planned terrorist attack. Some would like to construct a dilemma between the right to life of persons endangered by the attack and the prohibition on torture of the detained person. But the binding legal instruments do not leave any space for interpretation; the prohibition on torture and inhuman or degrading treatment is absolute. It is simply not possible to draw a line between a general practice of torturing or treating detainees inhumanely and exceptional single cases. It is also not possible to torture "a little". Investigators are required to use interrogation techniques similar to civil police forces without making use of physical or psychological coercion. If the results are unsatisfactory, it is forbidden to go further down the road of extracting information from a person unwilling to confess.[10]

---

[8] Çaycı, Sadi. Countering Terrorism and International Law: The Turkish Experience, presentation at the "Meeting of Independent Experts on Terrorism and International Law", San Remo, 30 May-1 June 2002.

[9] Hostettler, Peter.Human Rights and the "War" Against International Terrorism, presentation at the "Meeting of Independent Experts on Terrorism and International Law", San Remo, 30 May-1 June 2002.

[10] Ibid.

References

[1] Hastrup, Kirsten. Representing the common good. Human Rights in Global Perspective, Edited by Richard Ashby Wilson and Jon P. Mitchell. 203, Routledge, London.
[2] Legal Aspects of Combating Terrorism, Defense Institute of International Legal Studies, National Defense University School for National Security Executive Education, November 2004.
[3] Landman, Todd. Studying Human Rights, Routledge London and New York, 2006.
[4] Başeren, Sertaç. Terrorism and International Relations, Presentation at Symposium of Global Terror and Turkey", 29 May 2002, SAREM.
[5] Gambari, İbrahim A. United Nations Under-Secretary-General for Political Affairs, Commonwealth Ministers Reference Book, 2006.
[6] Hostettler, Peter. Human Rights and the "War" Against International Terrorism, presentation at the "Meeting of Independent Experts on Terrorism and International Law", San Remo, 30 May-1 June 2002.
[7] Çaycı, Sadi. Countering Terrorism and International Law: The Turkish Experience, presentation at the "Meeting of Independent Experts on Terrorism and International Law", San Remo, 30 May-1 June 2002.

Legal Aspects of Combating Terrorism
Centre of Excellence Defence Against Terrorism, Ankara, Turkey (Ed.)
IOS Press, 2008

doi:10.3233/978-1-58603-930-1-57

Combating Terrorist Financing: The Dichotomy between Formulating the Legal Bases and Effective Operational Intelligence

Dr. Nick RIDLEY
Senior Lecturer, John Grieve Centre for Police Studies, DASS, London Metropolitan University

Abstract. This paper is supportive of a presentation given regarding the legal basis of measures against the financing of terrorism. The central premise of this short paper is that anti-terrorist legal measures were actually compounding the problem of a strategic intelligence time lag involved in successfully identifying and acting against the various kinds of *modus operandi* used in terrorist financing in the half decade since 9/11.

Keywords. Counter-terrorism, terrorist financing, legal obstacles, FATF, charities funding terrorism, criminal activity to fund terrorism.

1. Legal Difficulties

In an attempt to disrupt terrorist activity and frustrate attacks, governments, law enforcement agencies, and financial regulators have been co-operating on an international scale in formulating measures to prevent terrorist groups obtaining funds, and to block the transfer and deployment of such funds. Unfortunately, this co-operation has been significantly hampered and delayed by a collective strategic mindset persisting from the pre-9/11 era.

Some problems have obstructed prosecutions for terrorist activities in general, whether in the area of financing or not. A particular legal difficulty facing counter-measures against terrorism and the financing of terrorism is that of 'double criminality',[1] especially concerning laws whereby a state deems any acts relating to terrorist activities as criminal. The legal process for bringing terrorists to justice in such cases is 'fraught with difficulties'.[2]

Another restriction on prosecuting terrorism is that the statutes and laws passed cannot always provide for all the possible types and modes of crimes which the

[1] 'Double criminality' is a principle which stipulates that the alleged crime for which extradition is being sought must be criminal in both the demanding and the requested countries.

[2] Chuckwuemerie, A., "International Legal War on the Financing of Terrorism," in Journal of Money Laundering Control, volume 9, no. 1, 2006.

terrorists may utilise and exploit. In Nigeria, for example, the blowing up of petroleum pipelines and installations is not in the criminal code, although the code abounds in regulations for preventing oil and commodity fraud. Yet pipelines criss-cross every part of Nigeria, and are an obvious target for terrorism.[3] The same difficulty applies to the financing of terrorism, in that a simple principal of 'blanket criminalisation' is insufficient to cover all types of *modus operandi*.

Another difficulty, more characteristic of the pre-9/11 era than today, was the tendency for certain countries to deal with terrorism on an individual basis, each specifically addressing an individual terrorist issue or organisation whose activities impacted upon that country. 9/11 was a significant event in that it placed terrorism, and the threat of terrorism, on a global scale.

In terms of combating terrorist financing, prior to 9/11 several arguments were made by regulators, the financial sector, and certain law enforcement organisations against deploying resources in the specific area of terrorist financing. One was that bankers and the banking sector could not and cannot identify terrorist financing due to the fact that they are not law enforcement agents, and have neither the expertise to identify, nor the powers to curb, terrorist financing.

However, although they cannot enforce the law, regulators can and are especially qualified to identify unusual transactional activities, create specialist business profiles of customers, and track financial activities that seem to have no business justification. Given that this is true, when their reports and other information are combined with ongoing intelligence from law enforcement agencies, links between potential terrorists and terrorist financing become stronger and can be corroborated.

2. Responding to the Challenges

In the immediate aftermath of 9/11 the potential of regulators' expertise was overlooked. Legislators reacting to the post-9/11 events constructed financial defence measures involving extra compliance regulations imposed upon banks and financial institutions. These measures cost large sums of money to implement in terms of equipment and staff training, and they resulted, and still result, in a great loss of revenue through time lost out of the business working day. The measures themselves were made more costly by being hastily promulgated with no input or advice sought as to what was practical and possible from banking practitioners. The overall result was that by 2003 over 209 international banks had stated that the compliance costs to their institutions had risen by over 60%. Wasteful economic damage to the international financial system became a factor of revenue loss, affecting the smooth running of business services, credit, and capital transfer.

It was only after a period of some years that the banking sector was properly consulted on regulatory and financial defence measures against the financing of terrorism, and meaningful, operational financial intelligence exchange between banking and law enforcement started to flow on a regular basis. In intelligence terms, this period of up to half a decade was crucial time lost in the area of terrorist financing.

[3] Ibid. The author cites examples from Nigeria, Canada, UK and US to illustrate the divergence of anti-terror perceptions and adequate levels of legislation.

International Counter-Terrorist Agreements

There have been several international legal and regulatory measures and agreements against terrorism. In the pre-9/11 era these consisted of:

- Convention for the Suppression of Unlawful Seizure of Aircraft, 1970;
- Convention on Suppression of Unlawful Acts Against Safety of Civil Aviation, 1971;
- Convention on Prevention and Punishment of Crimes Against Internationally Protected Persons, Including Diplomatic Agents, 1973;
- International Convention Against the Taking of Hostages, 1979;
- Convention on the Physical Protection of Nuclear Material, 1980;
- Protocol for the Suppression of Unlawful Acts of Violence at Airports Serving International Civil Aviation, 1988;
- Convention for Suppression of Unlawful Acts Against Safety of Maritime Navigation, 1988;
- Protocol for the Suppression of Unlawful Acts Against the Safety of Fixed Platforms Located on the Continental Shelf, 1988;
- International Convention for the Suppression of Terrorist Bombings, 1997;
- International Convention for Suppression of the Financing of Terrorism, 1999.

Only in 1999 were there specific measures enacted against terrorist financing. Even at this period, by 2001, of the 22 ratifications needed to bring the 1999 Convention against Terrorist Financing into force, only four had been deposited with the UN Secretary General.

The UN Security Council has passed a series of resolutions regarding terrorist financing. One in particular, Resolution 1373 of 2001, created a legally binding international obligation to prevent and suppress the financing of terrorist acts. This was an international action not taken against an individual country, or an individual, but a general 'blanket global action'. (By contrast, Security Council Resolution 1333 of 2000 was only specifically against Afghanistan and Bin Laden.)

The Financial Action Task Force

With the events of 9/11 international action against terrorist financing accelerated. The Financial Action Task Force (FATF), up to that time an international strategic anti-money laundering organisation, was galvanised into action in the post 9/11 period. From 2002 onwards, the swingeing nature of international anti-terrorist finance measures and conventions—and the potential threat of US sanctions—conditioned responses from countries. These responses took into account and adapted to regional conditions. At the time of writing there are no less than eight regional FATF bodies. These are: APG (Asia Pacific), CFATF (Caribbean), EAG (Eurasia), ESAAMG (East Africa), GAFISUD (South America), GIABA (Western Africa), MENAFTF (Middle East and North Africa), and MONEYVAL (Eastern and Central Europe). Such regional bodies perform an admirable task in facilitating information and experience exchange between countries, both within the same region and on an international scale, a task which is difficult due to cultural differences and the dual minefields of data protection and conflicting jurisdictions of criminal law and procedures.

In early 2001 the FATF considered the potential cross-overs and similarities between terrorism and money laundering.[4] The various experts and member states were unable to reach total unanimity, but did conclude that, for the most part, the *modus operandi* involved in money laundering and terrorist financing were similar, if not one and the same. As part of its deployment against terrorist financing, an Extraordinary Plenary Session of the FATF was convened and acted—with extraordinary speed—and their eight Special Recommendations against Terrorist Financing were formulated, and are binding on all member countries.

These Special Recommendations, covering the *modi* of illicit transfer, had their limitations. Unfortunately the measures, like all such financial measures promulgated in 2001, were conceived in the strategic mindset of the *modus operandi* of money laundering. Also, in the half decade that followed, certain types and *modi* in various regions—which will remain unspecified for intelligence reasons—were not covered, and other more *ad hoc* best practices had to be adopted between law enforcement and regulatory authorities in order to facilitate effective action against terrorist financing.

Within a month of the September attacks, the Financial Action Task Force convened an Extraordinary Plenary Session in Washington DC and formulated binding international recommendations. These were:

- Special Recommendation I, ratification of all existing UN instruments
- Special Recommendation II, criminalising of terrorist financing and money laundering
- Special Recommendation III, freezing and confiscation of terrorist assets
- Special Recommendation IV, reporting suspicious transactions
- Special Recommendation V, international co-operation
- Special Recommendation VI, reporting suspicious transactions re terrorist financing
- Special Recommendation VII, on alternative remittance systems
- Special Recommendation VIII, on charities and NGOs

Such measures are extremely laudable, but it is submitted that they may be vulnerable to the six possible dangers inherent in all anti-terrorist legislation, namely:

- Timing, as immediate and emotive reactions may lead to errors
- The political imperative of immediate action involving potential draconian provisions
- New legislation possibly duplicating such powers as already exist
- Unreal objectives
- Excessive powers
- Indirect applications, the later trend to use and pervert new legislation in applying it to other criminal offences

Also, with regard to the eight FATF Special Recommendations, it may be said that they were extremely laudable in concept but tended to suffer from the fact that they were the lowest common denominator of international agreement. Arguably, Special Recommendations I and II were merely repetition, while Special Recommendation V is, in stark terms, stating the obvious. The entities covered by Special Recommendation VIII are scarcely defined under a common international legal definition. Finally, and of extreme importance, the eight—and later nine[5]—Special Recommendations epitomise

---

[4] FATF Typology Report XII, February 2001.

[5] In late 2004/early 2005 a ninth Special Recommendation was added, encompassing the use of cash couriers.

a strategic intelligence time lag, in that they were perhaps formulated in, and perpetuate, the international strategic mindset of the anti-money laundering efforts of a previous decade.

3. Contexts for Legal Action

The Case of Saudi Arabia

The question of Saudi Arabia is one of the central issues of Islamic terrorism. Strategic analysts counsel constantly that, despite the fact that the 9/11 attacks were aimed at the United States, the true object of the implacable ire of al-Qaeda is the state of Saudi Arabia.[6] This hostility is reflected in the vitriolic allegations and accusations of Islamic extremists who claim that the country betrayed both its ethos as an Islamic state and its role as the location of the holy places by allowing a US military presence and engaging in subservient political and economic relations with the United States.

Saudi Arabia was the centre of a model of terrorist financing proposed by Brisard which highlights the potential terrorist finance trail.[7] The so called 'Brisard Model' takes into account the combined factors of the misdirection of *zakat* donations, transfers via the regular banking system, use of international charities and NGOs, subversion of localized relief organizations, *hawala* transfers, and the use by small terrorist groups of criminal activity to raise revenue. The significance of the model is that, according to its presentation of the flow of funds, terrorist abuse within the context of illicit transfers of money is not restricted to the financial sector. It reveals the wider abuse or exploitation of many organisations, including legitimate and illegitimate businesses, formal and informal financial systems, charities and NGOs.

The Saudi government has come under intense adverse publicity in the post-9/11 period on account of charities and NGOs registered in Saudi Arabia which were and are allegedly engaged in untrammelled fund transfers, potentially fully exploitable by those who wish to fund terrorists. However, on closer analysis, certain of the allegedly exploited charities, which were the subject of international controversy about regulation, and which had formed separate sub-charities in their fund-raising activities, presented difficulties in terms of effective supervision *not due to lack of political will or anti terrorist vigour* but due to legal difficulties involved in regions of the world including Saudi Arabia.

NGOs

The issue of the potential exploitation of NGOs has given rise to another change in trends in the perception of intelligence since late 2004. Up to that time, the *modi* of terrorist financing were addressed in the same terms as the money laundering *modus operandi*, that is, by identifying and concentrating on the main methods and ascertaining new trends and principle methods of fundraising and fund transfer.

NGO exploitation was perceived as one such principal *modus.* However, strategic intelligence revealed that such an approach was possibly flawed in that terrorist cells

---

[6] Bergen, P. (2002), "Holy War Inc., Inside the World of al-Qaeda," London Phoenix, conclusions in final chapter.

[7] Brisard, J. C. and Martinez, D. (2005), "Zarqawi, the new face of al Qaeda," Cambridge Policy Press.

and affiliated extremist groups were engaged in adaptable methods of raising and transferring potential funds.

Low Level Criminality

According to EU-wide intelligence indicators, this adaptability has manifested itself, since late 2004, in individual terrorist extremist cells within the EU having recourse to various forms of low level criminality in order to raise funds. The amounts in question are comparatively small, i.e. compatible with the normal amounts gained by low level criminality, and therefore they are unlikely to come to the attention of banking and financial regulatory authorities as they review amounts deposited or transferred. Such sources of criminal revenue for terrorist cells were reported in several EU member states and in South East Asia.

The methods and means vary considerably. The salient aspect for operational intelligence purposes is that the different terrorist cells quickly turn to short-term forms of criminality for revenue raising, which makes it difficult to identify intelligence patterns regarding both their sources of funds and their *modus*, and which compounds the difficulty of long-term strategic assessment of terrorist financing. This pragmatic and adaptable way of raising and transferring funds is important to terrorist financing, and part of the fundamental difference between money laundering and terrorist financing.

4. Conclusion

In the post 9/11 period of the 'new terrorism' it has taken over five years for law enforcement, inter-governmental initiatives, and international financial regulatory bodies to perceive fully these differences and formulate legal counter-measures. Given the continuing impact of terrorist attacks since 9/11, over a half-decade of failing to engage effectively in strategic intelligence oversight of terrorist financing is a time luxury that can we can ill afford.

Legal Aspects of Combating Terrorism
Centre of Excellence Defence Against Terrorism, Ankara, Turkey (Ed.)
IOS Press, 2008

doi:10.3233/978-1-58603-930-1-63

Legal Aspects of Cyberterrorism

Phillip W. BRUNST[1]
Senior Researcher, Max Planck Institute for Foreign and International Criminal Law, Freiburg i. B., Germany

Abstract. The Internet offers a wide range of possibilities for terrorists and terrorist organizations. This includes attacks that can be digitally launched and which can affect data, property or human lives. Other important aspects regard the spreading of terrorist-related contents and the conventional use of the Internet, e.g. for communication with each other. The legal framework that is available to the international community must address new possibilities for terrorists and at the same time respect the liberties of legitimate users.

Keywords. Cyberterrorism, Internet, terrorism, communication, propaganda, law.

Introduction

The separation between a physical "real" world and a digital "virtual" world is constantly vanishing. Computer systems can be used to control physical infrastructure, to communicate, and to prepare conventional attacks. Therefore, terrorists have started to make use of the Internet in many different ways [1], [2], [3]. This chapter will first briefly sketch some of the possibilities for terrorists and terrorist organizations to use the Internet for their purposes (1.). It will then focus on the legal aspects in fighting cyber terrorism (2.).

1. Use of the Internet by Terrorists

Terrorists have found many ways to use and abuse the possibilities of the Internet.[2] Results of such forms of use do not necessarily have to remain within the "virtual" sphere. On the contrary: Because of so-called SCADA systems, effects of cyber attacks can lead to the destruction of property or even the loss of life (1.1). However, the use of the Internet for attacks is not the only—and very probably not the most interesting—

[1] *Phillip W. Brunst* is a senior researcher at the Max Planck Institute for Foreign and International Criminal Law in Freiburg, Germany (http://www.mpicc.de). He heads the "information law" section at the Institute and can be contacted at p.brunst@mpicc.de. The author would like to thank *Nicolas von zur Mühlen* for valuable discussions on this paper.

[2] The following part can only roughly sketch the numerous possibilities that the Internet offers for terrorists and terrorist organizations. For a more thorough evaluation see [1], [2], and [3] with further references.

option for terrorists. Since everybody can freely access information that is stored on publicly available websites and forums, the spreading of terrorist-related contents over the Internet is of great interest to terrorist organizations (1.2). In this field, the line between neutral information, persuasive literature and texts with an explicit terrorist intent is sometimes very thin. Finally, the common use of the Internet, e.g. for communication, for storing and encrypting data, or for anonymous interaction, is open not only to legitimate users, but also to terrorists (1.3).

1.1. Attacks Launched over the Internet

If terrorists use the Internet to launch attacks, they do so in order to generate fear, to create economic confusion, or to discriminate a political opponent. A first step is often the illegal accessing of a computer system over the Internet, e.g. by using so-called “Zero-Day-Exploits”, i.e. software flaws that have not yet been disclosed to the manufacturer (and therefore have not yet been patched). These exploits can be either developed by talented members of a terrorist organization or they can be acquired on the black market.

Once an attacker has gained access to a computer system, several possibilities lie ahead. First, the system can simply be shut down, thereby making it unavailable to legitimate users. However, the system can (in most cases) easily be restarted by administrators, giving the attackers only a very short moment of success. Nevertheless, if the affected system is being used to control a power plant or in a medical environment, even a short interruption can be hazardous. Furthermore, the outage can be combined with a conventional attack.

Currently, large-scale bot-net attacks can be observed as a more effective weapon to render systems unreachable [2]. In 2006, more than 60,000 active bot-infected computers were observed per day. Furthermore, over 6 million distinct bot-infected computers were detected within a 6-month period. The fact that these “zombies” were controlled by less than 5,000 command-and-control-servers shows that the persons in control of these bot-nets are no longer hobby hackers, but well experienced and organized groups. Furthermore, botnets can be rented for attacks against any given target. Prices are reported to range from about 150 to 400 US dollars, depending on the target and the duration of the attack. The attacks on Estonia[3] in 2007 have shown that with bot-net attacks and the help of rented additional capacities a whole country can be brought to its knees.

Apart from these destructive types of attacks, terrorists who have gained access to a computer system can also alter information that is being stored, modify programs or simply monitor what information is being entered or processed via the altered system. Whether the access to the system is noticeable to administrators or users is often almost entirely dependent on the attacker. A so-called “defacement”, i.e. a changed web page, for example, will often be noticed shortly after the information has been altered. However, if Trojan horse programs have been installed or the e-mail communication is under surveillance, this might be unnoticed for a longer period of time [2].

Already the above-mentioned examples of control systems show that the results of a computer-based attack do not necessarily have to be within a computer network. Often, attacks on computer systems are considered less dangerous than conventional at-

[3] See http://en.wikipedia.org/wiki/Cyberattacks_on_Estonia_2007 [last visited: January 2008] for an overview.

tacks with bombs, because damage to computers are said to lead "only" to economic losses. This, however, is not true for SCADA systems.[4] These systems are used to measure and control other systems and can therefore lead to effects not only in the "virtual", but also in the "real" world. Often, these systems are—either knowingly or unknowingly—connected to the Internet. According to informal sources, 17% of SCADA malfunctions are caused by a direct Internet access to SCADA systems [1]. Other possibilities include VPN-, modem-, or trusted connections, e.g. remote access to allow maintenance work.

The possible effects of an attack against SCADA systems could be observed in the USA in the year 2003 when 21 power plants were brought down and other critically important institutions like Edwards Air Force Base (the test center for B-2 and B-1 bombers) were also affected. As far as is publicly known, these breakdowns were the result of the W32.Lovsan worm that was using the same port to exploit a weakness on individual personal computers being used by the plants to communicate with each other [4]. Other scenarios that are under discussion and that could directly result in lost lives have either not become known to the public or not yet taken place. Potential target scenarios with effects on human lives that are under discussion include launching attacks on hydroelectric dams, tampering with control systems for railways or air traffic, and gaining control over systems supervising power plants. For further discussion of these scenarios see [1], [2], [3].

1.2. Terrorist-Related Contents

The Internet was—from the very first days on—designed for communication. Apart from exchanging information between individuals, the WWW offers the possibility for everyone to disseminate information. Today, terrorists have begun to use the Internet not only to launch attacks, but also to exploit it for new possibilities in a "war of ideas" [7]. This can be found in the presentation of terrorist viewpoints, the propagation of threats and the use of the Internet to initiate fundraising.

In former times, terrorists had to spread their information and views through word-of-mouth propaganda and leaflets that were circulated on the quiet. Those alternatives were time-consuming and risky and did not reach a large group of people. With the help of the Internet, almost every underground organization can afford its own website. Many contain detailed information, and not only on leaders and the history of the group. Records of recent (successful) operations, suppression by opponent governments and victims are presented in an attractive (and usually one-sided) way. Additionally, the information is organized and specifically prepared for different "target groups", e.g. supporters, enemies, or mass media. Some websites even offer cartoon-style design and children stories in order to reach even the youngest. See [2] for further details and references.

Apart from the presentation of views, the Internet is also used by terrorists to send threats to enemies and spread propaganda. The assassination of *Daniel Pearl* showed impressively the impact of psychological warfare. Furthermore, recent threats against different countries have not been sent as mere text messages. Instead, professional-looking videos are being produced that are forwarded to news agencies and Internet forums. A high-ranking member of the German Office for the Protection of the Constitution is quoted as having said that these videos can be seen as a form of "psychologi-

---

[4] SCADA is an acronym for "Supervisory Control and Data Acquisition".

cal warfare", because they do not make direct threats, but, instead, they create an atmosphere of unease [8].

Finally, some organizations have started to use their websites not only to disseminate information, but also to use it as a source of income for financing and fundraising. Methods include the selling of CDs, DVDs, T-Shirts, badges, flags or books. Other websites give instructions on how to donate money to the organization. Since the websites of the organizations are often at the center of surveillance, terrorist organizations have started to create widespread webs of supporting websites. Each of these websites links to other sites and gives information on how to find further sites with additional information.

1.3. Other Uses

Apart from attacks carried out over the Internet and the dissemination of information, terrorists use the Internet also for seemingly harmless tasks, such as sending e-mails or visiting websites. However, the technical background of the Internet facilitates even such simple uses.

Text-based communication systems such as e-mail or IRC allow users to exchange information fast, encrypted, and largely anonymously. Especially with the help of Internet cafés most of these applications can be used without leaving any traces to the users. Voice-based systems, on the other hand, allow for real-time communication like on the telephone, however, with the advances of untraceability, anonymity and encryption. Online storage services on the Internet allow also for secret and sometimes encrypted possibilities to exchange files.

Other important uses of the Internet for terrorists concern the planning and supporting of conventional acts. According to a terrorist training manual, public sources can provide up to 80% of all required information on an opponent [9]. An example that is often being cited is the satellite maps that are provided free of charge for example by Google, Microsoft or NASA. In the eyes of governments around the world, at least part of such information poses a threat to national security, because it allows the examination of otherwise protected areas from a bird's eye view.

Furthermore, some information that is freely available on the Internet can be used specifically for terrorist purposes. For example, instructions on how to build bombs, chemical weapons, or on how to operate certain kinds of weapons are available to download for everyone. Some of these manuals remind one of school books or compilations for university students. Others, however, are specifically assembled with the intention of aiding terrorists and would-be terrorists in their plans. Already the titles of these works ("Terrorist's Handbook", "Encyclopedia of Jihad" or "Sabotage Handbook") indicate their intention. However, one has to keep in mind that not all of the instructions in those compilations seem to have been thoroughly tested. Therefore, the information contained within these texts is often dangerous not only for future victims, but in many cases also for the persons that want to put it into practice. Nevertheless, its mere existence has led many to believe that the Internet has become an open university for jihad. The extensive use that terrorists make of the Internet for these purposes (e.g. online libraries and terrorist's helpdesks) show that this option is being seriously considered by terrorists. See [2] for further details.

2. Legal Responses

The legal responses to cyberterrorism have—to a large extent—remained vague. One reason for this is that there is no common definition of what cyberterrorism is. Some authors claim that up to today not a single instance of cyberterrorism has been recorded, because only attacks on other systems in the Internet that result in violence against persons or property with a terrorist intention can be qualified as cyberterrorism. Others define the term more broadly and include any form of Internet usage by terrorists or even conventional attacks that are directed against IT infrastructures. Already for the term "terrorism" more than 100 different definitions with more than 20 definitional elements have been identified in a study carried out in 1988 [10]. The term "cyberterrorism" as well as similar concepts, like "cyber war" or "cyber attack" remain likewise uncertain.

With a view to the results of terrorist action on the Internet as outlined above, however, a framework of international law can be identified. Following below, the most important legal instruments and the possibilities they contain for action will be sketched. However, most parts of the international framework suffer from the same problems. Action against crimes committed over the Internet is only possible if all affected states work closely together and are able to react quickly. Otherwise traces can be lost and important information that is needed for the identification and for the routing of attacks will be irrecoverable. Many conventions and similar instruments that have been set up to allow the tracing and prosecution of cybercriminals, however, have only been ratified by a small number of countries. Additionally, even those countries that have introduced legal instruments on a country level often suffer from a lack of training and capable people within the investigating authorities. Therefore, the existence of international instruments is an important step. However, without as many signing and ratifying countries as possible and practical experience within the authorities of these countries, there will always be severe problems with the prosecution of cybercriminal and, especially, cyberterrorist attacks.

2.1. Attacks Launched over the Internet

From a technical point of view there is basically no difference between changing a program so that a website shows a different content and changing it so that a control system for an airplane gives out wrong data resulting in a crashing airplane. From a legal point of view, however, this difference is crucial. Some provisions take up the technical context and criminalize acts that infringe computer data or computer systems. Often, these instruments are worded in a general way so that, regardless of terrorist intent and of the results, actions are being criminalized. Other provisions focus on the results instead and leave the way in which the result was committed (i.e. with conventional or with digital tools) unconsidered.

2.1.1. Technical Approach

The technical approach, i.e. criminalization of digital methods of perpetrators, is mainly being followed by the Convention on Cybercrime by the Council of Europe and by the EU Council Framework Decision on Attacks against Information Systems. Both have the advantage that cybercrime in general is being made punishable, regardless if it was committed by cyberterrorists or by other cybercriminals.

Convention on Cybercrime

The Council of Europe Convention on Cybercrime[5] addresses several issues in the area of substantive criminal law (emphasis added by the author):

> **Art. 2 Convention on Cybercrime: Illegal Access**
>
> Each Party shall adopt such legislative and other measures as may be necessary to establish as criminal offences under its domestic law, when committed intentionally, the *access to the whole or any part of a computer system* without right. A Party may require that the offence be committed by infringing security measures, with the intent of obtaining computer data or other dishonest intent, or in relation to a computer system that is connected to another computer system.

Through Art. 2 of the Cybercrime Convention all kinds of intrusion techniques, especially hacking offences are covered. Therefore, the drafters of the Cybercrime Convention considered illegal access to computer systems to be a "basic offence" against the confidentiality, integrity, and availability of computer systems and data. Additionally, Articles 3, 4 and 5 of the Convention cover the interception of non-public transmissions of data as well as the damaging, deletion, deterioration, alteration or suppression of computer data and the hindering of the functioning of a computer system through the manipulation of computer data:

> **Art. 3 Convention on Cybercrime: Illegal Interception**
>
> Each Party shall adopt [...] measures [...][against] the *interception* without right, made by technical means, *of non-public transmissions of computer data* to, from or within a computer system, including electromagnetic emissions from a computer system carrying such computer data. A Party may require that the offence be committed with dishonest intent, or in relation to a computer system that is connected to another computer system.

> **Art. 4 Convention on Cybercrime: Data Interference**
>
> 1. Each Party shall adopt [...] measures [...][against] the *damaging, deletion, deterioration, alteration or suppression of computer data* without right.
> 2. A Party may reserve the right to require that the conduct described in paragraph 1 result in serious harm.

> **Art. 5 Convention on Cybercrime: System Interference**
>
> Each Party shall adopt [...] measures [...][against] the *serious hindering* without right *of the functioning of a computer system* by inputting, transmitting, damaging, deleting, deteriorating, altering or suppressing computer data.

In addition to these provisions, Article 6 criminalizes even some actions that take place in the forefront of actual cybercrime attacks. It was therefore highly disputed during the drafting process. Basically, Article 6 criminalizes the production, sale, procurement for use, import, distribution or otherwise making available of "a device, including a computer program" that is designed or adapted for the purpose of committing any act mentioned in the above cited articles of the Cybercrime Convention. Article 6 paragraph 1 lit. a. 2. extends this criminalization also to computer passwords, access codes, and similar data that is used to gain unauthorized access to a computer system. The provisions of the Cybercrime Convention are extended in scope by rules on attempts and aiding and abetting (Art. 11) and on corporate liability (Art. 12).

---

[5] Convention on Cybercrime, signed 23.11.2001 in Budapest, CETS No. 185.

EU Council Framework Decision on Attacks Against Information Systems
The EU Council Framework Decision on attacks against information systems[6] was explicitly driven by an increasing concern of terrorist attacks against information systems (recital (2)). The terminology differs slightly from that of the Council of Europe's Convention on Cybercrime. The latter refers to "computer systems" whereas the Framework Decision defines "information systems". Apart from that also the Framework Decision criminalizes also the illegal access (Art. 2), illegal system interference (Art. 3), and illegal data interference (Art. 4). There are, however, no provisions against the illegal interception of computer data or against the misuse of devices.

The Framework Decision also includes a provision on aggravating circumstances (Art. 7). Each member state is obliged to take necessary measures to introduce a certain range of punishment if the offence is committed within the framework of a criminal organization. The latter is defined in Art. 1 of the Joint Action 98/733/JHA[7] as a structured association, established over a period of time, of more than two persons, acting in concert with a view to committing offences which are punishable by deprivation of liberty or a detention order of a maximum of at least four years or a more serious penalty, whether such offences are an end in themselves or a means of obtaining material benefits and, where appropriate, of improperly influencing the operation of public authorities. Member States are asked to draft provisions according to the Framework Decision by 16 March 2007 at the latest.

2.1.2. Outcome Approach

Whereas the Cybercrime Convention and the Framework Decision focus on the technical issues of cyberterrorism, most of the international instruments stress the outcome of terrorist action. They therefore criminalize the results regardless of the way they were achieved. Both approaches—technical and outcome—do not compete against each other; instead, they add to each other and tackle the issue of cyberterrorism from two different angles.

EU Council Framework Decision on Combating Terrorism
The approach of tackling the outcome of terrorist action can be observed for example in the Council Framework Decision on Combating Terrorism.[8] Art. 1 of the Framework Decision rules that member states should take measures in order to ensure that acts like attacks upon a person's life which may cause death, attacks upon the physical integrity of a person, the causing of extensive destruction to a Government, or the seizure of aircrafts, ships or other means of public or goods transportation, should be deemed to be terrorist offences if they are committed with certain aims:

> **Art. 1 Framework Decision on Combating Terrorism – Terrorist offences and fundamental rights and principles**
> 1. Each Member State shall take the necessary measures to ensure that the intentional acts referred to below in points (a) to (i) as defined as offences under national law, which, given their

[6] Council Framework Decision 2005/222/JHA of 24 February 2005 on attacks against information systems, OJ 2005 L 69 (16.03.2005), pp. 67-71.

[7] Joint action of 21 December 1998 adopted by the Council on the basis of Article K.3 of the Treaty on European Union, on making it a criminal offence to participate in a criminal organization in the Member States of the European Union 98/733/JHA, OJ 1998 L 351 (29.12.1998), pp. 1-3.

[8] Council Framework Decision of 13 June 2002 on combating terrorism, 2002/475/JHA, OJ 2002 L 164 (22.06.2002), pp. 3-7.

nature or context, may seriously damage a country or an international organization where committed with the aim of:

- seriously intimidating a population, or
- unduly compelling a Government or international organization to perform or abstain from performing any act, or
- seriously destabilizing or destroying the fundamental political, constitutional, economic or social structures of a country or an international organization,

shall be deemed to be terrorist offences:

(a) attacks upon a person's life which may cause death;
(b) attacks upon the physical integrity of a person;
(c) kidnapping or hostage taking;
(d) causing extensive destruction to a Government or public facility, a transport system, an infrastructure facility, including an information system, a fixed platform located on the continental shelf, a public place or private property likely to endanger human life or result in major economic loss;
(e) seizure of aircraft, ships or other means of public or goods transport;
(f) manufacture, possession, acquisition, transport, supply or use of weapons, explosives or of nuclear, biological or chemical weapons, as well as research into, and development of, biological and chemical weapons;
(g) release of dangerous substances, or causing fires, floods or explosions the effect of which is to endanger human life;
(h) interfering with or disrupting the supply of water, power or any other fundamental natural resource the effect of which is to endanger human life;
(i) threatening to commit any of the acts listed in (a) to (h).

With a view to the threats that cyberterrorist attacks pose, especially when directed against SCADA systems, many of the outcomes enumerated in Art. 1 seem possible. This was relevant already at the time of the drafting of the Framework Decision: "Although terrorist offences committed by computer or electronic devices are apparently less violent they can be as threatening as the offences previously mentioned, endangering not only life, health or safety of people, but the environment as well. Their main characteristic is that their effect is intentionally produced at a distance from the perpetrators, but their consequences may also be much more far reaching."[9]

However, the Framework Decision covers only those attacks that are committed in the aims mentioned in Art. 1. Minor attacks that are directed against individual computer systems will usually not be covered. However, these can be prosecuted following the Cybercrime Convention. In turn, the Framework Decision takes the terrorist intention into consideration when it comes to penalties: according to Art. 5 of the Framework Decision, member states have to take the necessary measures to ensure that the offences mentioned above are punishable by custodial sentences heavier than those imposable under national law for such offences in the absence of the special intent.

UN Conventions and Protocols

The UN has worked out numerous multilateral conventions and protocols on combating violent acts and terrorism. Similar to the Framework Decision cited above, these cover the results that terrorist action can bring regardless of the way in which they have been conducted. Examples for such instruments are:

---

[9] Proposal for a Council Framework Decision on Combating Terrorism COM/2001/0521 final – CNS 2001/0217, OJ 2001 E 332 (27.11.2001), pp. 300-304.

- the Convention for the suppression of unlawful acts against the safety of civil aviation[10] which criminalizes the destruction and damaging of aircrafts and air navigation facilities. Additionally, the communication of false information with the effect of endangering the safety of an aircraft in flight is also covered;
- the "Airport Protocol"[11] extending the provisions of the Convention which adds a new Art. 1 paragraph 1 bis that criminalizes any person "using any device, substance or weapon" to destroys or seriously damages the facilities of an airport;
- the Convention for the suppression of unlawful acts against the safety of maritime navigation[12] that criminalizes the destruction or damaging of maritime navigational facilities or the interference with their operation. Furthermore, as with the Civil Aviation Convention, the communication of false information with the intention of endangering the safe navigation is prohibited;
- the Diplomatic Agents Convention[13] that criminalizes murder or other attacks upon as well as threats to commit such actions against internationally protected persons, e.g. Heads of State, certain Ministers, representatives and accompanying family members;
- the Nuclear Materials Convention[14] criminalizes the dispersal of nuclear material that causes or is likely to cause death or serious injury to persons or substantial damage to property. The International Convention for the Suppression of Acts of Nuclear Terrorism also addresses the possibility that damaging a nuclear facility (which could take place through digital channels) bears the risk of the release of radioactive material.

Other instruments of the UN, however, are not or are hardly applicable to acts of cyberterrorism due to their wording. The Convention for the Suppression of Unlawful Seizure of Aircraft,[15] for example, is applicable only to "any person who *on board* an aircraft in flight ... exercises control of that aircraft" (Art. 1 of the Convention, emphasis added by the author). Therefore, a cyberterrorist attack where the control system of either the aircraft or the airport is being disrupted from the outside of the aircraft would not be subject to the regulations of the convention.[16] Other conventions, like the Maritime Convention,[17] contain references to "force" or "acts of violence" where it is at least doubtful whether the manipulation of computer data and computer systems could be subsumed under these terms. Finally, some conventions, like the one on terrorist

[10] UN Convention for the suppression of unlawful acts against the safety of civil aviation (with Final Act of the International Conference on Air Law held under the auspices of the International Civil Aviation Organization at Montreal in September 1971), Concluded at Montreal on 23.09.1971, UN Treaty Series Reg. No. 14118.

[11] Protocol for the suppression of unlawful acts of violence at airports serving international civil aviation supplementary to the Convention No. 14118, Concluded at Montreal on 24.02.1988.

[12] UN Convention for the suppression of unlawful acts against the safety of maritime navigation, Concluded at Rome on 10.03.1988, UN Treaty Series Reg. No. 29004.

[13] UN Convention on the prevention and punishment of crimes against internationally protected persons, including diplomatic agents, adopted 14.12.1973, UN Treaty Series Reg. No. 15410.

[14] UN Convention on the physical protection of nuclear material, adopted at Vienna on 26.10.1979, UN Treaty Series Reg. No. 24631.

[15] UN Convention for the Suppression of Unlawful Seizure of Aircraft, signed at The Hague 16.12.1970, UN Treaty Series Reg. No. 12325.

[16] The same is true also for other conventions, e.g. Art. 11 (1) of the Convention on Offences and Certain Other Acts Committed on Board Aircraft, signed at Tokyo 14.09.1963, UN Treaty Series Reg. No. 10106 also expects the person interfering or otherwise taking control of an aircraft in flight to be on board.

[17] See n.12.

bombings,[18] can—in general—be thought to be connected to digital crime, e.g. if a bomb is being launched over the Internet. However, it is doubtful whether this can still be seen as a case of cybercrime. Most authors would probably qualify a case where a conventional bomb is placed and only the ignition is initiated over the Internet as conventional terrorism, because no specific characteristic of the Internet is being used. Furthermore, a distinction between conventional telephone lines, NGN,[19] or the Internet itself is often hardly possible and hardly in the hands of those who use these services. Regardless of this qualification, however, the case would be covered by the convention as there is no distinction on the way in which the detonation of a bomb is achieved.

2.2. Terrorist-Related Contents

The dissemination of terrorist-related contents is of great importance for any terrorist organization. With respect to the legal framework against such contents, most instruments do not distinguish between information that is being distributed by traditional carriers (e.g. printed publications), by data carriers (e.g. CD-ROM) or by computer networks (e.g. the Internet). Instead, a differentiation between the intentions that lie behind the contents can be observed. This, for example, can be seen in the Convention on the Prevention of Terrorism by the Council of Europe[20] which criminalizes contents that provoke others to commit terrorist offences, that are intended to solicit others to participate in the commission of terrorist offences, or that are intended to instruct others on the use of dangerous items and substances.

> **Art. 5 Convention on the Prevention of Terrorism – Public Provocation to Commit a Terrorist Offence**
>
> 1. For the purpose of this Convention, "public provocation to commit a terrorist offence" means the distribution, or otherwise making available, of a message to the public, with the intent to incite the commission of a terrorist offence, where such conduct, whether or not directly advocating terrorist offences, causes a danger that one or more such offences may be committed.
> 2. Each Party shall adopt such measures as may be necessary to establish public provocation to commit a terrorist offence, as defined in paragraph 1, when committed unlawfully and intentionally, as a criminal offence under its domestic law.
>
> **Art. 6 Convention on the Prevention of Terrorism – Recruitment for Terrorism**
>
> 1. For the purposes of this Convention, "recruitment for terrorism" means to solicit another person to commit or participate in the commission of a terrorist offence, or to join an association or group, for the purpose of contributing to the commission of one or more terrorist offences by the association or the group.
> 2. Each Party shall adopt such measures as may be necessary to establish recruitment for terrorism, as defined in paragraph 1, when committed unlawfully and intentionally, as a criminal offence under its domestic law.

---

[18] International Convention for the Suppression of Terrorist Bombings of 15.12.1997, UN Treaty Series Reg. No. 37517.

[19] Next Generation Networks (NGN) is a broad term for the description of the shift of conventional networks (e.g. telephone, mobile phone) towards combined networks. Often, services that in former times used dedicated networks are moved to the Internet.

[20] Council of Europe Convention on the Prevention of Terrorism, signed in Warsaw 16.05.2005, CETS No. 196.

Article 7 Convention on the Prevention of Terrorism – Training for Terrorism

1. For the purposes of this Convention, "training for terrorism" means to provide instruction in the making or use of explosives, firearms or other weapons or noxious or hazardous substances, or in other specific methods or techniques, for the purpose of carrying out or contributing to the commission of a terrorist offence, knowing that the skills provided are intended to be used for this purpose.
2. Each Party shall adopt such measures as may be necessary to establish training for terrorism, as defined in paragraph 1, when committed unlawfully and intentionally, as a criminal offence under its domestic law.

The applicability of these provisions to Internet-related offences is clearly mentioned in the Explanatory Report to the convention. According to this, for example, the term "making available" refers to an easy accessibility to the public "for instance, by placing it on the Internet or by creating or compiling hyperlinks in order to facilitate access to it" (para. 102 of the Explanatory Report). Refering to Art. 6 of the convention, the Explanatory Report explains that solicitation can take place by various means, "for instance, via the Internet" (para. 108).

Additionally, many of the UN conventions against specific terrorist acts also contain provisions that are applicable to terrorist threats. Again, the UN conventions and protocols do not define in what way the threat is being transported. Therefore, threatening by E-Mail or on a terrorist (or other) website is also encompassed by these conventions. This is true, for example, for the UN Convention on Diplomatic Agents (Art. 2 para. 1 lit. (c)), the UN Nuclear Materials Convention (Art. 7 para. 1 lit. (e)), the Maritime Convention (Art. 3 para. 2 lit (c)), or for the Nuclear Terrorism Convention (Art. 2 para. 2 lit. (a)). Other UN conventions, however, do not contain specific provisions against threatening to commit the acts described in those conventions (see [1] for further information on this issue).

Furthermore, some of the UN Security Council Resolutions also address the issue of the incitement to terrorist actions. Resolution 1624,[21] for example, calls upon all States to adopt "such measures as may be necessary and appropriate […] to: (a) prohibit by law incitement to commit a terrorist act or acts"; and to prevent such conduct.

A broad approach can finally be seen in the Council Framework Decision on Combating Terrorism. As cited above, Art. 1 para. 1 of the Framework Decision already covers a wide range of possible terrorist offences, e.g. attacks on person's life, kidnapping, extensive destruction, or the release of dangerous substances. Art. 1 para. 1 lit (i) of the Framework Decision puts the threatening to commit any offence listed in Art. 1 para. 1 on a par with the commission itself. Therefore, many of the possible terrorist-related contents are covered by this approach.

Apart from the use of the Internet to distribute threats and terrorist propaganda, organizations increasingly use the Internet to incite followers to contribute financially to the actions of terrorist organizations. Money trails can increasingly better be used to follow supporters and the groups themselves. Therefore, the priority is high on the agenda to create instruments for the freezing of funds, for the criminalization of those who support terrorism by pecuniary means, or to establish adequate procedural powers for monetary investigations. Examples for such instruments are the UN Convention for the suppression of the financing of terrorism,[22] UN Security Council Resolutions 1373

[21] UN Security Council Resolution 1624 (2005) of 14.09.2005.

[22] UN International Convention for the Suppression of the Financing of Terrorism, UN Treaty Series Reg. No. 38349, adopted by the General Assembly of the United Nations in Resolution 54/109 of 09.12.1999.

and 1617[23] or the Convention on Laundering, Search, Seizure and Confiscation of the Proceeds from Crime and on the Financing of Terrorism by the Council of Europe.[24] However, as the financing of cyberterrorism does not in principle differ from the funding of conventional terrorism, this issue will not be covered in more detail in this article.

2.3. Other Uses of the Internet

From a legal point of view the regulation of other uses of the Internet as outlined in the first part of this article is extremely difficult. This is mostly due to the fact that one and the same action would have to be judged differently based only upon the intention or the thoughts behind this activity. For example, the view of a webpage containing directions to a public building would have to be assessed as a terrorist use of the Internet if the request has been issued to plan a bomb attack on this building. However, all other— "legitimate" —accesses of the web page would have to be classified as safe and allowed. In most cases, such a differentiation will not be possible, unless the intent is clearly visible. This, for example, is true for the assembly of information explicitly for the training of terrorists. Therefore, the above-mentioned Art. 7 of the Convention on the Prevention of Terrorism by the Council of Europe explicitly covers all kinds of instructions "for the purpose of carrying out or contributing to the commission of a terrorist offence, knowing that the skills provided are intended to be used for this purpose". In "normal" (i.e. non-terrorist) cases the proof of such purpose as well as the knowledge about it will be difficult to obtain. However, many of the collections available on the Internet can clearly be identified as intended for terrorist use by their naming as well as by their design. Therefore, a distinction from other collections (e.g. notes on chemistry courses) that could also be abused for terrorist purposes will—at least in many cases—be possible.

Apart from the problems of identifying specific terrorist material, a number of safeguards for human rights have to be observed in legal instruments. Therefore, laws that want to tackle other uses of the Internet that can also be of interest for the generality of people will constantly have to keep the balance between human rights on the one hand and control mechanisms against terrorists on the other hand. This, for example, can be observed in the introduction to the UN Security Council Resolution 1624 which condemns the incitement of terrorist acts and any attempt to justify or to glorify terrorist acts. In the same document, however, the rights to freedom of expression are recalled:

UN Security Council Resolution 1624 (2005)

[…] *Condemning* also in the strongest terms the incitement of terrorist acts and *repudiating* attempts at the justification or glorification (*apologie*) of terrorist acts that may incite further terrorist acts, […] *Recalling* the right to freedom of expression reflected in Article 19 of the Universal Declaration of Human Rights adopted by the General Assembly in 1948 […], and recalling also the right to freedom of expression in Article 19 of the International Covenant on Civil and Political Rights adopted by the General Assembly in 1966 ("ICCPR") and that any restrictions thereon shall only be such as are provided by law and are necessary on the grounds set out in paragraph 3 of Article 19 of the ICCPR […]

---

[23] UN Security Council Resolution 1373 (2001) of 28.09.2001. UN Security Council Resolution 1617 (2005) of 29.07.2005.

[24] Council of Europe Convention on Laundering, Search, Seizure and Confiscation of the Proceeds from Crime and on the Financing of Terrorism, CETS No. 198, signed in Warsaw 16.05.2005.

The possibilities to effectively cover conventional uses of the Internet without constraining human rights are limited. The Parliamentary Assembly of the Council of Europe therefore warns that the fight against terrorism "must not be used as a pretext to restrict the fundamental rights and freedoms guaranteed under the European Convention on Human Rights and related legal texts."[25]

The best solution seems to be a general criminalization not of the technical acts, as these will often be difficult to prove and to control, but of the terrorist context of actions. This can be observed in many international instruments that cover the aiding and abetting of terrorist acts regardless of the tools that were used. A good example for this approach is the EU Council Framework Decision on Combating Terrorism which covers the direction of a terrorist group as well as the participation in any activity of a terrorist group "including by supplying information or material resources, or by funding its activities in any way" (Art. 2 para. 2). The same approach is taken by the UN Security Council Resolution 1373 (2001) which asks Member States to "ensure that any person who participates in the financing, planning, preparation or perpetration of terrorist acts or in supporting terrorist acts is brought to justice [...]" (Nr. 2 (e) of the Resolution). Since the Resolution is worded in a general way, also uses of the Internet for the planning of terrorist actions are covered, e.g. downloading maps for the planning of a conventional attack or testing of digital resources for electronic attacks.

Apart from this approach to criminalization it seems especially important to exchange information on current uses of the Internet by terrorists and terrorist organizations. Only the fast and frequent exchange can help states to identify possible security risks. It also—in some cases—gives the option of monitoring terrorist actions on the Internet and therefore might help in the identification of future targets and possible actions. This aspect is stressed, for example, in the Decision No. 3/04 of the OSCE on combating the use of the Internet for terrorist purposes:

Decision No. 3/04 of the OSCE – Combating the Use of the Internet for Terrorist Purposes[26]

The Ministerial Council [...] decides that participating States will exchange information on the use of the Internet for terrorist purposes and identify possible strategies to combat this threat, while ensuring respect for international human rights obligations and standards, including those concerning the rights to privacy and freedom of opinion and expression.

3. Summary and Conclusions

There is no common approach to fight all possible uses of the Internet by terrorists and terrorist organizations. Instead, several different solutions are being brought up. This is especially obvious in the area of terrorist attacks over the Internet. Some international instruments prefer a technical approach that tackles the technical side of such aggressions; others favor a way in which the outcome of attacks is being addressed. However, the two approaches do not compete—they add to each other instead. With respect to the dissemination of terrorist contents and other uses of the Internet by terrorists, many

---

[25] No. 3 of the Recommendation 1706 (2005) – Media and Terrorism – of the Parliamentary Assembly of the Council of Europe, adopted on 20.06.2005.

[26] Organization for Security and Co-operation in Europe, Ministerial Council, Decision No. 3/04 – Combating the Use of the Internet for Terrorist Purposes, MC.DEC/3/04 of 07.12.2004.

international instruments are applicable. Due to their general wording this is often the case even if cyber terrorist uses were not considered at the time of their creation.

However, even though many of the terrorist actions in connection with the Internet are covered by the international framework, some major problems still exist. One issue that can be identified is the number of countries that have signed, ratified and actually implemented the instruments contained in the various provisions [1]. Since cases of cyberterrorism are transnational in nature, only a broad international consensus and a global joint effort on the criminalization of terrorist actions in all of its forms of appearance can help to bring terrorists to justice and to establish a functional legal framework.

The second major aspect concerns more the practical than (only) the legal side. Without reasonable procedural rules for the investigation of computer-related offences in all countries convictions will often not be possible, even if a legal framework exists. Therefore rules on the cooperation in computer-specific cases and on investigation procedures are of uttermost importance. On the international level, especially the Convention on Cybercrime contains important instruments that can be fruitful in the investigation of all computer-related offences (see [1] for further details). Furthermore, the approach taken by the EC Directive on Data Retention[27] seems promising with respect to the prosecution of all digitally committed crimes. There is, however, a doubt concerning whether this instrument carries the aim to excess, as not only data of criminals, but also of all other law abiding citizens are being collected. This, as has been pointed out above, is an extremely important factor in the creation of an international legal framework against (not only cyber-) terrorism—and its acceptance by the international community: to establish functional measures against terrorists without constraining the freedom of others.

References

[1] U. Sieber/P. Brunst, Cyberterrorism and other use of the Internet for terrorist purposes, in: Council of Europe (ed.), Cyberterrorism – The Use of the Internet for Terrorist Purposes, Strasbourg 2008.

[2] P. Brunst, Use of the Internet by Terrorists, in: NATO Center of Excellence – Defense Against Terrorism (ed.), Responses to Cyber Terrorism, Amsterdam, forthcoming 2008.

[3] G. Weimann, Terror on the Internet, Washington, D.C., 2006.

[4] D. Bachfeld, War der Wurm drin? IT-Sicherheit in der US-Stromversorgung, at: http://www.heise.de/ct/03/18/034/default.shtml [last visited: January 2008].

[5] Symantec Corp., Internet Security Threat Report XI (March 2007).

[6] B. Bidder, Angriff der Cyber-Söldner, Der Spiegel 31/2007, pp. 74-76.

[7] G. Giacomello, Bangs for the Buck: A Cost-Benefit Analysis of Cyberterrorism, in: Studies in Conflict and Terrorism, Vol. 27 (2004), p. 387-408.

[8] A. Ramelsberger, Krieger im Internet, Süddeutsche Zeitung, 15 March 2007, p. 5.

[9] G. Weimann, www.terror.net. How modern terrorism uses the Internet. United States Institute of Peace Special Report 116, March 2004.

[10] J. Record, Bounding the global war on terrorism. Strategic Studies Institute of the U.S. Army War College, http://www.strategicstudiesinstitute.army.mil/pdffiles/PUB207.pdf [last visited: January 2008].

[27] Directive 2006/24/EC of the European Parliament and the Council of 15.03.2006 on the retention of data generated or processed in connection with the provision of publicly available electronic communication services of public communication networks and amending Directive 2002/58/EC. OJ 2006 L 105 (13.04.2006), pp. 54-63.

Legal Aspects of Combating Terrorism
Centre of Excellence Defence Against Terrorism, Ankara, Turkey (Ed.)
IOS Press, 2008

doi:10.3233/978-1-58603-930-1-77

Laws and Rules for Soldiers in Armed Conflicts, Crises and Counter-Terrorism[1]

Col. Osman AYTAÇ
Instructor, COE–DAT, Ankara

Abstract. The first part of this paper gives an overview of the Law of Armed Conflict. There are various international treaties governing armed conflicts: the main Hague Conventions (1907) and Geneva Conventions (1949), the Hague Cultural Property Convention (1949 and 1954), the protocols added to the Geneva Conventions, and the convention on certain conventional weapons (1977 and 1980). LOAC is described according to its basic principles and definitions. The second part of the paper concentrates on Rules of Engagement, one of the best tools available to policy-makers to help manage armed forces during a crisis. ROE are guidelines specifying under what conditions or circumstances force may be used to satisfy political and/or military demands. As these will vary greatly from situation to situation, this paper does not describe ROE, but discusses the principles of how ROE should be drawn up. Tension inescapably exits in a system that subordinates armed forces under civilian control while retaining military command. Managing this tension by delineating the boundaries of military action in support of political objectives is another major role of ROE. There are vital links between the strategic and tactical levels of conflict. The strongest of these links are often ROE. The ROE for counter-terrorist operations are different to war and crisis ROE in terms of applicable law and the political desire.

Keywords. International Humanitarian Law, LOAC, Hague Conventions, Geneva Conventions, Rules of Engagement, military operations other than war, crisis situations, ROE and counter-terrorism, mission accomplishment, force protection.

The Principles of LOAC and the Fight against Terrorism

The Law of Armed Conflict (LOAC, the Law of War, also called in some contexts International Humanitarian Law) is applicable in international and non-international armed conflicts, which may differ greatly from counter-terrorism operations. In countering terrorism the applicable law, depending on the area of operation, will mainly be domestic and international criminal law. Nonetheless, when planning and conducting counter-terrorism operations, the "basic principles, protection of cultural property and protection of works and installations containing dangerous forces" should

[1] In this paper the *Teaching File for Instructors in the Law of Armed Conflict* and *Fight It Right: Model Manual on the Law of Armed Conflict for Armed Forces*, both prepared by the International Committee of the Red Cross, were used extensively.

be taken into consideration, since they provide appropriate guidelines for all military conduct against the enemy.

LOAC is a branch of international law which governs relations between states during armed conflicts, but also applies to fighting within a state. The aim of LOAC is to reduce as much as possible the suffering, loss and damage caused by war. It places obligations on legal persons in the states involved, primarily the members of the armed forces. It contains the practical rules or codes of conduct which all military personnel can and indeed must understand.

In fact such laws have a long history. Every culture has customs determining the behaviour of soldiers towards the enemy and towards non-combatants, rules that were born on the battlefield, and was shaped and moulded gradually by military experience. Famously the ethics of the "just war" and proportionality in the use of weaponry were discussed during the Middle Ages. Developed alongside military experience and designed to be applied in time of armed conflict, the laws do not conflict with the principles of war, such as the need to maintain momentum, to concentrate efforts, to use the advantage of surprise, etc. While not impeding the conduct of war, however, they establish certain minimum standards of behaviour for combatants and their commanders. It is characteristic of humane and disciplined soldiers that they seek to reduce the suffering of the victims of the fighting. Furthermore, as one of the principles of war is simplicity of action, these laws tend to be straightforward and simple to grasp.

These humane norms began to be codified in their modern form in the international conventions of the early twentieth century. LOAC is compiled from customary international law and treaty law. The treaty law is based on the Geneva Law and the Hague Law. The Geneva Law, made up of the four 1949 Geneva Conventions, is aimed at protecting the victims of a conflict who are in the power of the adversary—it protects the wounded and sick on land and at sea, prisoners of war and civilians. The Hague Law concentrates on practical soldiering. It is designed to establish and universalize rules for the conduct of military operations, on how the fighting is to be carried out, and it determines (1) what you can attack and, (2) how you should attack it. Its rules limit the destructive effects of combat to what is absolutely necessary to achieve the aim of the operation, in such a way that excessive damage is avoided. Thus, the combat principle of concentration of effort is united with the demands of humane ethics.

An Overview of LOAC

Distinction between Combatants and Non-combatants

A fundamental distinction, indeed it may be called "the rule of distinction", is made between combatants and non-combatants. It is obvious that enemy combatants are what may be attacked, unless they are out of action. Non-combatants, civilians, are protected from attack, although they lose that protection if they participate directly in the hostilities, until such time as they cease to participate. The classic text for this law is as follows:

> In order to ensure respect for and protection of the civilian population and civilian objects, the Parties to the conflict shall at all times distinguish between the civilian

> population and combatants and between civilian objects and military objectives and accordingly shall direct their operations only against military objectives.[2]

A corresponding distinction is made between "military objectives", which of course may be attacked, and "civilian objects", which are to be respected and protected:

> Attacks shall be limited strictly to military objectives. In so far as objects are concerned, military objectives are limited to those objects which by their nature, location, purpose or use make an effective contribution to military action and whose total or partial destruction, capture or neutralization, in the circumstances ruling at the time, offers a definite military advantage.[3]

Damage Must Be Proportional

Another fundamental rule, particularly important in modern war and in the struggle against terror, is that civilians and civilian objects are to be spared from incidental (collateral) damage to the maximum extent possible. This means a commander must weigh up an attack's potential military importance and judge whether and how much incidental damage may be risked. The aim of avoiding excessive incidental damage comes within the principle of "proportionality".

> In the conduct of military operations, constant care shall be taken to spare the civilian population, civilians and civilian objects.[4]

To remain within this law careful planning and clear Rules of Engagement (ROE) are essential. This will require good training and high standards of professionalism, particularly in the types of combat and crisis intervention which have become widespread today.

Military Necessity

According to the principle that all combat activity must be justified on the basis of military necessity, activity which is not necessary for achieving a military aim is prohibited. In practice it is difficult to draw the boundaries, and the interpretation of the laws related to this principle is often a cause for tension and disputes.

More clear-cut is the rule that pillage, the unlawful taking of private property for private use, is forbidden, although civilian objects may be "requisitioned" if necessary for the war effort.

> It is forbidden to destroy or seize the enemy's property, unless such destruction or seizure be imperatively demanded by the necessities of war.[5]

LOAC does not limit any of the usual decisions the commanders and combatants must make, like choice of weapon, or the manner of the attack. However, it does set limits on the extent of the effect of those weapons and military tactics. Those which are destined to cause excessive suffering or unnecessary damage are to be avoided. The best, the most efficient, means possible should be used to put the enemy combatants out of action.

---

[2] Protocol 1 Additional to the Geneva Conventions of August 1949 Article 48.
[3] Protocol 1 Additional to the Geneva Conventions of August 1949 Article 52.
[4] Protocol 1 Additional to the Geneva Conventions of August 1949 Article 57.
[5] Hague Regulations IV 18 October 1907 Article 23.

There are, consequently, articles and clauses regarding certain classes of weapons, like those designed to cause untreatable injuries, or that result in a cruel and lingering death, under the following general rule:

> In any armed conflict, the right of the Parties to the conflict to choose methods or means of warfare is not unlimited. It is prohibited to employ weapons, projectiles and material and methods of warfare of a nature to cause superfluous injury or unnecessary suffering.[6]

Again, this law will not impede the conduct of a war. It is a matter of implementing the rules of distinction and proportionality described above, both of which take full account of the imperative to succeed militarily.[7]

Definitions Relating to Military and Associated Personnel

In order for soldiers to make the necessary distinction between combatants and non-combatants, the following definitions are used in the conventions and treaties:

Armed Forces

Armed forces are defined as all the organized units and personnel that are under a command responsible for the conduct of its subordinates; these units are subject to an internal disciplinary system that enforces compliance with the law of armed conflict.

> The laws, rights, and duties of war apply not only to armies, but also to military and volunteer corps fulfilling the following conditions:
> - To be commanded by a person responsible for his subordinates;
> - To have a fixed distinctive emblem recognizable at a distance;
> - To carry arms openly;
> - To conduct their operations in accordance with the laws and customs of war.[8]

Combatant

A related definition is that of combatants: They are members of the armed forces of a party to the conflict, except medical and religious personnel, are combatants, and in legal terms these are the ones entitled to take part in hostilities. There is an obligation upon these individuals to distinguish themselves from the civilian population, including through distinctive emblems, and to conform to LOAC.[9] This also applies to civilians who decide to become combatants and take a direct part in hostilities.

Persons under the age of fifteen years old cannot be recruited or become combatants.

Prisoner of War

Prisoners of war (POWs) are combatant in an international armed conflict who fall into the hands of the enemy, or more precisely, "[p]risoners of war are in the power of the

---

[6] Hague Regulations IV 18 October 1907 Article 35.
[7] "Fight It Right" Model Manual on the LOAC for Armed Forces Chapter 2 Article 203.1.
[8] Hague Regulations IV 18 October 1907 Article 1.
[9] "Dictionary of the International LOAC" by Pietro VERRI, p. 32.

hostile Government, but not of the individuals or formation which captured them". Prisoners of war are entitled to the corresponding status and treatment as set out in international law. They are subject to the laws, regulations and general orders in force in the armed forces of the detaining power.[10] Prisoners of war must always be humanely treated.[11] This means in detail that:

- Their honour and person must be respected;
- They must be protected from violence, indecency, intimidation, insults, abuse or public curiosity;
- Women must be treated with respect, with due regard to their sex and no less favourably than men;[12]
- They may not be subject to physical mutilation or scientific experiments;
- Reprisals may not be taken against prisoners of war.

Prisoners of war must be left in possession of:

- Military clothing and protective equipment such as combat helmets, body armour, gas masks and NBC protective clothing.
- Decorations, insignia badges of rank, eating equipment, ration packs and water bottles;
- Identity cards and discs;
- Personal possessions, including things such as spectacles and articles of sentimental value like family photographs.

POWs must be identified, so they are required to give their number, rank, name and date of birth. Other questions may be asked, since a POW could be a valuable source of intelligence, but no coercion or unpleasant or disadvantageous treatment may be used to obtain information.[13]

Medical and Religious Personnel Attached to the Armed Forces

Medical and religious members of the armed forces are associated personnel, and they have a special place within LOAC. Medical staff are allowed to be armed with light weapons for self-defence and for the defence of those they are caring for. Both medical officers and religious personnel should wear the insignia, for medical personnel this will be the red cross or the red crescent on their left arm as identification.

Medical and religious personnel, if captured, are not counted as POWs. If they are not required by their captors for medical and religious duties, under international law they must be repatriated. However, if the captors wish to make use of them, for example, for attending to the sick in a POW camp, or, in the case of religious personnel, looking after the prisoners' spiritual needs, they may be retained for those purposes.[14]

The White Flag and Negotiators

This is a tool of war arising from customary law and it is still widely used today. The white flag indicates an intention to negotiate, and it is to guarantee the protection of

---

[10] "Dictionary of the International LOAC" by Pietro VERRI, p. 88.

[11] Geneva Convention III Relative to the Treatment of POW 12 August 1949 Article 13.

[12] Geneva Convention III Relative to the Treatment of POW 12 August 1949 Article 14.

[13] Geneva Convention III Relative to the Treatment of POW 12 August 1949 Article 17.

[14] Geneva Convention I for the amelioration of the condition of the wounded, sick in armed forces 12 August 1949, Articles 8-9-24-25.

those who are negotiating. (It does not, in spite of the popular view, necessarily indicate an intent to surrender. There may be negotiations with an opponent for practical military reasons—to arrange a ceasefire to collect the dead and wounded or to exchange prisoners.) Clearly, the rule is that those using the white flag should not be harmed in the process of negotiation.[15]

Civil Defence Workers

Civil defence workers are those engaged in tasks that might include warning, rescue and fire-fighting operations, the construction of shelters, and emergency assistance in restoring and maintaining order in conflict or refuge areas. As the purpose of civil defence is to save and protect the civilian population from the effects of hostilities, it has no military relevance. Civil defence workers are not combatants and may not be attacked.

Civil defence workers may be armed with light individual weapons for their own protection, or if they have to maintain order among civilians, or to protect civilians, for example from the looting of equipment. Civil defence organizations must be respected and protected. These workers lose their protected status if they engage in acts which are outside their normal duties and are hostile to the adversary.[16]

Protection of Cultural Property

As stated above, civilian objects are protected from attack. Civilian objects are all objects which are not military objectives. Military objectives are limited to those objects which by their nature, location, purpose or use make an effective contribution to military action, and whose total or partial destruction, capture or neutralization in the circumstances ruling at the time offers a definite military advantage.[17] Special protection is extended in international law to cultural sites, which may not be brought into conflicts by either side.

Cultural Property

It is forbidden to attack historic monuments, works of art or places of worship which constitute the cultural or spiritual heritage of people. It is also forbidden to use such monuments, work or places in support of the military effort.[18]

It was decided to provide for the protection of cultural property in a separate treaty, the 1954 Hague Convention on Cultural Property, to which there is an additional protocol signed in 1999. Both instruments establish three forms of protection.:

- General protection;
- Special protection;
- Enhanced protection.

Attacks on clearly recognized cultural property are considered a grave breach of Geneva Protocol I[19] if the property is subject to special protection.

---

[15] Hague Regulations IV 18 October 1907 Articles 32-34.
[16] Protocol I Additional to the Geneva Conventions of August 1949 Articles 61-67.
[17] Protocol I Additional to the Geneva Conventions of August 1949 Articles 52 and 57.
[18] Protocol 1 Additional to the Geneva Conventions of August 1949 Article 53.

Works and Installations Containing Dangerous Forces

The law is specific in the definition of the term "dangerous forces". The term applies only to:

- Dams,
- Dykes, and
- Nuclear electrical generating stations.

These facilities and military objectives in their vicinity must not be attacked if doing so may result in the release of "dangerous forces". The effects of this release would be so catastrophic for the civilian population that it is judged that the military advantage would not justify them. The catastrophes envisaged are severe flooding, or the release of radioactive material.

By the same token, the opposing army may not abuse this law by deploying military objectives close to these installations. It is possible, however, to provide close or defensive protection for these sites, e.g. anti-aircraft guns, and guards against terrorist attack or sabotage. The protection of this law does not apply if the opponents break this law and use these installations to gain a military advantage.

The law also contains guidelines on how the installations must be marked so that they can be clearly seen as protected sites by ground and air forces. The markings are in the form of a grouping of three bright orange circles in a line, which are illuminated at night.[20]

Prohibited Methods of Warfare

Some methods of warfare are placed under an absolute ban by international law:

Starvation

It is prohibited to seek to starve civilians as a method of warfare, as happened, for example, at Leningrad during the Second World War. It is prohibited to attack, destroy, or remove objects vital to the survival of civilians, such as food, crops in fields, livestock, drinking water supplies, or irrigation works. This prohibition does not apply to objects that are being used solely by the opposing armed forces, or in direct support of their military action.[21]

Human Shields

Civilians may not be used to shield military objectives or to shield, promote or impede military operations. Military objectives must not be installed in a civilian area for protection. Civilians' movements should not be controlled in order to shield military objectives or operations. In other words, the responsibilities involved in avoiding the use of human shields apply to both sides.[22]

---

[19] Protocol I Additional to the Geneva Conventions of August 1949 Article 85, para. 4d.
[20] Protocol I Additional to the Geneva Conventions of August 1949 Article 56.
[21] Protocol I Additional the Geneva Conventions of August 1949 Article 54.
[22] Geneva Convention III Article 23 / Geneva Convention IV Article 28 / Additional Protocol I Article 12, 51.

Pillage

Pillage/plunder by soldiers is now universally prohibited. This applies to small acts of theft by soldiers in the course of a conflict, but above all it bans any order from a commanding officer permitting theft as a kind of reward to victorious soldiers.[23]

Perfidy

"Perfidy" is defined as a breach of good faith, or acts of treachery. This law prohibits deliberate and mendacious attempts to make an opponent think he may not attack because of a protection under LOAC. It is forbidden to commit a hostile act under the cover of legal protection with the intent to betray the confidence of the adversary.[24]

Improper Use of Enemy Uniform, Emblems, or Insignia

Related to the prohibition of perfidy is the law against using the flags, military uniform, emblems or insignia of your opponent during attacks, or for shielding or impeding military operations. One exception is that a POW may use enemy uniforms to help him escape. Another is that enemy uniforms can also be used for training purposes.[25]

Giving No Quarter

It is prohibited for an officer to order that no quarter will be given, e.g. to order that a military objective will be taken and no enemy survivors should be left.[26]

Torture

Torture and inhumane or degrading treatment or punishment are absolutely prohibited. The term torture includes rape and sexual assault. Torture is in any case a war crime in both international and non-international armed conflicts. It is universally prohibited, and the prohibition is stated just as unequivocally in human rights law. The argument of military necessity can never be used to justify torture.[27]

The Relationship between LOAC and Rules of Engagement

As has been noted above, modern warfare involves training, discipline and professionalism, particularly where soldiers are required to intervene in regional crises. Here the general principles of LOAC will be interpreted on a regular basis in the form of clear commands associated with each operation or series of operations. These instructions, called Rules of Engagement, are not part of international law. While they are guided by international law, they also aim to ensure the success of the political and

---

[23] Geneva Convention IV Article 33 / Hague Regulations IV Articles 28, 52, 53.
[24] Hague Regulations IV Article 23 / Protocol I Additional to the Geneva Conventions Article 37 and 85.
[25] Protocol I Additional to Geneva Conventions of august 1949 Article 39.
[26] Hague Regulations IV Article 23(d).
[27] Geneva Convention I Articles 12 and 50 / Geneva Convention II Articles 12 and 51 / Geneva Convention III Articles 17 and 87 / Commonn Article 3 to All Geneva Conventions.

military objectives of the military intervention. It is clear that in counter-terrorist operations, for example, ROE will often be the most direct and detailed connection between the active soldier and the laws which must govern his/her use of force.

General Introduction to ROE

Rules of Engagement (ROE) are concerned with the application of military doctrine. A commander in the field may know the doctrine, but he also needs to know immediately (1) the rules that govern how that doctrine is applied in each of the range of possible situations with which he may be faced, and in particular (2) what may trigger a change such that a different set of rules apply. The authorities therefore must decide the kind of ROE to issue to their commanders. In NATO member states, and countries with similar systems, those involved in issuing ROE are: government ministers, who give general guidance to commanders, and commanders, who may choose to re-write these rules with more specific details before issuing them to their troops.

The MC 362-1 NATO ROE Document officially defines ROE as: "Directives to military forces (including individuals) that define the circumstances, degree and manner in which force or actions which might be provocative may or may not be applied."[28]

The US Department of Defense officially defines ROE as: "Directives issued by competent military authority which delineate the circumstances and limitations under which United States forces will initiate and/or continue combat engagement with other forces encountered."[29]

ROE define the degree and the manner of application of force. When force is applied, its extent is clearly defined. The manner in which it is applied, involving consideration of what will give offense, etc., is also important.

ROE allow application of force to be controlled, and are distinct from orders about specific tasks, as they are not a means of issuing tactical instructions. In other words, effective ROE do not assign specific tasks or drive specific tactical solutions; they allow a commander to convey quickly and clearly to subordinate units a desired posture regarding the use of force. Thus, for example, ROE do not determine measures for determining the type of fire when an enemy is engaged, as fire control is a tactical consideration.

Although ROE are parameters detailing often tight constraints, they do not have the force of law. It remains the commander's responsibility in all circumstances to ensure that a given action is lawful. Effective ROE comply with domestic and international law, including the body of international law pertaining to armed conflict. ROE never justify illegal actions. In all situations, soldiers and commanders use force that is necessary and proportional.

General Character of ROE

The Rules of Engagement must clarify four issues:

- When military force may be used,
- Where military force may be used,

[28] MC 362/1 NATO Rules of Engagement Document.
[29] USDOD.DOD Dictionary of Military and Associated Terms: NATO Only Terms.

- Against whom force should be used in the circumstances described above,
- How military force should be used to achieve the desired ends.[30]

ROE are usually written in the form of prohibitions or permissions. Prohibitions set out certain actions which troops are forbidden to take. Permissions set out actions which may be taken. In this case the commander may judge whether the permitted actions are 'necessary or desirable' for carrying out the troops' tasks. No more force than is necessary and reasonable is to be applied. In practice these limits will be delivered to the troops as follows: (1) Actions a soldier may take without consulting a higher authority, unless explicitly forbidden (sometimes called "command by negation"), and (2) actions that may only be taken if explicitly ordered by a higher authority (sometimes called "positive command").

In addition to a typically large set of standing orders, military personnel will be given additional ROE before performing any mission or military operation. These can cover circumstances such as how to retaliate after an attack, how to treat captured targets, which territories the soldier is bound to fight in, and how the force should be applied during the operation. The ROE must evolve with mission requirements and respond to the realities of the threat.

The style of the instructions must be simple to understand and in keeping with established standards. Because of their importance, they should ideally be prepared during the planning process, and not left to just before the operation. If possible, all eventualities must be covered.

Purposes of ROE

These types of document are part of modern warfare, in which officers must always be aware of the legal and diplomatic dimensions of their orders, which will be followed closely, including in the press. Commanders need this tool to shape and control the actions of their soldiers.

Military actions must now be controlled in three dimensions: the political, the legal, and the military. A political consideration, for example, would include the rule that, in normal circumstances, an operation must stay within the boundaries of the Area of Operation. An example of a rule determined by law would be the forbidding of firing into hospitals, churches, schools, museums, and any other historical or cultural sites, except in self-defense.[31] Military considerations determine, for example, the rule frequently invoked in the field that engaging with the target should be preceded by observed indirect fire.

On the one hand, the purposes of ROE may contradict each other; typically, political considerations inhibit the accomplishment of tactical military goals, which may lead to complaints from the troops. On the other hand, there are many circumstances in which they coincide. For example, policy decisions and domestic and international law may support each other.

---

[30] Sagan, Scott D., Rules of Engagement, pp 443-470 in : George, A.; Avoiding War: Problems of Crisis Management.

[31] The Hague Convention for the Protection of Cultural Property in the Event of Armed Conflict (14 May 1954), Chapter 1; Art. 2-4; see especially: Chapter 2, Art. 8.

ROE Failures: Too Restrictive or Too Excessive

In preparing ROE before an engagement, two contrasting aims must be kept reconciled: force must be applied effectively so that the aims of the mission can be accomplished, but the force must not be excessive.

If this balance is not achieved, and not enough force is permitted by the ROE, the military mission will not be accomplished.

This kind of failure may well be the result of disputes and insufficient co-operation between military and political leaders. It is often the political decision-makers, aware of the sensitivities of other politicians, who argue that the army act within narrow limits.

An example of this first (1st) kind of error was the United Nations Mission's failure in Rwanda (UNAMIR). A mission made up of United Nations soldiers was in the country from 1993 to 1996 with the task of implementing the Arusha Accords, which were a peace agreement between the Hutu and Tutsi tribes. However, the UNAMIR soldiers could do little when hostilities broke out owing the severe limitations in the ROE set by the UN agreement. The UN troops were under fire for two days, after which they were forced to hand over their weapons to rebel forces. The United Nations forces, small in number and hampered by strict ROE, could not prevent the Rwandan genocide which resulted. Some force providing countries withdrew their troops in order to avoid further international embarrassment. Sagan provides a penetrating analysis of this topic.[32] The UN Peacekeeper's ROE during the Rwandan Genocide was a tragic example of too restrictive ROE.[33]

Excessive use of force is the second (2nd) common error with ROE. Here, loose rules facilitate an escalation in the conflict. Although the force is tactically effective, it in fact negates the political objectives that the use of force was meant to achieve. This is the "escalatory" error.

Types of ROE

Distribution of ROE: Force-wide, Operational or Tactical

There are three levels of ROE for land forces:

1. Force-wide guidance, or "Strategic ROE", includes: mandate limitations, operational boundaries, force size, structure, composition and capabilities. A NATO or national level ROE may be a good example of these widely-distributed rules.
2. Guidance for commanders, or "Operational ROE", includes: the "choice of weapons" to be deployed, and the reaction profile.
3. Commander's specific guidance to soldiers, or "Tactical ROE", includes: "choice of weapon/ammunition type to be used" (what kind of fire support, classic or precise systems), "weapon systems readiness" (weapons charged or uncharged/ammo in magazine or in weapon) and "orders for opening fire". At this level the so-called "soldier's card" would be a good example.[34]

---

[32] Sagan, Scott D., Rules of Engagement, pp 443-470, in :George, Avoiding War: Problems of Crisis Management.

[33] See: www.wisegeek.com/what-are -the-rules-of-engagement.htm.

[34] NATO 362-1 Rules of Engagement Document.

Types of Rule in ROE

The rules can be divided into many different types, according to the specific kinds of judgments which commanders must make in various situations:

Type I: Hostility Criteria. This category of ROE sets out the objective criteria and triggers to determine whether a possible enemy has hostile intent. They make clear whether firing is permitted even when the enemy has not yet engaged.

Type II: Scale of Force. Here the emphasis is on a graduated use of force when the situation is not clear. This ranges from verbal warnings, warning shots, up to deadly force. This category also sets out the situations in which pursuit is permitted. This often applies to public order disturbances.

Type III: Protection of Property. Clearly, force may be used in self-defense. It may also be used to defend people. However, this category of ROE sets out what kinds of property may also be defended with force. Also, it sets out what may be done about destruction or looting, and how much force may be used in preventing criminals' escape.

Type IV: Weapons Control Status. These rules, which also apply to air defense, set out situations in which fire-power can be used.

Type V: Arming Orders. These rules establish which troops are armed and how heavily. The type of ammunition is also specified. The commands for loading of firearms, and who gives them, are mentioned.

Type VI: Approval to Use weapons Systems. These rules designate the level of command at which approval for use of particular weapons must be given. The use of certain weapons may be forbidden by rules of this type.

Type VII: Eyes on Target. This is a rule which requires a check to be made that not just one soldier or piece of equipment has observed a target which will be fired upon.

Type VIII: Territorial or Geographic Restraints. This category of ROE set out the geographical limits in which the enemy may be engaged. It uses a system of zoning.

Type IX: Restrictions on Manpower. Here what is important is the number of troops which can be introduced into which areas of activity.

Type X: Restrictions on Point targets and Means of Warfare. Here rules specify certain people or places which may not be engaged.[35]

The Commander's Responsibilities

The commander is the person mainly responsible for establishing the ROE. They must ensure that operational aims are served by the ROE, and they must draw on the assistance of legal advisers in interpreting the guidelines provided by headquarters in the light of domestic and international law. They draft and distribute the ROE. In addition, they must provide training for their officers and troops in using the rules.

Interpret: Interpreting the ROE for the theater of operations is a difficult task, involving detailed political, legal, and military awareness. Legal support will provide opinions regarding the legal interpretation of general guidelines in detailed situations in the field. Ultimately the responsibility for uniting the political aims, the military objectives and the law will lie with the commander.

---

[35] www.globalsecurity.org/military/policy/army/fm/27-100/chap8.htm

Draft: The commander who is drafting the ROE may be from the highest ranks, for example the Land Forces Commander. These ROE are then issued to all forces under that senior commander, and remain unchanged. This method is called "top-driven" ROE. In practice the preference is for "top-fed" ROE, however. This is when the highest ranks give general rules, but the drafting is done by the subordinate commanders. Top-fed ROE have the advantage that they delegate responsibility, and also the subordinate commanders are able to tailor the ROE more to specific situations encountered in the field. In practice both top-driven and top-fed ROE are used.

It is important that the lower rank commanders, at theater or brigade level, are aware of the following general advice when drafting ROE: METT-TC summarizes the factors to consider. This is a mnemonic for "mission, enemy, terrain and weather, troops, time available, and civilian considerations" (whether the action will affect civilians and how). Secondly, if the ROE guidelines he/she has received contain elements which will not permit the mission to be accomplished, these problems must be referred back to headquarters. The commander deputed to draft the ROE should neither alter the guidelines, nor try to accomplish a mission when he/she is not satisfied that the ROE will permit success.

Avoid: There are various errors to avoid when drafting ROE. Avoid simple restatements: ROE produced at this level should not repeat the general statements of strategy and doctrine. ROE should not be used as the means to state strategy or doctrine. Avoid restating the law of war and the tactics. Avoid safety-related restrictions. Avoid excessively qualified language. ROE must be readily understandable.

Training: Training should be provided to reinforce ROE, and this must include exercises. Modern warfare is conducted in a glare of publicity, so maximum efforts must be made to ensure that each soldier understands and acts within the limits of the ROE provided. The best way to teach ROE is to rehearse real-life situations. Missions like peace-keeping and disaster relief will require great professionalism and restraint to avoid errors which may undermine the whole effort.

Counter Terrorism and Crises:

In recent years, because of the change in the global security threat assessment, 21st century's armed forces are tasked to perform their missions in a range from peace-keeping operations to combating terrorism which are completely different to classical warfare. The concept and doctrine for the armed forces have been also changed in order for them to adapt themselves to the new threat. Meanwhile, the roles of military forces have expanded, beyond traditional war fighting, to encompass a range of tasks related to different kinds of crisis. As one of the basic tools of modern armed forces, the concept of ROE has also changed, and new approaches are needed to fulfill the appropriate requirements for the new types of operation.

The operations that involve the use of military capabilities in a range of military operations short of war are called Military Operations Other Than War (MOOTW). MOOTW are more sensitive to political considerations, and often the military mat not be the primary player. More restrictive ROE and a hierarchy of national objectives are followed.

There are many types of MOOTW, several having multiple components: arms control, combating terrorism, enforcement of sanctions and exclusion zones, ensuring freedom of navigation and overflight, humanitarian assistance, national assistance, noncombatant evacuation operations, protection of shipping, recovery operations, show of force operations, strikes and raids. Almost all of them can be defined as crisis situations.

The ROE which are suitable for those crisis situations are different to wartime ROE, specifically in terms of the applicable law. In wartime ROE, as discussed above, the applicable law in addition to domestic law is the Law of Armed Conflict (LOAC), and the other instruments of international law. In crisis situations, depending on the area of operation (national territory/external theaters), the applicable law may vary. In domestic terrorist-based crisis LOAC is not applicable but the domestic law of that state is applicable. Legal and operational tools, and the rules of engagement cannot, be enforced over a national territory in the same way they can in external theaters, as the legal framework is different. There are two unique aspects of the crisis theater: the primacy of political objectives and the legal complexity.

Lead Role for Politicians

Crisis situations will be determined by over-arching political objectives, whether strategic or tactical. Although frequently a source of difficulty and tension in the army, it is necessary that political directives have the ultimate authority. Politicians will usually have the lead role, and ROE will have great importance because the fundamental goals of a mission can easily be undermined by military errors. Army commanders will have to have a detailed understanding of the political considerations, and an awareness of local sensitivities. In crisis situations it is often the lower-ranking commanders who will be expected to feed information about local reactions to headquarters, and junior commanders may also be asked to draft the ROE.

Specific Difficulties

Missions in crisis situations are always legally complex. Generally the intervention will be backed by international agreements, and it will be expected that internationally-agreed conditions as well as international and domestic laws will apply. It is notoriously difficult to develop ROE which allow the military to accomplish missions in legally complex situations, where the rights of contending groups must be respected.

In addition, there are several unique ROE concerns in crisis situations: "ROE in crisis are generally more restrictive, detailed, and sensitive to political concerns than in war. Restrained, judicious use of force is necessary; excessive force undermines the legitimacy of the operation and jeopardizes political objectives. During a crisis, ROE not only provide for self-defense, but prevent unauthorized and uncontrolled escalation, while simultaneously achieving national objectives. Crisis ROE considerations may include balancing force protection and harm to innocent civilians or non-military areas, balancing mission accomplishment with political considerations, protecting evacuees while not having the authority to preempt hostile actions by proactive military measures, enabling soldiers to properly balance initiative and restraint, determining the extent to which soldiers mat protect host nation or third nation civilians. In multinational operations, developing ROE acceptable to all troop contributing nations is important. Being responsive to changing ROE requirements is also important."[36]

---

[36] www.globalsecurity.org/military/polcy/fm/27-100/chap6.htm

Legal Aspects of Combating Terrorism
Centre of Excellence Defence Against Terrorism, Ankara, Turkey (Ed.)
IOS Press, 2008

doi:10.3233/978-1-58603-930-1-91

The Use of Force in Law Enforcement Practices in the Light of ECHR Case-Law

Inspector Ömer YILMAZ
Turkish National Police, Analyst, COE–DAT, Ankara, Turkey

Abstract. Among the diverse practical aspects of the law, the use of force is the one which is criticized most in democratic societies. Although national laws have developed the necessary control systems for the proper use of force, the growing importance of human rights has given rise to some additional international controls. The European Convention for the Protection of Human Rights and Fundamental Freedoms and its organs provide an important protection system in this regard. Especially, the case law of the European Court of Human Rights on the proper use of force is a valuable source for law enforcers in fulfilling their daily duties, as well as for the counter-terrorism strategies of the democratic countries.

Keywords. The use of force, European Court of Human Rights, right to life, prohibition of torture.

Individual-society-state relations have evolved in several historical phases. In many cases, the society was the determining element until the emergence of the state as an institutionalized structure in the late years of 18th century, which can also be read as the beginning of the modernity. The state, which almost completed its institutionalization period after the French and Industrial revolutions, mainly earned its superiority through its instruments, which regulated the life of the society. In particular, the effects of the division of labor, and related changes, on relations in the community and further technological developments enhanced the position of the state in relation to the society.

As a result of these developments, several tasks shaping the life of the society which had previously been carried out mainly by the communities in traditional ways passed through to the state. Some of these tasks were regarded as indicators of sovereignty, and among these the task of maintaining internal security and public order can be regarded as of primary importance. It is since the transition to the nation-state that the public order task can be said to be carried out by states in modern ways.[1]

Accordingly, the legitimacy criteria of the modern state are supplied to a large extent by the laws it enacts to establish the duties, the authorities and the responsibilities of the law enforcement agencies which are created to carry out this task. However, the way the agencies use force in carrying out their tasks has been subjected to various challenges, all relating to these legitimacy criteria, and therefore the

---

[1] Poggi, Gianfranco, *The Development of the Modern State*, Stanford, University Press, 1978, p. 90.

philosophy and the approach, as well as the tools, of policing, have evolved in parallel with social demands and political developments in the modern world.[2]

Some social demands have changed the conception of policing in a limited context, such as changes in the organizational structure, management policies and tactics.[3] Political developments, like two world wars, have had more profound effects on policing, as the atrocities the world experienced, particularly in World War II, strongly affected the individual-society-state relations. As a result of the will to avoid living through the same sufferings again, and to protect human dignity, the individual gained more concrete safeguards in these relations. The promotion of human rights, in both domestic and international politics, along with the establishment of international and regional bodies safeguarding these fundamental rights, has undoubtedly affected modern policing in democratic states substantially.

However, in some countries where the Cold War had a subversive effect, and even in some democratic countries, the political climate of the post-war era caused the promotion of human rights to be seen as *competing with or even compromising core issues of national security*.[4]

Although the promotion of human rights in both national and international politics became still more dominant after the Cold War, the 9/11 terrorist attacks in the United States and the subsequent international operations, as well as some other national/international counter-terrorism measures, have highlighted concerns over the interaction between human rights and national security.

Even some basic law enforcement practices have been subjected to criticism in many studies which examine the relationship between human rights and security, with the fear of a possible deterioration in some fundamental achievements of the individual and the conduct of his/her everyday life. In the light of the circumstances of the contemporary world, in which terrorism is accorded great attention, these criticisms (or would-be criticisms) of counter-terrorism strategies and practices have gained prominence, mainly due to the political characteristics of terrorism and the terrorists' exploitation of allegations of human rights violations to attract new recruits and political and foreign support for their causes. Accordingly, it is obvious that if counter-terrorism strategies are executed with a full awareness of their social, legal and international dimensions, the strategies will be able to serve the aims of those responsible for the fight against terrorism more.

From this point of view, in this essay, without arguing against the so-called 'negative interaction' between human rights and national security, which requires a more comprehensive study, the human rights criteria for the general law enforcement practices and particularly for the counter-terrorism practices in democratic countries will be studied in accordance with the case-law of European Court of Human Rights (Court), the leading, or one of the leading, regional institutions for the protection and promotion of human rights, which were established in parallel with the political atmosphere of the post-war period. As the terrorists, and their supporters in the legal field, eagerly exploit allegations of human rights violations by the security forces, and

---

[2] Kelling, George L. and Moore, Mark H. *The Evolving Strategy of Policing,* in Brandl, Steven G. and Barlow, David E., *Classics in Policing,* Cincinnati, Anderson Publishing Co., 1996, pp.71-95.

[3] *Ibid* and Menachem Amir, *Police, Policing, State and Society: Some Basic Problems in Protecting Human and Civil Rights* in Menachem Amir and Stanley Einstein, *Policing, Security and Democracy: Theory and Practice*, Huntsville, Office of International Criminal Justice, 2001, pp. 53-72.

[4] William W. Burke-White, *Human Rights and National Security: The Strategic Correlation*, Harvard Human Rights Journal, Vol. 17. Spring 2004, pp. 250-280.

as they focus on alleged police violations of the integrity of the human body, rather than other law enforcement practices, this essay will focus on practices that involve the use of physical force.

First of all, some important facts about the Court, such as its aim, position, and evidentiary standards, will be discussed. Secondly, the case-law of the Court on the use of force by the agents of the States will be examined within a classification of the lawfulness of the force used. The last section will try to define the general principles for the use of force by the security forces in democratic countries in the light of the case-law of the Court.

Some Facts about the Court

Allegations of human rights violations inflicted by security forces when using force are generally dealt with by the Court under the Articles 2 and 3 of the European Convention for the Protection of Human Rights and Fundamental Freedoms (Convention), as discussed below. In this regard, it can be argued that Article 2 of the Convention, which provides the right to life, and Article 3 of the Convention, which prohibits torture, should directly shape the counter-terrorism legislation and the practices of the law enforcement agencies in the Contracting States. Therefore, it is important to examine the way the Court establishes its case-law.

The Court will only deal with applications which have been subjected to prior legal proceedings in the domestic courts. In these terms, the Court has a secondary function, especially as it *relies on the findings of fact of those domestic tribunals*, in principle.[5] However, the Court is not bound by the findings of the domestic courts and in *highly exceptional situations* can send a delegation to establish the facts disputed between the parties:[6]

> The Court is sensitive to the subsidiary nature of its role and must be cautious in taking on the role of a first instance tribunal of fact, where this is not rendered unavoidable by the circumstances of a particular case [...]. Where domestic proceedings have taken place, it is not the Court's task to substitute its own assessment of the facts for that of the domestic courts and as a general rule it is for those courts to assess the evidence before them [...]. Though the Court is not bound by the findings of domestic courts, in normal circumstances it requires cogent elements to lead it to depart from the findings of fact reached by those courts [...]. The same principles apply *mutatis mutandis* where no domestic court proceedings have taken place because the prosecuting authorities have not found sufficient evidence to initiate such proceedings. Nonetheless, where allegations are made under Articles 2 and 3 of the Convention the Court must apply a particularly thorough scrutiny [...] even if certain domestic proceedings and investigations have already taken place.[7]

---

[5] Douwe Korff, *The Right to Life – A Guide to the Implementation of Article 2 of the European Convention on Human Rights*, Human Rights Handbooks, No. 8, Strasbourg, Council of Europe, 2006, p. 29.

[6] *Ibid*, p. 30. These situations are considered, by Korff, as; (a) serious defects in the respondent State's investigation of the events and (b) where it was an essential part of the applicants' allegations that these defects were such as to render the other domestic proceedings ineffective.

[7] *Adalı v. Turkey*, judgement of 31 March 2005, par. 213 with references (given as [...] in the quotation) to *McKerr v. the United Kingdom*, judgement of 4 May 2001; *Klass v. Germany*, judgement of 22 September 1993, *Ribitsch v. Austria*, judgement of 4 December 1995 and *Avşar v. Turkey,* judgement of 10 July 2001.

In addition, the aim of the Court's assessment is not to find or establish a criminal responsibility, but to ensure the Contracting States act in accordance with their international law responsibility under the Convention:

> When there have been criminal proceedings in the domestic court concerning those same allegations, it must be borne in mind that criminal law liability is distinct from international law responsibility under the Convention. The Court's jurisdiction is confined to the latter. Responsibility under the Convention is based on its own provisions which are to be interpreted and applied on the basis of the objectives of the Convention and in the light of the relevant principles of international law. The responsibility of a State under the Convention, arising for the acts of its organs, agents and servants, is not to be confused with the domestic legal issues of individual criminal responsibility under examination in the national criminal courts. The Court is not concerned with reaching any findings as to guilt or innocence in that sense.[8]

Accordingly, the Court makes its assessment on the basis of all material submitted by the parties, i.e. the oral evidence given by the witnesses, the documentary evidence adduced by the parties, in particular the documents submitted by the governments in respect of the legal proceedings carried out into the impugned incident, and the parties' written observations on the merits and, if necessary, the material obtained by its own motion, i.e. through the fact-finding missions of its own delegation.[9] The evidentiary standard adopted by the Court in assessing these materials is accepted as "beyond reasonable doubt" which is further explained by the Court as follows:

> Such proof may follow from the coexistence of sufficiently strong, clear and concordant inferences or of similar unrebutted presumptions of fact.[10]

The Court deals with two kinds of situation in determining the human rights framework for law enforcement practices envisaging the use of force: (i) the lawful use of force, and (ii) the unlawful use of force. In these terms, the lawful use of force is explicitly dealt with under Article 2 by the Court, while the unlawful practices, i.e. prohibited treatment in police custody, are provided under Article 3 without any explicit reference to use of force. Therefore, before discussing the decisions of the Court on the applications directly or indirectly related to the use of force by security forces, the objectives and the contexts of the provisions at issue will be examined below.

The Lawful Use of Force

At the core of law enforcement tasks lies the ability and the need to use force in fulfilling some of requirements.[11] Generally the public understand that in some situations force is necessary, unavoidable, and required.[12] Accordingly, in all countries, the police are given the legal authority to use force, and it is known that law enforcers use various forms of force in fulfilling some of their regular tasks. These tasks include

---

[8] *Matyar v. Turkey*, judgement of 21 February 2002, par. 109.

[9] *H. L. R. v. France,* judgement of 29 April 1997, par. 37.

[10] *Ireland v. the United Kingdom*, judgement of 18 January 1978, par. 161.

[11] Joel H. Garner et al. *Characteristics Associated with the Prevalence and Severity of Force Used by Police*, Justice Quarterly, Vol. 19 No. 4, December 2002, pp. 705-746.

[12] Noel Otu, *The Police Service and Liability Insurance: Responsible Policing*, International Journal of Police Science & Management, Vathek Publishing, Volume 8, Number 4, 2006, pp. 294-315.

the apprehension of the suspects and riot management, while above all security operations may require the use of force.

However, the legal use of force by authorized agents is usually subjected to criticism, which is not surprising as the ultimate level of the use of force is the deprivation of life. Actions were generally deemed excessive. As a result, various control measures were developed in many countries' national criminal justice systems. The growing importance of human rights in international politics, and the wish to ensure that countries show due respect to human rights, led to some supplementary international control systems, e.g. the protection system of the Convention.

The system of the Convention provides a partial protection in terms of the "legal use of force" as it mainly deals with the "use of lethal force", and very exceptionally with the "use of potentially lethal force" by the agents of the States. Not all forms of force are considered. The use of lethal force is the ultimate form of the legal use of force regulated in the domestic laws, and this is primarily dealt with under Article 2 of the Convention, which protects the right to life. This right, which is accepted as one of the most fundamental rights of an individual, is non-derogable in that it cannot be denied in any situation.[13] The article reads as:

> 1. Everyone's right to life shall be protected by law. No one shall be deprived of his life intentionally save in the execution of a sentence of a court following his conviction of a crime for which this penalty is provided by law.
>
> 2. Deprivation of life shall not be regarded as inflicted in contravention of this article when it results from the use of force which is no more than absolutely necessary:
>
> a) in defence of any person from unlawful violence;
> b) in order to effect a lawful arrest or to prevent the escape of a person lawfully detained;
> c) in action lawfully taken for the purpose of quelling a riot or insurrection.

Although the first paragraph of the article authorizes the execution of a death penalty as an exceptional situation, an indicator of the reality of Europe in 1950s, the dominance of anti-death penalty views in European public order systems led to the continent becoming a death penalty-free area with the ratifications of Protocol No. 6 (1983) and Protocol No. 13 (2002) to the Convention.[14] The second paragraph of the article lists certain situations in which the deprivation of life cannot be accepted as a violation of this protection, as long as the act which caused the loss of life meets certain criteria.

According to the case-law of the Convention organs, the provision imposes two obligations on the contracting States: the negative and the positive obligations. The negative obligation refers to the prohibition of deprivation of life unless certain situations are met, while the positive obligation requires both preventive measures of the State to protect life and some form of effective official investigation when individuals are killed as a result of the use of force.[15] These obligations are also examined by the Convention organs as the substantive and procedural requirements of the provision, respectively. In this context, the negative obligation of the States, or the substantive requirements of the article will be examined below, as they lie at the core of the concept of use of force.

---

[13] *McCann and Others v. United Kingdom*, judgement of 27 September 1995, par. 147.

[14] M. Bedri Eryılmaz et al. *The Analysis of European Court of Human Rights Decisions Related to Turkey (2002-2005)*, Review of International Law and Politics, Vol. 3, No. 9, 2007, pp. 28-59.

[15] *Kaya v. Turkey*, judgement of 19 February 1998, par. 89.

The second paragraph of Article 2 lists the situations which *may* legitimize the deprivation of life, however, the provision must not be read as if it is granting a *carte blanche* to those in authority to kill a person intentionally, as the Court states when explaining the aim of this paragraph in one prominent case, *McCann and Others v. United Kingdom*:

> (…) [T]he text of Article 2 (art. 2), read as a whole, demonstrates that paragraph 2 (art. 2-2) does not primarily define instances where it is permitted intentionally to kill an individual, but describes the situations where it is permitted to "use force" which may result, as an unintended outcome, in the deprivation of life. (…)[16]

As mentioned above, the Court is generally concerned with the use of lethal force by the agents of the State which resulted in the death of the victim. However, there are some exceptions in this regard and the Court examined some specific applications under Article 2, in which the applicants had not been killed in fact. These judgements are; *Osman v. the United Kingdom,* judgement of 28 October 1998, *Yaşa v. Turkey,* judgement of 2 September 1998, *L.C.B. v. the United Kingdom,* judgement of 9 June 1998, *İlhan v. Turkey,* judgement of 27 June 2000 and *Makaratzis v. Greece,* judgement of 20 December 2004. Among these judgements, the *Makaratzis* is the sole one related to the use of force by the agents of the State.

The case, *Makaratzis,* concerned an apprehension of the applicant subsequent to a police pursuit. The applicant, Christos Makaratzis, had driven through a red traffic light in the centre of Athens, near the American embassy and accelerated afterwards, prompting a police chase. After breaking through five police roadblocks, the police officers started firing at his car and the applicant was finally stopped at a petrol station. Following his arrest, the applicant was taken to hospital. According to the medical reports, the applicant was injured on the right arm, the right foot, the left buttock and the right side of the chest. One bullet was removed from his foot and another one is still inside his buttock. The applicant was unarmed at the time of the incident and subsequently sentenced to a forty-day imprisonment *inter alia* for bodily injury and harm to others by negligence, while the police officers, who were prosecuted for causing serious bodily harm and unauthorized use of weapons, were acquitted. Consequently, the applicant applied to the Court and alleged that the police officers who had tried to arrest him had used excessive firepower against him, putting his life at risk.

The very first issue the Court addressed in the *Makaratzis* case was whether cases brought before the Court alleging a breach of Article 2 could still be examined under Article 2 when the victim had not been killed but had in fact survived the use of potentially lethal force by the State agents. The Court discussed the previous cases (mentioned above) brought before it with the allegation of a breach of Article 2 when the victims had survived. It reiterated that the first three applications were related to the positive obligation on the State, under the first sentence of Article 2 §1, to protect the life of the individual from third parties or from the risk of life-endangering illness. The last one was related to physical ill-treatment by State agents which did not result in death. The Court noted that the key to deciding whether Article 2 was applicable in the case under consideration was to determine whether the force used against the applicant was potentially lethal, and what kind of impact the conduct of the officials concerned had, not only on his physical integrity but also on the interests the right to life is intended to protect. Consequently, the Court concluded that Article 2 was applicable to

---

[16] *McCann and Others*, par. 148.

the case as the applicant was the victim of conduct which put his life at risk, even though, in the event, he survived.[17]

In assessing the situations which resulted in the deprivation of life by using force, the Court applies a triple-examination. This examination consists of the criteria of legality, legitimacy and necessity in a democratic society, which is also applied by the Court in assessing the applications made under Articles 8 to 11.

The legality criteria primarily require the Contracting States to protect the right to life effectively in their national legislations and to set out the conditions for the use of force by their agents. As for the legitimacy examination, the Court refers to the aims set out in the second paragraph of the Article 2 and also notes that there must be a balance between the aim pursued and the means employed to achieve it.[18] Finally, an inquiry is conducted into whether the use of the means which are specified by law to achieve the aims at issue are necessary in a democratic society. However, in the light of the importance of the right to life in democratic societies, this test requires a stricter scrutiny than when it is applied to Articles 8 to 11. At this point the test of necessity of the Court requires the act to be "no more than absolutely necessary", and also examines all the circumstances surrounding the actions of the agents of the States which resulted in the deprivation of life. In brief, it can be assumed that the last two aspects of the Court's examination are primarily related to the law enforcement practices and policies and the first criterion is more related to legislative regulations.

In the case-law of the Court on the use of force by the agents of the States, the judgement in *McCann and others v. the United Kingdom* is one of the most illustrative ones for law enforcers who wish to observe how a lawful arrest and a security operation should be carried out in compliance with human rights criteria and especially with a full respect for the right to life. This prominent case concerned the killings of three Irish Republican Army (IRA) terrorists by British Special Forces soldiers in Gibraltar. According to the intelligence received, the three IRA terrorists were planning a terrorist attack against a British target in Gibraltar and the authorities of the United Kingdom, Spain and Gibraltar took some required measures to prevent such an attack.

At the time, the IRA terrorists had parked a car next to their planned target and left the scene. After the inspection of the car, the authorities were convinced that a bomb had been placed on the car and it could be detonated by a radio-controlled device by either suspect. The authorities gave instructions to the military to conduct the arrests of the suspects. The military personnel were also informed that the car had a bomb inside and the suspects would not hesitate to detonate it when they were confronted. In the course of the attempt to arrest, the soldiers approached the suspects, who noticed their presence. The soldiers judged that the terrorists were in threatening positions due to their sudden movements, and they shot all three at close range until the suspects were no longer a threat. The subsequent search of the suspects and the car revealed that the suspects were unarmed and the car did not contain a bomb, although a bomb and a detonator were found in their hideout.

The Court ruled out the allegations of the applicants concerning the compatibility of national law and practice with Article 2 (art. 2) standards, the adequacy of the inquest proceedings as an investigative mechanism, and the premeditation of the killings.[19] It also mentioned that the actions of the soldiers did not, in themselves, give

---

[17] *Makaratzis v. Greece*, judgement of 20 December 2004, par. 49-55.
[18] *Güleç v. Turkey*, judgement of 27 July 1998, par. 71.
[19] *McCann and Others*, par. 151-184.

rise to a violation of the second paragraph of Article 2.[20] However, it concluded that there was a violation of Article 2 (art. 2) of the Convention regarding the control and organization of the operation due to the decision of the authorities not to prevent the suspects traveling into Gibraltar, as well as the failure of the authorities to make sufficient allowances for the possibility that their intelligence assessments might be flawed, and their failure to prepare for the possibility of an automatic recourse to lethal force when the soldiers opened fire.[21] In taking this decision, the Court relied on its consideration given below, which requires the States show the "absolute necessity" of any killing, not only in respect of the actions of the agents who actually carried out the killing, but in respect of all the surrounding circumstances including the planning, control and organization of the an operation:[22]

> In keeping with the importance of this provision (art. 2) in a democratic society, the Court must, in making its assessment, subject deprivations of life to the most careful scrutiny, particularly where deliberate lethal force is used, taking into consideration not only the actions of the agents of the State who actually administer the force but also all the surrounding circumstances including such matters as the planning and control of the actions under examination.[23]

In conclusion it can be argued that the *McCann* case is important for the law enforcers in two respects: first, for the way lethal force is used in the course of a lawful arrest, and second for the planning and conduct of a security operation. The first one clarifies that law enforcers who honestly believe that a suspect is in a position to threaten life, according to the information provided to them or the movements of the suspect, are entitled to use lethal force proportionately. The Court concluded that the use of lethal force by soldiers who, on the basis of sudden movements interpreted as actions to detonate a bomb placed in a car next to an intended target, as well as on previously provided information, shot and killed IRA terrorists, did not in itself give rise to a violation of Article 2/2. On the other hand, the latter aspect of the case should guide security forces in democratic societies to plan and conduct their further operations in compliance with due respect for the fundamental human rights of suspects, including terrorists, especially their right to life.

As for policing operations, the Court expanded its case-law in a further case, *Makaratzis v. Greece*, and it commented that policing operations must be sufficiently regulated by national law, within the framework of a system of adequate and effective safeguards against arbitrariness and abuse of force, and even against avoidable accidents, and the police officers should not be left in a vacuum when performing their duties, whether in the context of a prepared operation or a spontaneous chase of a person perceived to be dangerous.[24] [That is to say] a legal and administrative framework should define the limited circumstances in which law-enforcement officials may use force and firearms, in the light of the international standards which have been developed in this respect.[25] In addition, the Court ruled in its judgement of *Şimşek and Others v. Turkey* that the States should undertake to provide effective training to the police force with the objective of complying with international standards for human rights and policing in order for the police officers to cope with the great stress and

---

[20] *Ibid*, par. 200.
[21] *Ibid*, par. 213-214.
[22] Korff, p. 31.
[23] *McCann and Others*, par. 150.
[24] *Makaratzis*, par. 58.
[25] *Ibid*, par. 59.

psychological pressure they may face in performing their duties.[26] Specifically for large-scale lawful policing operations, i.e. quelling a riot or dispersing crowds, the Court noted that a clear and a centralized command[27] is a requirement in order not to increase the risk of police officers using disproportionate force, while the supply of necessary equipment, such as tear gas, plastic bullets, water cannons, etc., to disperse the crowd, which may prevent the security forces resorting to use of lethal force, or at least make such force not absolutely necessary, is also essential.[28]

The Unlawful Use of Force

In the performance of their duties, the law enforcers sometimes resort to unlawful practices. They may also use their legally given powers to commit such acts. Generally, when such acts are related to the unlawful use of force, the officials act with the intention of better serving their causes, societies or countries, although they know that the acts they are committing are illegal and banned, at least by their national legislations. In the system of the Convention these acts arise in the form of ill-treatment, and are dealt under Article 3 which prohibits torture and other types of ill-treatment.

The prohibition of torture is non-derogable and is an absolute prohibition in the protection system of the Convention, and it is regarded as one of the most fundamental values of democracy. Although some of the provisions of the Convention can be derogated in extraordinary situations, such as in the fight against terrorism, organized crime, or in cases of public emergency threatening the life of the nation, in accordance with the Article 15, this provision cannot be applied to Article 3 in any situation.[29] In brief, the Contracting States do not have any authority to derogate the Article 3, which reads:

> "No one shall be subjected to torture or to inhuman or degrading treatment or punishment."

As mentioned in the text of the provision, there are three kinds of ill-treatment: torture, inhuman treatment and degrading treatment. Not all kinds of ill-treatment can be regarded as torture, but every act of torture constitutes inhuman and a degrading treatment at the same time. The reason is the difference in the severity of the types of ill-treatment, and torture is the most severe type in the Convention system. According to the case-law of the Court, ill-treatment must reach a level of severity in order to be regarded as a violation of Article 3; that is to say, even treatment which is undesirable or illegal will not breach Article 3 unless it causes sufficiently serious suffering or humiliation to the victim.[30] The assessment of this threshold depends on all the circumstances of the case, such as the duration of the treatment, its physical or mental effects and, in some cases, the sex, age and state of health of the victim.[31] However, having reached the required level, it remains for the Court to decide which form of ill-treatment is constituted by the actions complained of, with reference to the intensity of the suffering inflicted. Having said this, the classifications of the ill-treatment are not

---

[26] *Şimşek and Others v. Turkey*, judgement of 26 October 2005, par. 109.
[27] *Ibid*, par. 110.
[28] *Ibid*, par. 111.
[29] *Ireland*, par. 163.
[30] Francis G. Jacobs and Robin C. A. White, *The European Convention on Human Rights*, Oxford, Oxford University Press, Second Edition, 1996, p.49.
[31] *Ireland*, par. 162.

fixed, and can change in parallel with the increasingly high standards being required in the area of the protection of human rights and fundamental liberties in democratic societies.[32]

The Court's first judgement that defines the difference between the torture and other kinds of ill-treatment is the judgement of *Ireland v. the United Kingdom* of 18 January 1978.[33] The Court decided that the five interrogation techniques the British security forces applied to Irish detainees, in the relevant time period, did not constitute torture and the Court defined them as inhuman or degrading treatment. Those techniques which were regarded as inhuman or degrading treatment, in contrast to the decision of the Commission that concluded that these techniques amounted to torture, are:

1. hooding the detainees except during interrogation;
2. making the detainees stand continuously against a wall in a spread-eagled and painful posture for prolonged periods of some hours;
3. subjecting the detainees to continuous and monotonous noise;
4. depriving the detainees of sleep; and
5. restricting the detainees to a diet of one round of bread and one pint of water at six-hourly intervals.[34]

According to the Court, the application of these techniques in combination does not cause suffering enough to be named torture. The Court was of the opinion of that there is only sufficient reason to name any treatment reaching a specified level of severity as torture when it occasions suffering of the particular intensity and cruelty implied by the word torture as so understood.[35]

The first judgement of the Court in which it named the disputed treatment as torture, was the judgement of *Aksoy v. Turkey* of 18 December 1996. In this judgement, the applicant alleged that he was strung up by his arms in the form of torture known as "Palestinian hanging" and subsequently lost the movement of his arms and hands as a result of, *inter alia,* this treatment, and he provided the Court with some medical reports confirming his allegations. Despite the Government's objections to several aspects of the evaluation of the facts and the evidence, and her argument that the allegations were unfounded, the Court decided that the treatment, which was confirmed by medical reports, was of such a serious and cruel nature that it could only be described as torture.[36]

A similar decision was given by the Grand Chamber of the Court in the judgement of *Selmouni v. France* of 28 July 1999, in which the responsible Government accepted that the types of treatment the applicant had been subjected to amounted to inhuman and degrading treatment but argued that they were not torture. Ahmed Selmouni, the 49 year-old applicant, a Netherlands and Moroccan national arrested by French police for drug-trafficking, alleged that he had been subjected to various forms of ill-treatment while in police custody, such as being repeatedly punched, kicked, and hit with objects, being sexually abused and raped with a small black truncheon. His allegations were also partly confirmed by medical reports. Having examined the facts of the application, the Court concluded that the physical and mental violence the applicant had suffered

---

[32] *Selmouni v. France*, judgement of 28 July 1999, par. 101.
[33] Eryilmaz et al.
[34] *Ireland v. the United Kingdom.*
[35] *Ibid*, par. 167.
[36] *Aksoy v. Turkey*, judgement of 18 December 1996, par. 64.

caused "severe" pain and suffering and was sufficiently serious and cruel to be regarded as acts of torture for the purposes of Article 3 of the Convention.[37]

Although it is one of the basic rules of the law that the burden of proof lies with the claimant, in cases when an applicant is taken into police custody in good health and is found to be injured on release, Article 3, just like Article 2, requires the responsible Governments to provide a plausible explanation of how those injuries were caused.[38] It means that the burden of proof lies on the respondent Governments when an applicant alleges that he/she was subjected to ill-treatment in police custody and received medical attention afterwards or sustained some kinds of permanent or short-term injuries. Besides this, the Court does not always find explanations of the Governments to be convincing or consistent, as was the case with *Biyan v. Turkey*, in which the applicant alleged that he was subjected to ill-treatment in police custody and obtained a medical report indicating some injuries. In reply the Government provided the Court with a statement, signed by the applicant, saying that the injuries were self-inflicted. Noting that the applicant was still in police custody when the record was made, and he was under pressure from police officers, the Court found that the Government's explanation was neither plausible nor satisfactory in view of the applicant's vulnerability as a prisoner in police custody and concluded that the treatment amounted inhuman and degrading treatment.[39]

Conclusion

In democratic countries the whole range of law enforcement practices are criticized, and the issue of the use of force has a prominent place in these criticisms. In addition to the fact that the issue is deeply associated with individual-society-state relations, it earns this position mainly from its practical consequences, which, when force is taken to extremes, may include undesirable situations and illegal acts. Although the national authorities in democratic societies take many steps to avoid such circumstances, some additional control systems have been developed in international law, especially in view of the growing importance of human rights.

Among these international systems, the system of the Convention is undoubtedly regarded as one of the most effective and efficient systems in the world. Therefore, the case-law of the European Court of Human Rights on the issue of the use of force has an important and illustrative role for law enforcers as they fulfill their tasks in compliance with the primary values of the societies they serve, namely the rule of law and respect for human rights.

As discussed above, and according to its contemporary case-law, the Court deals with the issue of the use of force by agents of the States in two aspects: (i) explicitly as the lawful use of force, and (ii) implicitly as the unlawful use of force. The cases concerning the first aspect are examined by the Court under Article 2 of the Convention, and the latter aspect under Article 3.

However, in the case of the lawful use of force, the guidance of the Court remains limited as it mainly deals with the use of lethal force, and only in very exceptional situations with the use of potentially lethal force. In this context, the examination by

---

[37] *Selmouni*, par. 105-106.
[38] *Ibid*, par. 87.
[39] *Biyan v. Turkey*, judgement of 3 February 2005, par. 45-46.

the Court of situations in which the use of force by the agents of the Contracting States resulted in deprivation of life is divided into three parts: the legality, legitimacy and necessity of the authority used. This means that the lethal force exercised by the security forces can only be accepted as compatible with the Convention, as well as with the respect due to human rights, insofar as that force is used in accordance with the law, which must adequately protect the right to life. To achieve the aims defined in the second paragraph of Article 2 it must be determined whether actions are absolutely necessary in a democratic society. The Court further explains these theoretical requirements with reference to the examination of the actual events brought before it.

As for the unlawful use of force, which arises in the form of ill-treatment in the system of the Convention, the Court takes a solid stance by prohibiting such acts in all circumstances, even in the fight against terrorism or organized crime, or in case of public emergencies threatening the life of a nation.

In the light of the fact that terrorists eagerly exploit alleged human rights violations of the security forces, and use them for their aims, compliance with the human rights criteria of the Court becomes critically important for the security forces in democratic countries in their fight against terrorism. Taking into consideration the very thought-provoking warning of the U.S. Supreme Court, namely *"nothing can destroy a government more quickly than its failure to observe its own laws, or worse, its disregard of the charter of its own existence",*[40] the conformity of the security forces to the values of the societies they serve will surely be their most operative instrument in fulfilling their tasks, and especially in denying the terrorists any field to survive in the global fight against terrorism.

References

[1] M. Amir, Police, Policing, State and Society: Some Basic Problems in Protecting Human and Civil Rights in M. Amir and S. Einstein, Policing, Security and Democracy: Theory and Practice, Huntsville, Office of International Criminal Justice, 2001.

[2] W.W. Burke-White, Human Rights and National Security: The Strategic Correlation, Harvard Human Rights Journal, Vol. 17. Spring 2004, pp. 250-280.

[3] G. Poggi, The Development of The Modern State, Stanford, University Press, 1978.

[4] M. B. Eryılmaz, B. Çiçekli and Ö. Yılmaz, The Analysis of European Court of Human Rights' Decisions Related to Turkey (2002-2005), Review of International Law & Politics, Vol. 3, No. 9, 2007, pp. 28-59.

[5] J. H. Garner, C. D. Maxwell and C. G. Heraux, Characteristics Associated with the Prevalence and Severity of Force Used by Police, Justice Quarterly, Vol. 19 No. 4, December 2002, pp. 705-746.

[6] F. G. Jacobs and R. C. A. White, The European Convention on Human Rights, Oxford, University Press, Second Edition, 1996.

[7] L. G. Kelling and M. H. Moore, The Evolving Strategy of Policing, in G. S. Brandl and D. E. Barlow, Classics in Policing, Cincinnati, Anderson Publishing Co., 1996.

[8] D. Korff, The Right to Life – A Guide to the Implementation of Article 2 of the European Convention on Human Rights, Human Rights Handbooks, No. 8, Strasbourg, Council of Europe, 2006.

[9] N. Otu, The Police Service and Liability Insurance: Responsible Policing, International Journal of Police Science and Management, Vathek Publishing, Volume 8, Number 4, 2006, pp. 294-315.

[10] ECHR, *Adalı v. Turkey*, judgement of 31 March 2005.

[11] ECHR, *Aksoy v. Turkey*, judgement of 18 December 1996.

[12] ECHR, *Avşar v. Turkey,* judgement of 10 July 2001.

[13] ECHR, *Biyan v. Turkey*, judgement of 3 February 2005.

[14] ECHR, *Güleç v. Turkey*, judgement of 27 July 1998.

[15] ECHR, *H. L. R. v. France*, judgement of 29 April 1997.

---

[40] U.S. Supreme Court, MAPP v. OHIO, 367 U.S. 643 (1961).

[16] ECHR, *Ireland v. the United Kingdom*, judgement of 18 January 1978.
[17] ECHR, *Kaya v. Turkey*, judgement of 19 February 1998.
[18] ECHR, *Klass v. Germany*, judgement of 22 September 1993.
[19] ECHR, *Makaratzis v. Greece*, judgement of 20 December 2004.
[20] ECHR, *Matyar v. Turkey*, judgement of 21 February 2002.
[21] ECHR, *McCann and Others v. the United Kingdom*, judgement of 27 September 1995.
[22] ECHR, *McKerr v. the United Kingdom*, judgement of 4 May 2001.
[23] ECHR, *Ribitsch v. Austria*, judgement of 4 December 1995.
[24] ECHR, *Selmouni v. France*, judgement of 28 July 1999.
[25] ECHR, *Şimşek and Others v. Turkey*, judgement of 26 October 2005.
[26] U.S. Supreme Court, MAPP v. OHIO, 367 U.S. 643 (1961).

Legal Aspects of Combating Terrorism
Centre of Excellence Defence Against Terrorism, Ankara, Turkey (Ed.)
IOS Press, 2008

doi:10.3233/978-1-58603-930-1-105

A Study of UK Anti-Terror Law

Maj. J. P. I. A. G. CHARVAT
SO2 Course Director, Centre of Excellence – Defence Against Terrorism, Ankara

Abstract. This paper discusses the development of the UK's terrorism law from the emergency powers of the Northern Ireland Troubles to the law's recent developments in the face of contemporary terrorist threats. The paper looks in detail at the London attacks of July 2005 and other events, and at how the laws have been applied in countering the terrorists' threat and their activities in the UK.

Keywords. Terrorism, legal aspects of terrorism, UK anti-terror laws, Terrorism Act 2000, Anti-terrorism, Crime and Security Act 2001, Prevention of Terrorism Act 2005, Terrorism Act 2006.

Introduction

In 1969 the United Kingdom faced the threat of domestic terrorism when the Provisional Irish Republican Army (PIRA) began its campaign of violence. This meant a new and challenging security threat for Her Majesty's Government and the British legal system. The combating of terrorism creates many strains on the law, as urgent security situations may drive the authorities to explore every avenue in the search for solutions. Ordinary criminal law struggles to make adequate provision for the unique situation that terrorist campaigns can bring. The British Governments throughout the 1970s, 80s and 90s addressed this situation with a series of Emergency Powers for the security forces and authorities, to equip them with a legal basis to deal with the situation. The powers were annually approved or updated to allow the authorities to develop along with the situation. Although the laws provided a firm legal basis, learning from mistakes, and providing a balance between security and the expected safeguards a democratic state enjoys, they did not enter the statute books and were transient in their design and nature. It was not until the year 2000 that the British Parliament brought in a statutory act, the Terrorism Act 2000, to deal with the terrorist threat with statute legislation. This act was designed to deal with the internal threat of Irish Republican and Loyalist terrorist groups associated with the ongoing troubles in Northern Ireland. It was soon overtaken by events after the dramatic attacks on New York, Washington and Flight 93 on 11 September 2001.

British legislation during the Northern Ireland troubles was characterized by both success and failure. The fact that these were emergency powers allowed for the simple repeal of those that were unsuccessful in their application. The fundamental aim was to establish a legal system that was robust enough to prevent or prosecute terrorists under circumstances where the existing law did not give sufficient power to the police and security forces for prompt or pre-emptive action.

The Northern Ireland Troubles

The troubles in Northern Ireland gave a real and stern test to the British legal system. It suddenly had to evolve to cope with the situation of British citizens committing acts of terror in the UK. While the acts themselves, once carried out, would constitute a statutory offence, terrorism was not a circumstance covered by existing legislation. The increased level of organized violence in the United Kingdom prompted change.

The troubles in Northern Ireland began in the 1960s. The large Catholic minority was feeling aggrieved at its treatment from the Protestant dominated Parliament of Northern Ireland, the regional government. Although the province was ruled from London, the Parliament of Northern Ireland based in Belfast was responsible for the day-to-day running of most matters. Although there was no legal basis for the differential treatment of the Catholic minority, the Protestant majority could use its powers to impose disadvantage without raising great concern on the mainland. By the late 1960s the elements of the Catholic minority formed the Northern Ireland Civil Rights movement, campaigning for better and fairer treatment. Part of their grievance was that the fabric of Northern Irish public administration was biased against them, including the police and local government. With some justification they began a campaign of largely peaceful and legitimate protests to raise awareness of their plight. These marches were often attacked by Protestant youths and were afforded little protection by the police. The violence increased and by mid-1969 Catholic areas were being attacked quite openly by large Protestant gangs. The police had lost control and the British Army deployed on Operation Banner to restore law and order. This caused changes in the Irish Republican Army, which saw an opportunity to capitalize on the political situation and make a bid for their aim of a united Ireland in a social republic. They resorted to violence and a campaign of terrorism that would last almost 40 years.

The situation created a new type of crime and therefore needed a new type of solution. One of the first initiatives was the development of a Stop and Search system by the security forces to stop the movement of illegal weapons and munitions. Since the early part of the 20th Century guns had been controlled in the United Kingdom. The Pistols Act (1903)[1] brought in basic controls for certain pistols, but the more significant Firearms Act (1920), which "was substantially the modern scheme of control",[2] tightened weapon ownership in the United Kingdom. Through a series of developments from 1920 to 1967[3] the situation was that in 1969 automatic, rifled guns and pistols required a Firearms Certificate where the holder had to prove he/she had a good reason to own each gun and that they were not a danger. Shotguns over 24 inches (60cm) only required a license and did not require registration individually. Consequently when the Provisional IRA began their campaign, weapons that would be of use to terrorists were not legally available to them.

With the legitimate ownership of weapons denied to the Provisional IRA they had to use illegal weapons. The Stop and Search Policy was highly successful in targeting

---

[1] The 1824 Vagrancy Act introduced the first controls for owning a weapon with intent.
[2] Gabb, S: Gun Control in Britain p. 2.
[3] Firearms Act 1937, Firearms Act 1965 and Criminal Justice Act 1967.

the movement of illegal weapons on the streets of Northern Ireland, and legislation readily provided a legal basis for prosecution of those in possession of them. However the application of this policy was unsuccessful as it targeted the young male Catholic demographic group in particular and was a major source of resentment against the authorities on the part of this element of the population, as innocent young men, unconnected to terrorism, were frequently targeted for searches, whereas their Protestant counterparts were not. The policy, with improved methodology, was included in later acts.

Article 39 of the Magna Carta gave Englishmen (and later Irishmen) the inherent right of trial by jury:

> No free man shall be captured, and or imprisoned, or disseised of his freehold, and or of his liberties, or of his free customs, or be outlawed, or exiled, or in anyway destroyed, nor will we proceed against him by force or proceed against him by arms, but by the lawful judgement of his peers, and by the law of the land.[4]

In Northern Ireland this became a problem during the Troubles. The population was deeply divided on sectarian lines and the jury system meant that for cases relating to terrorism there was an intrinsic bias. This was compounded by the fact that those selected for jury service in terrorist-related cases were subject to intimidation and threats from the terrorist organizations. Consequently a fair jury trial was almost impossible in the province in a terrorist-related case.

The Diplock Courts[5] were introduced to give accused persons a fair trial without the risk of a partisan or intimidated jury. They consisted of a judge sitting on his or her own, who conducted the trial, decided the verdict and issued the sentence. In order to ensure fairness the judge had to issue reasons for his guilty verdicts, and as a matter of routine would usually also issue reasons for not guilty verdicts. While this system was a break from the fundamental basis of British law it was established in order to ensure the basic intent of the Jury system, the fairest possible system of trial. Diplock was only used in specific circumstances and was never seen as more than a temporary solution to specific terrorist-related offences, and it was never intended to replace trial by jury.

Terrorism Act 2000

This act sought to make the response to terrorism a permanent feature of British Law. While it was written specifically for the situation in Northern Ireland it was reasonably general in its approach to terrorism, and it did not confine its scope so that it would be inapplicable to other forms of terrorism, should they become a threat in the United Kingdom. The act defined terrorism as follows:

> (1) In this Act "terrorism" means the use or threat of action where
> (a) the action falls within subsection (2),

---

[4] Translated by Lysander Spooner from the original: "Nullus liber homo capiatur, vel imprisonetur, aut desseisetur de libero tenemento, vel libertatibus, vel liberis consuetudinibus suis, aut utlagetur, aut exuletur, aut aliquo modo destruatur, nec super eum ibimus, nec super eum mittemus, nisi per legale judicium parium suorum, vel per legem terre."

[5] These special courts were introduced in 1972 after a report by Lord Diplock in an attempt to overcome widespread jury intimidation.

(b) the use or threat is designed to influence the government or to intimidate the public or a section of the public, and
(c) the use or threat is made for the purpose of advancing a political, religious or ideological cause.
(2) Action falls within this subsection if it
(a) involves serious violence against a person,
(b) involves serious damage to property,
(c) endangers a person's life, other than that of the person committing the action,
(d) creates a serious risk to the health or safety of the public or a section of the public, or
(e) is designed seriously to interfere with or seriously disrupt an electronic system.
(3) the use or threat of action falling within subsection (2) which involves the use of firearms or explosives is terrorism whether or not subsection (1) (b) is satisfied.[6]

The Act proscribed specific terrorist organizations of which membership and support was made illegal. This included financing the proscribed groups. Although the list only included terrorist groups active in Northern Ireland at the turn of the millennium, it did make provision for the list to be amended as appropriate. The list included fourteen organizations from both the Republican and Loyalist elements in the Province.[7] This proscription meant that the security forces had increased scope in prosecuting terrorists, i.e. for membership of the organizations. The leadership, who may commission terrorist acts but keep themselves sufficiently distant from the crime itself and therefore avoid prosecution, could therefore be subject to charges if their membership was proven. Furthermore, anyone professing to be a member of a proscribed organization was also guilty of an offence.[8] Membership or profession of membership carried a tariff of up to 10 years.[9]

Support for a proscribed organization was also an offence under the act. This included furthering the activities of a proscribed organization or making an address at a meeting with the purpose of encouraging support for a proscribed organization.[10]

Terrorist finances and funding were criminalized under the Terrorism Act 2000. It became an offence to use finances for terrorist purpose or to raise funds for proscribed organizations. The act further covered the duty of people to disclose their suspicions to the police if they believed that they had become aware of arrangements that were providing funds for terrorists.[11]

Investigation of Terrorism

As well as proscribing organizations and dealing with terrorist funds, the Terrorism Act 2000 dealt with the unique circumstances of how terrorism investigations need to be

[6] Part 1 Section 1 of the Terrorism Act 2000. Crown Copyright reprinted with permission.
[7] Schedule 2 of the Terrorism Act 2000 listed all organizations banned as terrorist under this act.
[8] Terrorism Act 200 11 (1).
[9] Terrorism Act 2000 11 (3).
[10] Terrorism Act 2000 12 (3).
[11] Terrorism Act 2000 19 (2).

conducted. Unlike ordinary crimes, terrorism, especially in a situation like Northern Ireland, may be supported by significant elements of the population who may, through political persuasion or fear, hamper the investigation of terrorist acts.

One measure that aided the police in the investigation of a terrorist incident was the inclusion of a cordon area in which the police had special power, to allow an unhindered investigation. A cordon area should be clearly marked and its designation made by a senior police officer (at least a Superintendent), although in an urgent situation it could be designated by a constable.[12] In addition to this offences were created under the Act which made the hampering of an investigation of a terrorist act a crime.[13]

The Stop and Search powers were confirmed under the Terrorism Act 2000. A search could be done by a policeman working on reasonable suspicion to see if a suspect had any evidence indicating that he/she may be a terrorist. Weapons training and inciting terrorism were also covered briefly under the Terrorism Act 2000.

Anti-terrorism, Crime and Security Act 2001

On 11 September 2001 the attacks on New York, Washington and Pennsylvania changed the world, and the problem of dealing with terrorism altered significantly. The United Kingdom's initial legal response to the attacks was in the Anti-Terrorism, Crime and Security Act 2001. While the previous 2000 act was still valid the threat of international terrorism and religious extremism were not sufficiently dealt with. The 2001 legislation sought to address this.

The 2001 act sought to tighten the legislation on terrorist property. Previously the United Kingdom's legislation had been designed with the primarily domestic problem of Northern Irish terrorism in mind. However since 11 September the concept of International terrorism presented new dilemmas, especially if funds or property were outside British jurisdiction. The 2001 act introduced Freezing Orders, which allowed the government to freeze the assets of persons or organizations suspected of being involved in terrorism. These required frequent review, but did allow suspects property and funds to be held pending examination. The new power enabled the Treasury to freeze the assets of overseas governments or residents who had taken, or were likely to take, actions to the detriment of the United Kingdom's economy, or actions constituting a threat to the life or property of a national or resident of the United Kingdom.[14]

The Act further dealt with the issue of religion. The United Kingdom already had laws dealing with racial hatred and racially motivated crimes. The 2001 act made the amendment that the racial offences did not have to occur in the UK.[15] The 2001 act now included religiously motivated crime.[16] Thus, for the first time under British Law, religious groups were mentioned and not specific religions. The tariff for religiously motivated crimes was increased to seven years maximum.

The most controversial aspect of the Anti-terrorism, Crime and Security Act 2001 was the introduction of control orders and the ability of the Home Secretary to order

---

[12] Terrorism Act 2000 34 (1).
[13] Terrorism Act 2000 39 (2).
[14] OPSI Explanatory note to 2001 Anti-terrorism , Crime and Security Act.
[15] It removed the wording "in Great Britain" from Section 17 of the Public Order Act 1986.
[16] This amended section 28 of Part 2 of the Crime and Disorder Act 1998.

the detention of asylum seekers and immigrants who were suspected of involvement in International Terrorism for an indefinite period. These control orders could be very specific in their application and could be issued on the approval of the Secretary of State without requiring a conviction. Those held under these orders were detained at Belmarsh or an equivalent high security prison, unless the individuals took the option of being deported from Britain.[17] Although only 16 orders were issued[18] they were challenged in the European Courts. As they only applied to non-UK nationals the appeal was upheld and this form of control order was replaced in later legislation.

There were allegations that those held under the control orders were subject to a British 'Guantanamo Bay'. However these detainees were held pending deportation and were denied access to the UK. In his ministerial written statement Mr Blunkett confirms that 2 of the 16 detainees had left the UK of their own choice and the other 14 had elected to stay. Although these orders detained some people while in the UK they did not deny them the right to return freely to their country of origin or to a third country.

Prevention of Terrorism Act 2005

The 2001 act had established a form of control orders but these were only applicable to non-UK nationals. This was challenged as legally unfair and the control orders as allowed under the 2001 act were deemed illegal. The Prevention of Terrorism Act 2005 sought to redress this by introducing a new form of control order which was applicable to British Citizens as well as foreign nationals. Two types of control order were introduced, the non-derogation and derogation from the European Convention on Human Rights Article 5 (ECHR).[19]

Control orders have been seen as an effective and acceptable method of preventing terrorists having the freedom to plan and carry out attacks without the controversy and legal conundrum of internment. Control orders can limit a person's liberty in the areas they are considered to be dangerous and allow them to pursue a normal life within the scope of the order.

Non-derogation control orders are the normal type to be issued to individuals. These can limit or prevent someone from certain actions if it is considered that allowing them these actions could entail the risk of terrorist action. Control orders may prevent the subject from attending certain meetings or meeting up with specific groups or individuals should it be considered a risk to allow them to do so. It could restrict mobile telephone use or access to the internet. Unless the control order derogates from Article 5 of the ECHR it can be approved by the Home Secretary. The order is valid for up to twelve months[20] and can be reviewed and renewed by the Secretary of State.

Control orders can derogate from the ECHR. In order to do this the Home Secretary must apply to a court and gain judicial approval for the order to be issued.

[17] Belmarsh Prison was the main detention facility for immigrants suspected of terrorism as they awaited deportation after failed asylum bids. While kept in secure facilities, these detainees may leave to return to their country of origin or a willing third party at any time. Those who stay are usually pursuing an appeal to stay in the UK, claiming that they would be in danger or refused entry elsewhere.

[18] Written Ministerial Statements by Mr David Blunkett, Home Department, 18 Nov 03.

[19] The ECHR was first adopted in 1950 to protect human rights and fundamental freedoms.

[20] Prevention of Terrorism Act 2005 2 (4).

Derogation orders are designed only to be issued in the most extreme circumstances and are subject to very strict procedures in their application phase.

Terrorism Act 2006

Having covered a great deal of ground in the three acts on terrorism since 2000, the Terrorism Act 2006 looked at areas that were evidently an aspect of terrorism but where the law remained at a disadvantage in the fight against them. The 2006 act looked at the aspects of training and encouragement of terrorism. This was in many ways a very broad and useful law as it criminalized those who stopped short of aiding and abetting terrorism but used rhetoric and propaganda that could cause others to commit terrorist acts. It also creates offences regarding the dissemination of terrorist literature that encourages people to terrorism, including disseminating this on the Internet.[21]

The act covers the glorification of terrorism. There had been an increasing problem since the 2001 attacks on the United States that certain individuals were promoting terrorist causes by glorifying the acts. The posting of terrorist attacks or actions on websites had become a significant issue, and the 2006 act was designed to criminalize these actions and deny terrorists this publicity tool.

The act also covered the preparation and/or training for a possible terrorist act. This legislation covers the growing problem of attending ‘terrorist training camps’ or the seeking or purchase of equipment intended for a terrorist act. The preparation required to make certain types of terrorist tools is now covered, which gives the authorities greater scope to act before an attack takes place.

The period of pre-charge detention was further increased by the 2006 act. The 2000 act had give police up to 7 days to hold a suspect before charge or release. Any detention above the normal time would require frequent review and court approval. The 2006 act significantly increased this time to 28 days. This was not designed to be a normal practice but sought to allow additional time to conduct an investigation while keeping a potential terrorist off the streets. This extended period is only used *in extremis*.

Closed-Circuit Television

There is always a debate about the level of protection that should be applied by the authorities and the level of invasion of privacy that is acceptable to a nation. One area where the UK has accepted a reasonable invasion of that privacy is in the area of surveillance and closed-circuit television. London alone has over 10,000 CCTV cameras across the city.[22] There are also cameras on most buses and in train stations. This has meant that the police have been able to view crimes and produce key evidence or even to call patrols to an ongoing incident in order to prevent the full commission of a crime. There have even been some cameras that have been fitted with speakers, and this has allowed the operator to inform someone committing or about to commit a crime that they are on film in the hope of preventing further crime.

---

[21] Terrorism Act 2006 2.(2) (e).

[22] Figures from thisislondon.co.uk article by Justin Davenport 19 Sept 07.

The attacks on the London Underground and bus network on 7 July 2005 are an example of how the UK's balance has helped in terrorist investigation. The attacks took place without warning and it was not immediately known who had carried them out. Closed-circuit television (CCTV) was viewed and the bombers were seen getting onto the tube trains prior to their attacks. The footage was then reverse tracked which allowed the police to build up a clear picture of the bombers' movements on 7 July 2005. It led them to Luton, about 35 miles from King's Cross train station in London, where they found the bombers' car and further to their flat in Leeds, where they had made the bombs. These links were vital in the police investigation. Having found the bombers' hideout and gained detailed forensic evidence as to how the crimes were carried out, the police were able to establish a clear picture of what happened. This could have taken the police to any surviving accomplices but no such evidence was left.

Just two weeks later CCTV footage was needed for another terrorist attack on the London transportation network. A group of six men had conspired to carry out suicide bombings in London on 21 July 2005 but their attempts were unsuccessful as their bombs failed to detonate. Four of the group, Yassin Omar, Muktar Said Ibrahim, Ramzi Mohammed and Hussein Osman attempted to blow themselves up on the transport system, which gave the police some CCTV footage to start the manhunt for them. This footage helped identify the perpetrators and build a picture of the events of 21 July. This footage clearly showed the attempted bombings and the reaction of the would-be bombers which negated some of the defences that they tried to use.

The four men who attempted the bombings were found guilty and sentenced to life imprisonment. One man, Manfo Asiedu, who panicked and discarded his bomb, was found guilty of a lesser offence, and the sixth man, Adel Yahya, was imprisoned for a shorter term for conspiracy. He had not planned to carry out an attack himself but had been heavily involved in encouraging the others.

Other Uses of the Legislation

There have been some high profile cases involving the Terrorism Acts. One of the most notable is that of the Egyptian-born cleric Abu Hamza. Abu Hamza frequently preached in mosques in the United Kingdom, specifically look for more radical congregations. He preached an anti-Western message and was seen by those young people who were sympathetic to al-Qaeda as a voice to listen to. Abu Hamza was open in his remarks and frequently stirred ill feeling among elements of the Muslim community in the United Kingdom towards non-Muslims.

Abu Hamza's sermons and speeches would often be listened to by the police and were scrutinized for breaches of anti-terror law. In some of his addresses Abu Hamza used language which was clearly designed to incite radical Muslims to commit acts in breach of the anti-terrorism and other legislation. The cleric was charged with nine counts of soliciting to murder, four counts of using threatening, abusive or insulting words or behaviour, and two counts of possession of threatening, abusive or insulting sound recordings. He was found guilty of eleven of these charges and sentenced to seven years imprisonment.

The UK's terrorism laws had allowed the police to investigate someone who was actively trying to create hatred in the Muslim community towards non-Muslims. Clearly Abu Hamza was promoting violence and celebrating attacks on the West. As the UK's law had been developed to tackle terrorism in the *mens rea* as well as the *actus reus*, the cleric was guilty as charged. By stopping those who promote and incite terror, the problem can be tackled before lives are ruined by terrorist acts.

In 2006 there were protests in many countries about the publication of a cartoon depicting the Prophet Mohammed. London saw multiple protests, during which feelings ran high. While the majority of protesters were only exercising their legal and moral right to protest about a grievance, some members of the radical Muslim community used this as a vehicle to promote hatred and, given the charged atmosphere of the protests, to seek and encourage potential terrorists into action. Police videoed and observed the protests and found that some elements of the protesters were using the events as a forum to incite violence and stir up hatred.

While many protesters carried placards saying "Massacre those who insult Islam" there were four men who were identified of going further and inciting terror. Mizanur Rahman from London called for British soldiers in Iraq to come home in body bags,[23] while Adul Muhid was sentenced to six years for soliciting murder,[24] and Umran Javad was guilty of the same offence as well as inciting racial hatred. The terrorist laws were used to charge those men identified by the police with various offences and convictions were duly secured after due process.

Conclusion

The United Kingdom dealt with terrorism through existing laws and specific emergency powers during the Northern Ireland Troubles until the year 2000. Since then it has developed its terrorism laws through a series of acts to deal with the specific problems of terrorism. Although most acts of terrorism are offences under ordinary criminal and common law they differ in their rationale and intent. It is therefore necessary to deal with these aspects to ensure that a comprehensive approach is taken to the matter through the legal system.

The Terrorism Act 2000 and subsequent legislation has been reactive to some terrorist incidents and proactive in anticipating others. It has given the police the appropriate legal tools to investigate and prosecute terrorism in all its stages. It has concentrated on many pre-emptive and preventative measures while balancing the rights and safety of British citizens.

However, the writing of the law is only part of the solution. The law needs to be applied in both its enforcement by the police and its execution by the judiciary. It is only by a fair and just application, as robust as necessary, that laws such as these have the use for which they were intended. It is also essential that they retain public support. Civil liberties and rights are often infringed in the fight against terrorism and the public need to accept the balance of these infringements compared to the additional safety they bring. Inventions such as CCTV are useful tools in fighting terror but will only work with public support.

There must also be a trust from the public in both how the police will enforce these law and how the courts will use them. Areas such as prolonged detention will always be a difficult issue. Pre- or no charge detention effectively means an internment, which Northern Ireland showed to fail against terrorism. However, due to the nature and complexity of most terror investigations, this additional time is often deemed necessary.

---

[23] http://news.bbc.co.uk/2/hi/uk_news/6903445.stm

[24] He distributed placards calling people to 'Annihilate those who insult Islam'.

Indeed, at the time of writing, the topic of a further increase in pre-charge detention in terrorist related investigations is the most controversial topic among the planned amendments to Britain's terrorist legislation.

References

Alonso, Rogelio: The IRA and Armed Struggle, London, Routledge, 2006
Bennetto, J: Controls on firearms tighten over 170 years, The Independent (London), 1 Aug 1996.
Gabb, S: Gun Control in Britain, Libertarian Alliance Political Notes No 33, Libertarian Alliance, 1988.
Hansard: Written Ministerial Statements by Mr David Blunkett, Home Department, 18 Nov 03.
Hoffman, Bruce: Inside Terrorism, Columbia University Press, New York, 2006
Northern Ireland Office: Replacement Arrangements for the Diplock Court System. A consultation paper, August 2006
Sinclair, Andrew: An anatomy of Terror, London, MacMillan, 2004
www.nio.gov.uk
http://en.wikipidea.com
www.thisislondon.co.uk
www.theyworkforyou.com
www.publication.parliament.uk

Legislation, Common and Case Law

The Magna Carta 1215
Habeas Corpus Act 1679
Public Order Act 1986
Terrorism Act 2000
Anti-terrorism, Crime and Security Act 2001
Prevention of Terrorism Act 2005
Terrorism Act 2006

Legal Aspects of Combating Terrorism
Centre of Excellence Defence Against Terrorism, Ankara, Turkey (Ed.)
IOS Press, 2008

doi:10.3233/978-1-58603-930-1-115

Institutional and Legal Aspects of EU Counter-Terrorism

Davide CASALE
The author is a founding member of a new EU policy think-tank in Brussels

Abstract. The 9/11 terrorist attacks in New York and Washington lifted counter-terrorism to the top of the European security agenda. The bombings in Madrid of March 2004 and in London of July 2005 proved that Europe is also a target of the new forms of international terrorism. The EU has since been trying to react to the terrorist threat with a comprehensive strategy grounded on four core objectives: prevent, protect, pursue and respond. The Union has also reshaped its institutional and legal counter-terrorist framework. The role of some EU bodies has been strengthened, while new institutional actors have been set up. The most important EU institutions in the fight against terrorism have proved to be the European Commission, Europol and Eurojust. Despite some good results achieved, lack of co-ordination and difficulties in information sharing are weaknesses that still hamper the realization of effective intelligence and judicial co-operation. A new common European definition of terrorist offences, the introduction of the European Arrest Warrant and the use of biometrics are pioneering legal instruments in counter-terrorism. Such legal tools have enhanced the efficacy of the EU action in preventing and suppressing terrorism. On the other hand, they have raised concerns with fundamental rights and civil liberties. This paper is aimed at providing an initial evaluation of both institutional and legal aspects of the EU fight against terrorism. Whilst acknowledging the achievement of many positive results, this assessment leads also to the conclusion that the European Union has to step up further its efforts to remedy a number of inadequacies and weaknesses arising in both the institutional and legal frameworks of the EU counter-terrorism response.

Keywords. European Commission, Europol, Eurojust, definition of terrorism, European Arrest Warrant (EAW), biometrics.

The origins of European co-operation on counter-terrorism can be identified in the 1970s with the establishment of the Terrorism, Radicalism, Extremism, and International Violence group (TREVI group) in 1975, and with the European Convention on the Suppression of Terrorism (ECST) of 1977. The TREVI group set up a forum for information exchange and mutual assistance on terrorism and related international crimes. It consisted of high level gatherings of Interior and Justice Ministers and national top security officials. The TREVI group lasted until 1992, when it was replaced by the provisions of the Maastricht Third Pillar on immigration and asylum, policing, customs and legal co-operation.[1] Beyond TREVI, unified Europe

[1] Peek J., International police cooperation within justified political and judicial frameworks: Five theses on TREVI, in J. Monar, & R. Morgan (eds), The third pillar of the European Union, Brussels: European Interuniversity Press, 1994, pp. 201-207.

created additional co-operative arrangements to combat terrorism, such as the Police Working Group on Terrorism. In 1993, the TREVI Group and other European institutions dealing with judicial, customs, and immigration issues were brought together in one new structure under Title VI of the Treaty of European Union.[2] The Maastricht Treaty also mandated the creation of the European Police Office (Europol). In 1997, a counter-terrorism preparatory group was created to formulate Europol's role in matters of counter-terrorism and Europol became operational one year later.[3]

In spite of efforts made during the 1980s and 1990s, European co-operation in the field of counter-terrorism remained quite limited until the September 11 attacks. This was due to the reluctance of the EU Member States to cede to the EEC (and then to the EU) part of their sovereignty in a delicate field, such as security.[4] The plane attacks on New York and Washington moved international terrorism to the top of the European political agenda. Although the attack was directed against the US, it was perceived as an aggression against the West as a whole. Consequently, all European leaders condemned at once the terrorist atrocity and promptly gave their support to the US declaring the firm intention to "stand shoulder to shoulder with America" since the fight against terrorism "is not a battle between the United States of America and terrorism, but between the free and democratic world and terrorism".[5] The attacks on America in 2001 and, more recently, the Madrid and the London bombings in 2004 and 2005, showed that Europe must face a new threat. The emergence of international terrorism as a new security threat made it necessary to elaborate a new counter-terrorist strategy. The goal was to fight a menace very different from the previous (mainly domestic) terrorism that Europe had faced in the past.[6] Following the 9/11 attacks the Member States of the EU adopted a range of measures, in an effort to provide a vigorous long-term response to the Al-Qaeda international terrorist threat. On 21 September 2001, the European Council stated that "Terrorism is a real challenge to the world and to Europe and that the fight against terrorism will be a priority objective of the European Union".[7] This was followed by the adoption of a first comprehensive EU Action Plan to Fight Terrorism.[8] A further instrument to respond to the threat of terrorism was the Council Framework Decision on Terrorism, aimed at improving legal harmonisation of Member States' legislations.[9]

---

[2] Treaty on European Union (TEU), Maastricht, 7 February 1992, available at: http://eur-lex.europa.eu/en/treaties/dat/11992M/htm/11992M.html#0001000001.

[3] Rauchs G., and Koenig D. J., *Europol*, in Koenig D. J. and Das D. K., (eds), *International Police Cooperation*, New York: Lexington Books, 2001, pp. 43-62.

[4] Wilkinson P., *International Terrorism: The Changing Threat and the EU's Response*, Institute for Security Studies *Chaillot Paper*, n. 84, October 2005 pp. 29-31.

[5] Blair T., *Prime Minister Tony Blair's Statement in Response to Terrorist Attacks in the United States* – 11 September 2001, available on www.number-10.gov.uk/output/Page1596.asp.

[6] To underline the different kind of terrorism the Europe started facing after 9/11, EU Commissioner A. Vitorino noted that "We had national terrorism, that is true, but up to 11 September we never had suicide attacks" – quoted in Szyszkowitz T., *The European Union*, in von Hippel K. (ed.), *Europe confronts Terrorism*, Houndmills, Basingstoke [etc.], Palgrave Macmillan, 2005, p. 171.

[7] Council of the European Union, *Extraordinary Council Meeting: Justice, Home Affairs and Civil Protection*, Brussels, 20 September 2001; available at: http://ue.eu.int/uedocs/cmsUpload/1201 9.en1.pdf.

[8] *EU Action Plan on Combating Terrorism*, last update is available at: http://register.consilium.europa.eu/pdf/en/06/st05/st05771-re01.en06.pdf.

[9] Council Framework Decisions on Combating Terrorism of 13 June 2002, available at: http://www.eur-lex.europa.eu/pri/en/oj/dat/2002/l_164/l_16420020622en00030007.pdf.

In the wake of the terrorist attacks in Madrid in March 2004, the European Council adopted an ambitious Declaration on Combating Terrorism[10] and endorsed the revised EU Action Plan on Combating Terrorism on 18 June 2004. The EU Action Plan identifies a series of measures such as joint investigation teams of police and magistrates from throughout the EU, routine exchange of information among the Member States, a specialist anti-terrorist team within Europol and a co-operation agreement between Europol and the relevant US authorities. The Action Plan establishes high level Strategic Objectives for the EU action in preventing and combating terrorism. These include, among others:

- Deepening the international consensus and enhancing international efforts to combat terrorism;
- Reducing the access of terrorists to financial and other economic sources;
- Maximising capacity within EU bodies and Member States to detect, investigate and prosecute terrorists and prevent terrorist attacks;
- Enhancing the capability of the European Union and of Member States to deal with the consequences of terrorist attacks;
- Addressing the factors which contribute to support for, and recruitment into, terrorism;
- Targeting actions under EU external relations towards priority Third Countries.

In the aftermath of the London bombing in July 2005, an extraordinary meeting of the Ministers of Interior of Member States identified the implementation of a series of measures already adopted as matter of urgency: the European Arrest Warrant; strengthening of the Schengen and visa information system; biometric details on passports; combating terrorism financing; prevention of recruitment and radicalisation; greater controls over trade, storage and transport of explosives.[11] In December 2005 the Justice and Home Affairs Council approved a new European Union Counter-Terrorism Strategy,[12] which aims at covering four strands of work: *Protect*, *Prevent*, *Pursue*, *and Respond*. Across these four categories, the strategy seeks to link strands from different policy areas and emphasise close interaction of measures at the Member State, the European and international levels.

The first objective is to *prevent* people from turning to terrorism by tackling the root causes which can lead to radicalisation and recruitment, in Europe and internationally. The second objective of the EU Strategy is to *protect* citizens and infrastructure and to reduce Europe's vulnerability to attacks, including through improved security of borders, transport and critical infrastructure. The third objective is to *pursue* and investigate terrorists across EU internal borders and globally; to impede planning, travel and communications; to disrupt support networks; to cut off funding and access to attack materials and to bring terrorists to justice. The fourth objective of the EU Counter-Terrorism Strategy is to prepare Member States, in the spirit of solidarity, for managing and minimising the consequences of a terrorist attack, by improving capabilities to deal with the aftermath, the coordination of the *response*, and the needs of victims.

---

[10] Council of the European Union, *Declaration on Combating Terrorism,* Brussels, 25 March 2004; available at: http://ue.eu.int/uedocs/cmsUpload/DECL-25.3.pdf.

[11] Council of the European Union, *Extraordinary Council Meeting, Justice and Home Affairs*, Brussels, 13 July 2005; available at: http://ue.eu.int/ueDocs/cms_ Data/docs/ pressdata/en/jha/85703.pdf.

[12] Council of the European Union, *EU Counter-terrorism Strategy*, 2697th Council Meeting, Brussels 1-2 December 2005, doc. 14390/05 (Presse 296), available at http://www.consilium.europa.eu/uedocs/cmsUpload/JHA,1-2.12.05.pdf.

The EU Counter-Terrorism Strategy is not only a set of almost 200 counter-terrorism measures, grouped around the above mentioned four key concepts. It is also an attempt to set out the EU policy in the fight against terrorism in a comprehensive and consistent fashion, which is comprehensible also for the general public.[13]

The Role of the European Institutions

The most relevant institutions in the EU Counter-Terrorism Strategy are the European Commission, Europol and Eurojust. In fact, these three institutions play a major role at a legislative level (the Commission) and at the operational level (Europol and Eurojust), these two latter having as top priority in their mandate the fight against terrorism.[14]

The **European Commission** (EC) plays an active role in a large number of fields related to counter-terrorism policy. Primarily, the EC is the main actor in proposing new legislative tools in the areas of the Third Pillar. These proposals are the ground for the EU legislation on counter-terrorism (i.e.: the EC proposals for the Framework Decision defining the crime of terrorism and the European Arrest Warrant). The activity of the Commission in counter-terrorism is subjected to many criticisms. It is maintained that the Commission lacks in coherence as well as a consistent political guide. Furthermore, it seems that an overlapping of the roles in the area of Justice and Home Affairs does not allow the EC to act efficiently. A possible response to these criticisms would come from the modifications to the Justice and Home Affairs area entailed in the proposed European Constitutional Treaty,[15] once it enters into force. In fact, this Treaty would design a new institutional scenery, rationalising the roles of different EU bodies involved in the Third Pillar areas. Furthermore, the Commission would be enabled to play its traditional role of "guardian of the treaty" also in matters concerning Justice and Home Affairs. This means that the EC would have the power to take a Member State to the Court of Justice if the State does not implement EU legislation or is late in the implementation process. Most importantly, in the decision-making process, unanimity would no longer be a requirement for the adoption of legislation concerning matters of the Third Pillar. Thus, qualified majority voting would render the legislative process much swifter and more efficient.[16]

The European Police Office, **Europol**, established by the Maastricht Treaty in 1992, is an international police organisation whose objective is promoting co-operation among law enforcement authorities of the EU Member States in the fight against

---

[13] Den Boer M., *The EU Counterterrorism Wave: Window of Opportunity or Profound Policy Transformation?*, in Van Leuween M. (ed.), *Confronting Terrorism. European Experiences, Threat Perceptions and Policies*, 2003, p. 189.

[14] A number of other institutions also take part in the EU counter-terrorism activities (e.g.: the *European Counter-Terrorism Co-ordinator,* the *European Joint Situation Centre* SitCen and FRONTEX). Nonetheless, the little availability of data on their work or their recent establishment do not allow to carry out a comprehensive analysis of the activities of such institutions.

[15] The text of the *Treaty establishing a European Constitution* (Rome, 29 October 2004) is available at: http://eur-lex.europa.eu/JOHtml.do?uri=OJ:C:2004:310:SOM:EN:HTML.

[16] Nunes de Almeida J., Head of Directorate D1 of the Directorate General of the European Commission: Fight against Terrorism, *The European Commission in the Fight against Terrorism*, in ICLN (International Criminal Law Network, The Hague) and EULEC (European Institute for Freedom, Security and Justice, Brussels), joint co-operation, *European Co-operation Against Terrorism*, Wolf Legal Publishers, Nijmegen, 2004, pp 38-39.

serious organised crime, including terrorism.[17] The main task in Europol's mandate is the collection and exchange of intelligence information with national agencies, which can then translate this information into operational actions. It plays the role of "intelligence gatherer" within what is called "intelligence-led law enforcement" at the European level.[18] The instruments of Europol in the fight against terrorism are essentially the Counter-Terrorism Unit and, more recently, the Counter Terrorism Task Force (established as a response to the attacks of 11 September 2001) that collects and analyses data on suspected terrorists, recorded in an Analytical Work File (AWF), a record of information on international terrorists provided by Member States. In addition, Europol's mandate includes the collection of other forms of data, such as legislation on counter-terrorism, and a glossary of terrorist groups. Alongside the establishment of the Counter-Terrorism Task Force, Europol created a number of functionally specialized programmes. Among these, a Counter-Terrorism Programme was set up in order to co-ordinate better all Europol activities against terrorism, including information gathering and threat assessments. In its crucial task of co-ordination, Europol also sustains operational investigations by EU police and joint investigation teams.[19] Europol also issues an Annual Terrorism Situation and Trend Report (TE-SAT).[20] Furthermore, in the aftermath of the attacks on 11 September 2001, the Europol Operational Centre was established, with the task of providing a 24-hour service for the exchange of information.[21]

Europol, especially through its Counter-Terrorism Task Force, has certainly achieved some good results in its counter-terrorist activities. Among these, most remarkable are the production of threat assessments with regard to terrorist groups and cells in EU Members States and a constantly updated overview of counter-terrorism measures and legislation in Europe. However, sensitivity and confidentiality of information concerning criminal investigations and a certain degree of reluctance to make available such information make it difficult to assess the work of Europol in counter-terrorism.[22] In 2005, an EU effectiveness study of European counter-terrorism policies was published, but no information from Europol was mentioned in the report.[23] From the data provided it emerges that the Member States have been increasingly

---

[17] According to the Europol Convention (art. 2.1) the objectives of Europol are "preventing and combating terrorism, unlawful drug trafficking and other serious forms of international crime where there are factual indications that an organised structure is involved". Europol Convention, 26 July 1995, available at: http://www. europol.europa.eu/legal/Europol_Convention_Consolidated_version.pdf.

[18] Nunes de Almeida J., *The European Commission in the Fight against Terrorism*, *op. cit*., p. 41.

[19] See Schalken, T. and Pronk M., *On joint investigation teams, Europol and supervision of their joint actions*, in *European Journal of Crime, Criminal Law and Criminal Justice*, no. 10, 2002, pp. 70 ff.

[20] Last updated report in 2007: *EU Terrorism Situation and Trend Report TE-SAT* 2007; available at: http://www.europol.europa.eu/publications/EU_Terrorism_Situation_and_Trend_Report_TE-SAT/TES AT2007.pdf.

[21] For a more in-depth analysis of organisation and activities of Europol see: Deflem M., *Policing World Society: Historical Foundations of International Police Cooperation*. Oxford; New York: Oxford University Press, 2002; Lavranos, N., *Europol and the fight against terrorism*, in *European Foreign Affairs Review*, 8(2), 2003, 259-275; Rauchs G., and Koenig D. J., *Europol*, in Koenig D. J. and Das D. K., (eds), *International Police Cooperation*, New York: Lexington Books, 2001, pp. 43-62.

[22] Deflem M., *Europol and the policing of international terrorism: Counter-terrorism in a global perspective*, in *Justice Quarterly*, vol. 23 n. 3, September 2006; also available at: http://www.cas.sc. edu/socy/faculty/ deflem/zeuroterror.htm.

[23] Council of the European Union, *EU counter-terrorism clauses: Assessment*, Brussels, May 11, 2005. Available at: http://www.statewatch.org/news/2005/may/eu-terr-clauses.pdf.

making use of the services of Europol in their investigative activities.[24] Europol has played an active role in some significant investigations, and large-scale police operations have been supported by Europol and a large number of national investigations use terrorism analysis carried out by Europol.[25]

"Europol's main problem is the imperfect flow of information from national intelligence services."[26] In fact, Europol can be able to fulfil the tasks in its mandate only if the relevant authorities in the Member States provide it with the necessary information. Nonetheless, in practice Member States are too frequently reluctant to share intelligence with Europol, to the detriment of an efficient European police co-operation. As a result, the European Police Office has a limited capacity of fulfilling its tasks due to the difficulties encountered in collecting and sharing information with relevant national authorities. The latter often make too little information available, showing limited trust in Europol, in spite of the fact that trust should be a key element of European co-operation. As a consequence, it appears that often Europol cannot be blamed for the inefficiency of co-ordination and co-operation among EU Member States agencies. Rather, it is national agencies that hinder the development of effective European law enforcement co-operation. The reason for this attitude is mistrust, since "intelligence collectors are concerned about the security of their sources and their methods of collecting information. They fear that if these are uncovered access to future information will be jeopardised."[27]

Eurojust is a permanent network of national judicial authorities of the EU Member States. It was established in 2002[28] with the following core objectives:

- To improve co-operation between national authorities in the investigation and prosecution of serious crime;
- To stimulate and improve co-ordination of investigations and prosecutions in Member States; and
- To provide expertise to Member States and the Council.

Each Member State appoints at Eurojust a representative or "National Member" (usually a judge or prosecutor). In fact, Eurojust can be described as a team of senior lawyers, magistrates, prosecutors, judges and other legal experts seconded from every EU country. Being a permanent network of judicial authorities, Eurojust has a key role to play in the European counter-terrorist action. After the attacks of 11 September 2001,

---

[24] Europol, *Annual Report* (2006); available at: http://www.europol.europa.eu/publications/Annual_Reports/EuropolAnnualReport2006.pdf; and Europol, *EU Terrorism Situation and Trend Report TE-SAT* 2007; available at: http://www.europol.europa.eu/publications/EU_Terrorism_Situation_and_Trend_Report_TESAT/TESAT2007.pdf.

[25] Council of the European Union, *EU Plan of Action on Combating Terrorism - Update*. Brussels, May 23, 2005; available: http://www.statewatch.org/news/2005/may/eu-terr-action-plan-may05.pdf.

[26] Dittrich M., *Facing the Global Terrorist Threat: A European Response*, European Policy Centre Working Paper, n. 14, January 2005, p. 32; available at: http://www.epc.eu/TEWN/pdf/606965316_PC%20Working%20Paper%2014%20Facing%20the%20global%20terrorist%20threat.pdf.

[27] Hojbjerg J. H., *Building Trust and Developing More Efficient Sharing of Intelligence in Response to and Prevention of Terrorist Attacks. The Europol Perspective*, in ICLN (International Criminal Law Network, The Hague) and EULEC (European Institute for Freedom, Security and Justice, Brussels), joint co-operation, *European Co-operation Against Terrorism*, Wolf Legal Publishers, Nijmegen, 2004, p. 53.

[28] Council of the European Union, Council Decision of 28 February 2002, *Setting up Eurojust with a View to Reinforcing the Fight against Serious Crime*, available at: http://eurojust.europa.eu/official_ documents/Eurojust_Decision/l_06320020306en00010013.pdf.

the Council Decision of 19 December 2002[29] redefined the tasks of Eurojust in the EU fight against terrorism.[30] According to article 3 of the Council Decision, each Member State should designate a *National Correspondent for Terrorism* and ensure that the National Correspondent has access to all relevant information concerning and resulting from criminal proceedings conducted under the responsibility of its judicial authorities.

The tasks of Eurojust in the field of counter-terrorism, according to the Council Decision, can be divided into the following areas:

1. Organisation of National Correspondents at national level (and access to information).
2. Transmission of information.
3. Eurojust's methods of processing the information; and
4. Assistance and feedback from Eurojust to Member States.

Since the execution of most of the tasks resulting from the Council Decision is regrettably still in a preparatory stage, so far there has been little exchange between National Correspondents and National Members. Furthermore, a number of obstacles are encountered in the course of the practical realisation of these tasks.[31]

All Member States have appointed a National Correspondent, most of whom are prosecutors. Difficulties arise when it comes to the matter of access to, and collection of, all relevant information according to the Council Decision. Currently, such information is not accessible to all National Correspondents. There are several obstacles that hamper access to relevant information. The first is a lack of legal provisions for access and collection in some Member States. In such cases National Correspondents are not allowed to forward information to Eurojust unless there is a specific request in a criminal case from one Member State to another country. Moreover, there are several restrictions on access that arise at the practical level. For instance, sometimes national authorities are simply unaware of their duty to inform the National Correspondent. In other cases investigating judges may decide not to transmit relevant information to the National Correspondent, without any possibility of checking if they fulfil their duty of transmission of information when their activities are covered by the secrecy of an investigation. A further difficulty related to the transmission of information from National Correspondents to Eurojust arises from different interpretations of the tasks of the Council Decision by Member States. In accordance to the Council Decision, information concerning and resulting from criminal procedures pertaining to terrorism and conducted under the responsibility of judicial authorities should be forwarded. But this has resulted in many differences at the stage of the trial and in the kind and means of transmission of information to Eurojust, due to the

---

[29] Council Decision of 19 December 2002 *on the implementation of specific measures for police and judicial co-operation to combat terrorism in accordance with article 4 of the Common Position 2001/931/CSFP*, available at: http://eur-lex.europa.eu/LexUriServ/site/en/oj/2003/l_016/l_0162003012 2en00680070.pdf.

[30] On the role of Eurojust in the fight against terrorism: Kennedy M. (Eurojust President), Eurojust and the Fight against Terrorism, in *European Cooperation against Terrorism: The Peace Palace, The Hague*, 13 October 2004: *Conference Proceedings*, Nijmegen: Wolf Legal Publishers, 2004, pp. 59-64; Coninsx M. (Belgian Member of the College of Eurojust), *Eurojust and EU Judicial Cooperation in the Fight against Terrorism, in Legal Instruments* in *The Fight against International Terrorism: a Transatlantic Dialogue*, Leiden (etc.), Nijhoff, 2004, pp. 181-186; Dittrich M., *Facing the Global Terrorist Threat: a European Response*, op. cit., pp. 34-35; Kenndy M., Faletti F., Knut K., Eurojust, speech at the AIPP Conference, Paris, 31 August 2006; available at:
http://www.iap.nl.com/speeches_11th_annual_conf_2006/speech_eurojust_members_case_presentation.pdf.

[31] EUROJUST, *Eurojust's Tasks in the Area of Preventing and Combating Terrorism, Gaps between Formal Decisions and Actual Practice*, unpublished document, 2005.

differences of the 27 national systems of Member States.[32] Consequently, it should be clarified what information is to be transmitted from National Correspondents to National members and at what stage of the criminal proceedings (or investigations) it is to be transmitted. Furthermore, provisions concerning the means by which the usually highly sensitive information will be communicated to Eurojust are needed.

The recent Council Decision of 20 September 2005 on "the exchange of information and co-operation concerning terrorist offences"[33] tried to respond to the need for greater exchange of information at all stages of criminal proceedings in the area of counter-terrorism. This Decision requires a more extended exchange of information during investigations and prosecutions concerning terrorist offences. According to the provisions of this Decision, Member States have the obligation to make sure that "information (...) concerning prosecutions or convictions for terrorist offences which affect or may affect two or more Member States (...) is transmitted to Eurojust and to Europol" (article 2) and made "*available as soon as possible to the authorities of other interested Member States, taking account of the need not to jeopardise*" (article 6). The rapidity and effectiveness of the process of implementation of this Decision by Member States will make it possible to assess whether the mentioned problems in the exchange of information have been overcome.

Beyond the transmission of information to Eurojust, it should also be clearer how Eurojust should handle the collected information. In fact, an unambiguous policy on processing the information by Eurojust has yet to be set out. It should be clarified what kind of assistance Eurojust is requested to provide to the Member States. To fulfil its task of co-ordination of cases of serious cross-border crime and to improve the effectiveness of activities to prevent and combat terrorism, Eurojust should be able to know in more detail how it should help ongoing investigations and what kind of feedback national authorities expect. In fact, too often it is not yet clear whether Member States need co-ordination or simply advice. Furthermore, information received by Eurojust needs to be duly stored and analysed, but currently Eurojust has no secured connection with the Member States and does not have the technical resources to analyse large amounts of information. A closer co-operation with Europol, which is in possession of a secured system and a group of analysts, would be a possible solution.[34]

Legal Aspects of EU Counter-Terrorism

As a response to the attacks of 11 September 2001, and again after the attacks in Madrid and London, the EU has created a large legislation to help the national and European institutions better combat international terrorism within a coherent legal framework. The most innovative and controversial tools have certainly been the definition of the offence terrorism provided by the Council Decision of 13 June 2002, the European Arrest Warrant, and the use of biometrics as a counter-terrorism tool.

Several problems come into consideration with regard to the **definition of terrorism** in international law. These include a major concern with the exact legal definition of the phenomenon and of the offence of terrorism. Secondly, it arises the

---

[32] *Ibidem*.

[33] Council Decision of 20 September 2005 *on the exchange of information and co-operation concerning terrorist offences*, available at: http://eur-lex.europa.eu/LexUriServ/site/en/oj/2005/l_253/l_25320050929en00220024.pdf.

[34] EUROJUST, *Eurojust's Tasks in the Area of Preventing and Combating Terrorism*, *op. cit.*.

question of how largely the definition of the offence of terrorism should be extended. The main difficulty is to identify which behaviours have to be covered by the legal definition of terrorism and the perpetrators of which shall consequently be pursued as terrorists.[35] After 11 September 2001, the need for a common definition became vital[36] and the Framework Decision on Combating Terrorism of 13 June 2002 bridged this gap introducing a comprehensive and harmonised definition of terrorism in the EU legislation. This decision finally established minimum criteria describing the constituent elements of the offence of terrorism.[37]

The Decision defines terrorism, differentiating it from common or ordinary crimes, focusing on the intent pursued by the criminal act, while national "common law" and "continental" systems usually define the incrimination of terrorism (and other offences) regardless of its aim and focusing instead on the (prohibited) acts.[38] Article 1 of the Framework Decision defines terrorist offences as "offences under national law, which, given their nature of context, may seriously damage a country or an international organization where committed with the aim of: (1) *seriously intimidating a population, or* (2) *unduly compelling a Government or international organization to perform or abstain from performing any act, or* (3) *seriously destabilising or destroying the fundamental political, constitutional, economic or social structures of a country or international organization*". Alongside this set of terrorist offences, the Decision also defines three other categories of offences. Firstly, article 2 defines *offences relating to a terrorist group*, emphasizing the necessity of punishing participants in a terrorist group (by supporting, funding, or contributing to the activities of the group). Article 3 describes *offences linked to terrorist activities*, namely preparatory acts to terrorist acts, such as extortion or forgery of documents. Finally, article 4 calls upon Member States to take measures also against further activities, such as *inciting*, *aiding and abetting*, and *attempting* terrorist offences.[39]

Scholars have pointed out that the language used for such definitions appears "somewhat complex and uncertain"[40] and leaves room for opposing interpretations of the same fact. For instance, it seems that the riots in Paris and other French cities in November 2005 entailed all constituent elements of the definition of terrorism provided by the Framework Decision. Indeed, there certainly was intimidation of the population, the government was compelled to act, and social, political and constitutional structures

---

[35] For a discussion on the definition of terrorism in international law, especially with regard to the UN response tackling this question, see Shaw M., *International Law*, fifth edition, Cambridge University Press, 2003, pp. 1048-1053, and Cassese A., *Terrorism is also Disrupting Some Crucial Legal Categories of International Law*, in *American Journal of International Law*, n. 95, 2001, pp. 993 ff..

[36] As it is remarked in the *Framework Decision on Combating terrorism* of 13 June 2002, Preamble (6): "The definition of terrorist offences should be approximate in all Member States, including those offences relating to terrorist groups"; Council of the European Union, Council Framework Decisions on Combating Terrorism of 13 June 2002, available at:
http://www.eur-lex.europa.eu/pri/en/oj/dat/2002/ l_164/l_16420020622en00030007.pdf.

[37] Den Boer M., *9/11 and the Europeanisation of anti-terrorism policy: A critical assessment.* Notre Europe, Policy Papers No. 6, 2003, p. 5.

[38] Saul B., *International Terrorism as a European Crime: The Policy Rationale for Criminalization*, in *European Journal of Crime, Criminal Law and Criminal Justice*, n. 11, 2003, p. 323.

[39] Troosters R., *The European Union Framework Decision of 13th June 2002 on Combating Terrorism*, in ICLN (International Criminal Law Network, The Hague) and EULEC (European Institute for Freedom, Security and Justice, Brussels), joint co-operation, *European Co-operation Against Terrorism*, Wolf Legal Publishers, Nijmegen, 2004, pp. 68-72.

[40] Guillaume G., *Terrorisme et Droit International*, Lecture at the British Institute for International and Comparative Law (BIICL), London ,13 November 2003, published on *International and Comparative Law Quarterly*, Vol. 53, n. 3, 2004, p. 537.

were endangered. Nonetheless, those events were "not *perceived* as terrorism either in France or abroad".[41] This example illustrates some of the difficulties in contextualising terrorism into a legal definition. Despite these criticisms, it is remarkable that for the first time in the history of European counter-terrorism, the Framework Decision of 2002 has provided Member States and EU institutions with a common (although to some extent vague) definition of the offence of terrorism. Such a definition will probably be refined in future legislation, but it constitutes a legal basis for upcoming legislation and gives political and judicial authorities dealing with terrorism the essential guidelines for a common understanding of the constituent elements of terrorism as a criminal offence.

The **European Arrest Warrant** (EAW) has probably been the most important piece of legislation in the EU fight against terrorism after the attacks in New York and Washington in 2001 and the most innovative legislative tool in the areas of the Third Pillar. A first political agreement was reached in December 2001 and the Framework Decision on the EAW was finally adopted on 13 June 2002.[42] The EAW came into force on 1 January 2004, replacing the previous extradition procedures among Member States. The objective of the EAW is to improve judicial co-operation in the EU creating a simplified system of surrender of sentenced and suspected persons for the purposes of execution or prosecution of criminal sentences, removing the delay of bilateral extradition procedures. The EAW is grounded on the trust of every Member State in the legal system of each other Member State and on the mutual recognition of national courts' decisions. Hence, the European Council referred to the EAW as to a cornerstone of EU judicial co-operation, in view of the realization of a more efficient area of freedom, security and justice in the European Union.[43]

At the practical and operational level, the implications of the introduction of the EAW are very significant. In fact, a national judicial authority can issue a request for the arrest and the return (namely, a European Arrest Warrant) valid throughout the EU for a person accused of a serious criminal offence[44] or for a person sentenced to at least 4 months imprisonment.[45] Consequently, the requested person has to be arrested and surrendered without delay to the requesting Member State.[46] For the offences listed in the Framework Decision, the EAW has not abolished the "dual criminality principle" (or "double criminality"), according to which, traditionally, extradition can be denied if the offence in question is not a criminal offence in the executing country.[47] Hence, the

---

[41] Saul B., *Defining Terrorism in International Law*, Vaughan Lowe ed., Oxford University Press, 2006, pp. 164-166.

[42] Council of the European Union, Framework Decision *on the European arrest warrant and the surrender procedures between Member States* of 13 June 2002, available at: http://europa.eu.int/eur-lex/pri/en/oj/dat/2002/ l_190/l_19020020718en00010018.pdf.

[43] Framework Decision on the European Arrest Warrant, Preamble (6).

[44] Article 2 of the Framework Decision on the EAW lists 32 categories of criminal offences for which a EAW can be issued, including, *inter alia*, terrorism, trafficking in human being, sexual exploitation of children and child pornography, and fraud.

[45] Framework Decision on the European Arrest Warrant, article 1.

[46] Nonetheless, article 3 and 4 of the Framework Decision define some exceptions in which the surrender can be denied. The most relevant grounds for non-execution of an EAW are: 1. The offence is covered by amnesty in the executing State; 2. The person has already been tried in respect of the same acts (*ne bis in idem* principle); 3. The person is a minor or has not reached the age for criminal responsibility in the requested State.

[47] Blekxtoon R., *The European Arrest Warrant*, in ICLN (International Criminal Law Network, The Hague) and EULEC (European Institute for Freedom, Security and Justice, Brussels), joint co-operation, *European Co-operation Against Terrorism*, Wolf Legal Publishers, Nijmegen, 2004, esp. p. 78.

objection to the extradition that a conduct is considered a crime in a country but might be legal in a different Member State has not been ruled out, and a co-operation system based on the mutual recognition of the conduct of the suspected or sentenced person as unlawful and criminal has been established.[48] Nonetheless, since the Member States have the general obligation to execute the EAW and surrender the person, they can no longer refuse to surrender their own nationals. All EU citizens are held responsible not only before national judicial authorities, but before courts in all Member States. As a result, an EU country will not have the right to ground the denial of surrender on the fact that the alleged person is its national.

In assessing the effectiveness of the EAW, the European Commission has repeatedly stated that the introduction of the EAW has been a success. A first report evaluating the implementation and the impact of the Framework Decision on the EAW was released by the European Commission on 23 February 2005. The Commission underlined that, although with some delay, all Member States implemented the Framework Decision and that from the available data (2,603 warrants issued) the EAW seemed to have acquired a widespread use among national judicial authorities. Most importantly, the average time taken to execute a warrant was estimated to have decreased from more than 9 months to 43 days.[49] In a more recent report, the EC highlighted how the use of the EAW by Member States has grown year by year, making easier the surrender of persons between national judicial authorities in a much shorter time than in the previous conventional system of extradition. In 2005 the number of requests of EAW rose up sharply, whilst conflicts of national laws that impeded a complete application of the Framework Decision seem to have been overcome by the adoption of new national legislative measures.[50]

Criticisms of the common EAW have been particularly strong. In fact, the introduction of the EAW seemed to render it easier for the United States to obtain extradition of a suspect, and potentially use the death penalty against him/her, which all European states oppose. A partial solution to this controversial matter has been provided by the Council Framework Decision: "No person should be removed, expelled or extradited to a State where there is a serious risk that he or she would be subjected to the death penalty, torture or inhuman or degrading treatment or punishment" (Preamble 13). Nonetheless, there remains a certain ambiguity since this provision seems to be more a declaration of principle rather than an obligation on Member States. More importantly, the adoption of the EAW has raised many constitutional issues is several Member States, with the necessity for some countries to amend their constitutions.[51] The German Constitutional Court declared void the German Act provisions that implemented the framework decision on the EAW

---

[48] See European Commission, Justice and Home Affairs Directorate, *European Arrest Warrant Replaces Extradition between EU Member States*; available at: http://ec.europa.eu/justice_home/fsj/ criminal/extradition/fsj_criminal_extradition_en.htm.

[49] European Commission, *Report based on article 34 of the European Council Framework Decision of 13 June 2002 on the European Arrest Warrant and Surrender Procedures among Member States*, Brussels, 23 February 2005, available at: http://ec.europa.eu/justice_home/doc_centre/criminal/doc/ com_2005_063_en.pdf.

[50] European Commission, *Report based on article 34 of the European Council Framework Decision of 13 June 2002 on the European Arrest Warrant and Surrender Procedures among Member States*, Brussels, 11 July 2005, available at: http://eur-lex.europa.eu/LexUriServ/site/en/com/2007/com2007_ 0407en01.pdf.

[51] House of Lords, European Union Committee, 30th Report of the 2005-2006 Session, *European Arrest Warrant—Recent Developments*, pp. 10-12; available at http://www.publications.parliament.uk/ pa/ld200506/ ldselect/ldeucom/156/156.pdf.

(decision of 18 July 2005), for they were assumed to be against fundamental rights and guarantees. It seems that the improvements to the efficiency of the judicial co-operation, especially through simplified and quicker procedures of surrender, might reduce the basic rights of defence and the right to a fair trial, guaranteed in Member States in their constitutional charters (besides being fundamentals principles recognized in international law).[52] This might presumably lead in short to a conflict between the German Constitutional Court and the European institutions on the constitutional implications of judicial co-operation among Member States.[53]

Such difficulties probably arise from the fact that the co-operation model adopted for the introduction of the EAW is more similar to a system based on mutual recognition (of judicial decision) rather than to a process of harmonisation of legislation in Member States, which has been the traditional model of juridical integration and development in the European Communities first, and then in the EU.[54] Most likely, this is due to the attempt of Member States to preserve a strong control on criminal law matters. As a result, the practical model of the EAW, based on the simple abolition of legal barriers between Member States (negative integration) will narrow and reduce the necessary guarantees of the right of citizens to defence, to the detriment of the principle of due process, unless it is countervailed by specific trade-off measures (that have not been undertaken in the case of the EAW). In short, in the Framework Decision establishing the EAW, the Council has ruled out the option of traditional harmonisation. Instead, it has preferred to follow the path of the mutual recognition, based on co-existence and reciprocal trust among national judicial authorities. Hence, the system is based on a sort of "*full faith and credit clause*" between national courts like in the US judicial system, but without necessary counterweights as there are in the US Bill of Rights.[55]

Another counter-terrorist tool raising concerns with fundamental rights is the use of biometric technology in the fight against the terrorist threat. **Biometrics** are the most innovative technological tool among the counter-terrorist methods, but their efficacy in the fight against terrorism and implications with regard to civil liberties are controversial. A biometric is a physical or biological feature or attribute that can be measured and biometric identification can be defined as the "automatic recognition of a person using distinguishing traits".[56] Through the technology of biometrics individuals are recognised by means of individual traits, such as voice, eyes or fingerprints. Biometric identification technologies selected by the European Commission are face recognition, fingerprint recognition, iris recognition and DNA as a biometric identifier.[57] Following the attack of 11 September 2001, the EU began to develop a coherent strategy for the improvement of the security of identity documents using

---

[52] Centre for European Policy Study (CEPS), *The European Arrest Warrant, A Good Testing Ground for Mutual Recognition in the Enlarged EU?*; available at: http://www.ceps.be/Article.php? article_id=295.

[53] Satzger H. and Pohl T., *The German Constitutional Court and the European Arrest Warrant, 'Critical Signal' from Karlsruhe*, in *Journal of International Criminal Justice*, n. 4 (4), 2006, pp. 686-701; See also Euractiv, *European Arrest Warrant ruled unconstitutional in Germany*, 19 July 2005, available at: http://www.euractiv.com/en/security/european-arrest-warrant-ruled-unconstitutional-germany/article-142674.

[54] Palladino G., *Il Mandato d'Arresto Europeo, tra Appiattimento e Preservazione della Tutela Personale*, in *Diritto e Diritti*, 2 August 2007, available at: http://www.diritto.it/art.php?file=/archivio/ 24508.html.

[55] Palladino G., *Il Mandato d'Arresto Europeo*, *op. cit.*.

[56] Woodward J. D., Horn C., Gatune J. and Thomas A., *Biometrics: A Look at Facial Recognition*, Rand Documented Briefing prepared for the Virginia State Crime Commission, 2003.

[57] European Commission's Joint Research Centre (JRC) Report*: Biometrics at the Frontiers: Assessing the Impact on Society'*, released on 30 March 2005, available at ftp://ftp.jrc.es/pub/EURdoc/ eur21585en.pdf.

biometric identifiers. The European Council of Laeken (December 2001) and Seville (June 2002) decided that the Visa Information System (VIS) shall also include biometric identifiers with the aim of preventing "visa shopping", improving the administration of the common visa policy and contributing to internal security and fighting terrorism. In September 2003 the Commission presented proposals to introduce biometrics in visas and residence permits for third national countries.[58] In November 2005 the European Council presented the Draft Conclusions of the Representatives of the Government of the Member States on common minimum security standards for Members States' national identity cards.[59] This document aims at giving an impetus to the development of common standards for security features and secure issuing procedures for national ID cards.

Critics of biometrics worry that such a system, as it is usually connected to a large centralised database, will lead to an erosion of personal freedoms. Concerns are that the use of biometrics will inevitably expand both in the amount of data that will be collected and in the ways it will be used in everyday life, endangering the balance between liberty and security. Worries about the protection of basic rights are present also within the EU institutions. The European Parliament's Rapporteur on biometrics in visas Ole Sorensen remarked in 2004 that the proposals on the use of biometrics could be a step towards systematic and centralised storage of sensitive personal data, "which would be like using a sledgehammer to crack a nut".[60] He observed that from a data protection point of view, such a central storage of biometric data might jeopardize the protection of civil rights, especially the right to privacy. The fundamental concepts of trust seem to be challenged by the governmental aspirations to security. The risk is that "the emphasis changes to ordinary citizens being almost treated as criminal suspects"[61] and the right to privacy and anonymity being withdrawn. If in the short term citizens might agree to a certain extent on sacrificing their personal liberties for a more secure world, in the long term this sacrifice would become unpopular and lead to an erosion of trust in governments.

It is argued that through the introduction of biometric passports and ID cards, as well as new EU health cards and driving licences using biometric technology, and, within the foreseeable future, one single biometric chipped card integrating an EU passport, ID card, driving license and health card, we are moving towards a surveillance society.[62] Hence, a particularly strong need for effective privacy and data protection emerges. In this perspective, the Commission's Report points out that a reinforced legal framework for privacy and data protection may be needed in order to prevent biometrics from becoming a tool in the service of surveillance. If, on the one

---

[58] European Commission *Proposal for a Council Regulation amending Regulation (EC) 1683/95 laying down a uniform format for visas and amending Regulation (EC) 1030/2002 laying down a uniform format for residence permits for third-country nationals*, COM (2003) 558 Final, 24 September 2003, Brussels; available at: http://www.statewatch.org/news/2003/sep/combiometrics.pdf; See, in particular, the Explanatory Memorandum.

[59] Council of the European Union, *Draft Conclusions of the Representatives of the Government of the Member States on common minimum security standards for Members States' national identity cards*, 14351/2005, Brussels, 11 November 2005, available on http://www.statewatch.org/news/2005/nov/eu-biometric-ID-Cards-Conclusions. pdf.

[60] Euractiv, *'Biometric Era' raises fears over privacy*, 15 August 2004, available at: http://www.euractiv.com/en/justice/biometric-era-raises-fears-privacy/article-111988.

[61] EC's Joint Research Centre (JRC) Report: *Biometrics at the Frontiers*, *op. cit.*, (fn 57).

[62] Bunyan T., *Unaccountable Europe: Unknown to most of its citizens, behind the closed doors of Brussels the European Union is making serious inroads on their privacy*, in *Index of Censorship*, No 3/2005, Special Issue, pp. 52-53.

hand, the data protection directive of 1995[63] gives general protection for the use of personal data on individuals, on the other hand there is recognition that technology is outstripping existing legislation. In this view, the European project BITE (Biometric Identification Technology Ethics) was launched in 2005 to analyse social, legal and the ethical implications of the increasing use of biometric technology.[64]

It is now possible to draw some **conclusions** on EU counter-terrorism. The European legal and institutional structure in the area of Justice and Home Affairs has been able to adapt quickly to the increased demand it faced in the wake of 11 September 2001. Many efforts have been undertaken and important steps forward have been made by the European countries. European states and the European Union have responded to the terrorist attacks in Madrid and London by reshaping the institutional architecture in the area of Justice and Home Affairs and by introducing innovative legislation against terrorism. Whilst acknowledging the enhancement of effective co-operation between states to counter terrorism, it is also worth considering that the European Union has to further step up its efforts to remedy gaps and shortcomings arising in both the institutional and legal frameworks of the EU counter-terrorism policies.

As for the institutional level, more co-ordination is utterly necessary. Specific criminal and anti-terrorist measures are within the competence of the Member States only. The main role of the EU is, therefore, co-ordination. But, to be successful in this task, the EU primarily needs a comprehensive and coherent institutional counter-terrorist framework within itself. Instead, the European institutional architecture of counter-terrorism consists of too many actors, with duplication of overlapping tasks. In consequence, the process of taking the necessary decisions becomes complex and cumbersome. Paradoxically, before co-ordinating the actions of its Member States, the EU has first to reach a much higher level of co-ordination and coherence among its own institutions. A disjointed and sometimes incoherent governance of counter-terrorist activities and initiatives produces inconsistencies and contradictions, weakening the effort in the fight against terrorism. One possible solution would be the reinforcement of the role of the EU Counter-terrorism Co-ordinator, whose powers and competences are at present very narrow. Enabling the Co-ordinator actually to pursue the statutory objective of co-ordination would be a major step towards increasing the efficiency of the EU counter-terrorism institutional network. Further, the introduction of the European Constitution would be a major step towards coherence of the system for it would delineate a clear asset of roles and competences of EU institutions in charge of countering terrorism.

As for the legal aspects of the EU counter-terrorism, the Council Framework Decision of 13 June 2002, approximating the definition of terrorist offences, facilitates police and judicial co-operation and aligns criminal law in Member States so that terrorism is fought and prosecuted in the same manner all over Europe. Nonetheless, the wide definition of offences in anti-terrorism legislation could result in undue restrictions of fundamental freedoms (e.g.: persons engaged in legitimate political or social dissent being branded as terrorists). The EAW has replaced the traditional

---

[63] European Parliament and Council Directive 95/46/EC of 24.10.1995 *on the protection of individuals with regard to the processing of personal data and on the free movement of such data*, available at: http://eurlex.europa.eu/smartapi/cgi/sga_doc?smartapi!celexplus!prod!DocNumber&lg=en&type_doc=Directive&an_doc=1995&nu_doc=46.

[64]Euractiv, *Biometrics & Democracy*,13 May 2005, available at: http://www.euractiv.com/en/justice/ biometrics-democracy-archived/article-139471.

system of extradition with faster and simpler surrender procedures. But concerns with fundamental rights have emerged. Similar worries surface over biometric technology. Since counter-terrorist measures and the protection of human rights are not conflicting goals, but complementary and mutually reinforcing, the EU should seek to fulfil its tasks in preventing and suppressing terrorism while complying fully with fundamental rights. Therefore, adequate safeguards have to be established to guard against the possible erosion of fundamental civil liberties in the fight against terrorism.

Legal Aspects of Combating Terrorism
Centre of Excellence Defence Against Terrorism, Ankara, Turkey (Ed.)
IOS Press, 2008

doi:10.3233/978-1-58603-930-1-131

Military Response to Terrorism and International Law on the Use of Force

Dominika SVARC
Researcher at the Institute for Comparative Law, Ljubljana, Research Assistant to Prof. Christopher Greenwood QC, London School of Economics

Abstract. In the post-Cold War security environment there have been factual developments and ambiguities that pose important challenges to the basic concepts, principles and rules of international law, especially concerning the use of force. The first part of this paper considers the option of multilateral employment of military force to prevent or to respond to acts of terrorism, and looks particularly at the Security Council's gradual enlargement of the notion of threat to international peace and security with respect to (international) terrorism. The second, and central, part of the paper then proceeds to examine the complex issue of a unilateral military response to terrorism, focusing on some its most murky features, such as: (a) the appropriate interpretation of the concept of 'armed attack' in the context of terrorist activities; (b) the requirement of attributability to States of terrorist attacks; and (c) the doctrines of anticipatory and preventive self-defence.

Keywords. International law, terrorism, *jus ad bellum*, multilateral military response to terrorism, unilateral military response to terrorism, armed attack, attributability, anticipatory self-defence, preventive self-defence.

Introduction

International law offers States a variety of tools to combat terrorism—mechanisms of law enforcement and criminal justice, as well as diplomatic, economic and financial measures. But especially in recent years, leaders have increasingly considered the use of military means in confronting terrorist groups abroad and, occasionally, governments that harbour them.

That is why the subject on which I have been asked to speak, "The Military Response to Terrorism and International Law", is central to any contemporary consideration of international law and security. At the same time, it is a very large, complex, and occasionally foggy topic, which legal academics, practitioners and politicians debate for days on end. We are not here today to debate the controversial issues, but to try and understand the basic features of the international legal framework governing States' decisions to respond to terrorist threats with military force. What I therefore propose to do is to make an overview of the existing international rules regulating decisions to use of force in the international arena, while at the same time still at least touching upon some recent challenges and developments in this area, prompted by the specifics of terrorism and counter-terrorist military operations.

The fundamental framework of international law on the use of force, its basic principles and rules, have been articulated in an international agreement that nearly all States have signed and ratified: the Charter of the United Nations, adopted in 1945. Article 1 of the Charter stresses that the maintenance of international peace and security is one of the principal goals of the new world organization and it should be preserved if at all possible. Building on this underlying value, Article 2(4) then articulates the almost absolute and general prohibition of the use of force in the international arena. The provision requires that:

> "All Members shall refrain in their international relations from the threat or use of force against the territorial integrity or political independence of any State, or in any other manner inconsistent with the purposes of the United Nations."

This prohibition is also a part of customary international law, which means that it is binding not only upon State parties to the Charter, but upon all States. In 1984, in the famous case between Nicaragua and the United States, the International Court of Justice also described this prohibition as a rule of *jus cogens,* a peremptory norm of international law, from which States cannot derogate by virtue of bilateral or multilateral agreements. This does not mean that a State cannot be militarily present or active on another State's territory with that State's prior consent, for example with the purpose of carrying out counter-insurgency or counter-terrorist operations along the common border. But any such agreement cannot have as its purpose or effect, political subordination or occupation of the consenting state's territory, neither can it be *in any other manner inconsistent* with the purposes of the UN Charter. The purpose of the phrase "or in any other manner inconsistent with the purposes of the UN" is to strengthen the prohibition and to close any potential gaps, not to open them. The legal effect of such wording is that *any* use or threat of force by one State against another will be considered unlawful, unless it can be justified on the grounds of an expressly articulated legal exception.

The UN Charter itself envisaged only two such exceptions. The first is a collective military enforcement action taken or authorized by the UN Security Council, acting under Chapter VII of the Charter, in case of a threat to the peace, breach of the peace, or act of aggression. The second exception is the exercise of individual or collective self-defence in case of an armed attack, as outlined in Article 51. That means, in effect, that the legality of any military action of one State against another will depend on the applicability of either of these exceptions in a given situation. Or if we translate this to the language of our course topic: whether or not the use of military force may be a legally valid response to terrorist activities in the *international* arena depends on whether it can be justified on the basis of either of these two exceptions. Thus, we need to look at both of these exceptions a bit more closely and try to answer two main questions: (a) Can the Security Council take or authorize military action in response to terrorism and under what conditions? and (b) May States resort to military measures against terrorism unilaterally, without a Security Council approval, and if so, under what conditions?

Collective Military Action against Terrorism

Under Article 39 of the Charter, the Security Council has the exclusive authority to 'determine the existence of any threat to the peace, breach of the peace or act of aggression', and upon having made such determination, it may decide either to take measures *not* involving the use of armed force as exemplified in Article 41 (economic, diplomatic, other sanctions), or it may even decide to authorize collective enforcement action involving the use of armed force under Article 42. The provisions of this Article stipulate: "Should the SC consider that measures provided for in Article 41 would be inadequate or have proved to be inadequate, it may take such action *by air, sea, or land forces* as may be necessary to maintain or restore international peace and security (IPS). Such action may include demonstrations, blockade, and other operations by air, sea, or land forces of Members of the UN."

The Council has very broad (although not unlimited) political discretion when determining whether a particular situation or issue is a threat to international peace and security. It does not matter whether the threat is emanating from a State or a non-state actor, whether it is immediate or more remote in time, what matters is that the Council is convinced that a certain situation constitutes a threat to the international peace and security (or a breach of peace, or an act of aggression). Indeed, since 1992, the Council has frequently condemned specific acts of terrorism as well as specific cases of state support for terrorist activities as threats to the peace. On that basis, it has often authorized non-military sanctions under Chapter VII, for instance against Libya, Sudan and the Taliban regime in Afghanistan. More recently, the Council members have begun to characterize terrorism in general as a threat to international peace and security. They first characterized "international" terrorism as such as a TIPS in the post-9/11 resolution 1373, where they stated that "this attack, like *all acts* of international terrorism, constitutes a threat to international peace and security". A few years later, the Council expanded its view to include all acts of "terrorism", not limited to "international" terrorism, as a threat to international peace and security, in its resolution 1566 of 2004.

In the aftermath of the 9/11 attacks, the Council even expressed its readiness to take *'all necessary steps'* to combat all forms of terrorism, but it has so far stopped short of actually authorizing a collective *military* action in that respect. However, these recent steps at least indicate the Council's growing belief that collective military action might be necessary when dealing with this global security threat.

Unilateral Use of Force in Response to Terrorism

Without a Security Council authorization, States may only use force in individual or collective self-defence to repel an armed attack as articulated in Article 51 of the Charter[1] and further refined in customary international law. When applying this right in the context of terrorism, at least three questions must be considered: (a) Can a terrorist attack constitute an 'armed attack' within the meaning of Article 51?, (b) If so, does

---

[1] Article 51 reads in part: "Nothing in the present Charter shall impair the inherent right of individual or collective self-defence if an armed attack occurs against a Member of the United Nations, until the Security Council has taken measures necessary to maintain international peace and security."

such an attack give rise to a right of self-defence as understood in international law?, and (c) If so, what are the conditions of a legitimate response in self-defence?

Terrorist Attacks as Armed Attacks

The language of Article 51 clearly states that self-defence is lawful only where there is an armed attack. The phrase 'armed attack' was *traditionally* understood as referring to the attacks by States, but in fact nothing in Article 51 or elsewhere in the Charter indicates that an armed attack can emanate *only* from States. In fact, a prevailing view in contemporary state practice, jurisprudence and legal scholarship is that the concept is broad enough to include armed acts by private actors such as terrorists, whether they are acting as a tool of another State or on their own, under condition that such acts are sufficiently grave, or, in other words, where such acts are equivalent, by their 'scale and effects', to an armed attack by a State. This standard was first developed by the International Court of Justice (ICJ) in the *Nicaragua* case in 1986, where the majority of judges agreed that the concept of armed attacks covers the non-state acts of armed force 'of such gravity' that they would be considered as actual armed attacks if they were conducted by regular armed forces.

At least since the 9/11 attacks, most States also seem to support this view. Many States have explicitly expressed their understanding that the incident of 9/11 amounted to an 'armed attack' against the United States, most notably the NATO Member States, and the members of the Security Council that carefully worded resolutions 1368 and 1373 so as to support the existence of the right of self-defence within a context of a broader response to terrorism. At the same time, most other States have not objected to the US-claimed right of self-defence in response to this particular attack. Something similar can be said about the Israeli military intervention in southern Lebanon in July 2006, where most States have criticized Israel's military action as being '*disproportionate*', but did not deny or oppose its right to military self-defence in response to acts by Hezbollah, in principle.

Selecting the Target: The Attributability Requirement

Although terrorist armed activities may amount to an 'armed attack', the right of the victim State to respond with military force does not follow automatically. As a fundamental rule, measures of self-defence can only be directed against the attacker. Yet most defensive military measures in response to a terrorist armed attack will, as a matter of fact, involve incursions into another sovereign State (the rare exceptions would be military actions on the high seas or in the international air space). If this latter State did not previously consent to the military incursion by the State that claims to be the victim of terrorist attack, the main question in legal terms remains *whether and under what conditions* could the victim state justify its military incursion as an exercise of its right to self-defence against a terrorist attack. The prevailing view in international law is that the victim State would have to prove that the initial terrorist armed attack can be somehow attributed to another State, before it could lawfully launch a defensive military action on its territory. General international law does offer some guidance on when private acts may be attributed to a State.

The only clear-cut scenario involves an attack committed by private actors acting in the capacity of *de jure* or *de facto* organs of another State, which would be actually regarded as an attack committed by that State, thus rendering it a potentially legitimate target of defensive strikes. However, when no such 'organic' connection between the attackers and the target State can be established, the situation becomes far more murky. Yet the *prevailing* view in contemporary international law is that a specific terrorist attack can be attributed to another State only if that State a) had exercised 'effective' control over *that* particular attack, or b) if it had subsequently acknowledged the operation in question as its own. This rather restrictive test of 'effective control' has been developed by the ICJ in its 1986 *Nicaragua* decision, and despite some critiques it remains the most widely accepted standard in jurisprudence, scholarship and State practice. The International Criminal Court for Former Yugoslavia (ICTY) applied a much looser standard in its 1999 decision in the *Tadić* case, and concluded that the acts of the Bosnian Serb Army could be attributed to Serbia because the latter exercised *'overall control'* over them, which did not necessarily require that each illegal operation had to be controlled by the particular State (ICTY, 1999: paras. 116-145). But this alternative approach had little impact on the stringent 'effective control' test: the ICJ explicitly dismissed the *Tadić* standard as too broad in its most recent decision in the *Bosnia Genocide* case (ICJ, 2007) and again applied its *Nicaragua* standard, which has also been accepted as valid by the International Law Commission in its Draft Articles on State Responsibility of 2001 (Art 8). Accordingly, it would not be enough to prove that the State had exercised 'overall' control over the activities of the terrorist group, but not over the specific attack.

Moreover, state assistance to terrorists in the form of arms supplies, financial or other support, does not by itself make their specific attacks attributable to the supporting State and it does not render that State a legitimate target of a defensive strike. *A fortiori*, mere harbouring of terrorists, while a violation of international law, does not justify a military invasion of the host State's territory, when that State was otherwise not substantially involved in the attack. Similarly, a State that fails to control or prevent illegal terrorist activities on its territory might be in violation of its international obligations regarding international terrorism, but such a violation is not by itself tantamount to an armed attack attributable to that State; thus the victim State has no right to direct its defensive military actions *against* that State.

The US military response to the 9/11 terrorist attacks was regarded by some authors as extending the right of self-defence so as to justify actions against States which have been actively supporting or willingly harbouring terrorists. Although it might seem that by securing the advance support of a large number of other States for its military action in Afghanistan the US has effectively lowered the traditionally required high threshold of involvement, it is difficult to determine the exact impact of this one-off support for the US legal position on the emergence of a new international norm. A number of international legal scholars have rightly noted that, while the international reaction to the 9/11 events might be indicating an emerging *trend* towards such an expansion of the concept of self-defence, it could hardly be interpreted as an 'instant custom', changing the standard of attributability overnight. Apparently, the ICJ shares this view: in two of its post-9/11 decisions, the *Legal Consequences of the Wall* and *DRC v. Uganda*, the Court essentially reconfirmed the *Nicaragua* standard and considered the current state of international law to permit self-defence in the case of an armed attack by a non-state actor only if the attack is attributable to another State.

One must admit that this traditional approach fails to answer one very important question, namely, what kind of action a victim State *is* entitled to take in response to a large-scale terrorist attack that cannot be attributed to any foreign State. This question is of utmost relevance in the context of contemporary terrorist threats that are emanating from largely independent armed groups, often operating in a territory with no effective governmental presence or authority. A minority of authors and States (primarily Israel, Turkey, and the US) have suggested that the victim State might be justified in carrying out defensive military strikes directed only against terrorist targets from such territory within a State which had failed to take adequate measures to prevent terrorists from carrying out the specific attack. Although there are signs that States might be increasingly supporting this position (e.g. in the context of the Israeli strikes in Lebanon in 2006), this view is far from being widely accepted.

Conditions of Lawful Self-defence

Even if the victim State is in principle entitled to a military action in self-defence, its action will be legally acceptable only if all other classic conventional and customary legal requirements of self-defence are satisfied. Thus, Article 51 of the Charter requires that the measures planned or taken in alleged self-defence be immediately reported to the Security Council; once the Council has taken over, any defensive measures must cease. Customary international law further requires that defensive military measures must be taken only when absolutely necessary. That means they can only be taken as a last resort, after all non-military means of redress have been exhausted or have proven futile. The action taken in self-defence must also be an *immediate* reaction to aggression; any unreasonably delayed response might be viewed as dangerously close to armed reprisals, unlawful in contemporary international law. However, it seems to be widely accepted today that a *reasonably delayed* response might be seen as legally acceptable, for instance, where there is a need to gather evidence of the attacker's identity and/or collect the intelligence and [organize the] military force in order to strike back in a targeted manner.

In addition, any armed response against terrorist attacks must be proportionate to its sole legitimate objective: to repel an armed attack and its consequences. Accordingly, only such force may be used as is absolutely necessary to repel the attack. In the context of terrorism, the legitimate purpose of self-defence might extend to the detention of persons allegedly responsible for the attacks, and the destruction of the legitimate military objectives, such as infrastructures, training bases and similar facilities used by the terrorists. What is crucial, though, is to keep in mind that the purpose of self-defence cannot be retribution, general deterrence, punishment or any other non-defensive motive.

Pre-empting an Anticipated Terrorist Attack

Another complex question in relation to the right of self-defence in the context of terrorism is whether unilateral military action against a *threat* of a (terrorist) armed attack may ever be justified. Before the Second World War, international customary law endorsed the idea that a State can respond to an impending attack leaving no sufficient alternative choice of means. But the applicability of this customary law doctrine after the entry into force of the Charter and its general ban on unilateral force is arguable. The language of Article 51 makes it clear that self-defence is lawful only when an armed attack *occurs* and not as a first strike option. However, the Charter does not define at which point in time an 'armed attack' begins and nothing in this provision itself implies the legality or illegality of the use of force in cases when an armed attack is *about to occur*.

In practice, States have mostly refrained from invoking the doctrine of anticipatory self-defence to justify their military actions after 1945 and in those rare cases when the argument was actually used to justify recourse to force,[2] very few other States have explicitly endorsed it. The views in scholarship are likewise split with some progressive writers (primarily UK, US and Israeli) supporting the validity of the doctrine in the case of an *imminent* threat of an attack.[3] Although in the aftermath of 9/11 some of the key actors (such as the US, the UK, France, and Russia) have also supported this view, the doctrine of anticipatory self-defence remains largely unsupported in both state practice and scholarship. However, as I said, views are heavily split on this issue and from my own point of view there seems to be some room for the argument that a unilateral military response to an *imminent* threat of a terrorist attack might be acceptable even in post-Charter international law.

In the light of the rising threat of terrorism coupled especially with a potential use of non-conventional methods and weapons for attack, States might increasingly feel compelled to use force without having previously dialed-up the 911 at the Security Council, even when a terrorist armed attack is not near, but the threat of it is very serious, credible, and could materialize in an attack without a reasonable degree of warning and time for defence. It might be prudent to discuss seriously the options and conditions for such action in order to reduce the danger of abuse of the right of self-defence. But it must be clear that this argument is a matter of legal policy, an argument about the law as, perhaps, it should be, and not the law as it *is*.

In practice, some States have developed an argument that, in assessing the right of self-defence, terrorist armed attacks should be reviewed, especially with regard to attacks originating from private actors. In particular, the existence of past attacks has been relied on to affirm the credibility of future attacks, thus building up the image of a continuing attack. This view seems to make sense especially in the context of terrorist campaigns, which generally consist of a series of actions that occur periodically over extended periods of time. Mainly Israel and the United States have asserted that the right to self-defence includes the right to disrupt ongoing terrorist attacks in some circumstances, where it appears to be necessary to prevent further attacks that are anticipated on the basis of previous experience. Some leading scholars have also suggested that self-defence against future terrorist attacks may be justified where *prior* attacks have occurred and there is *clear and convincing evidence* that more attacks are planned. On the other side, while the UK and France have also consistently supported that view, most other members of the Security Council seem to reject the 'accumulation of events' theory in the context of counter-terrorist military actions.

Preventive Strikes as a Counter-terrorist Measure?

In the aftermath of the 9/11 attacks, the most radical challenge to the existing international law on the use of force has been posed by the Bush administration's doctrine of unilateral preventive war as a means of reduction or prevention of terrorist threats, which has been formally articulated in the 2002 US NSS (reconfirmed in 2006). Denying terrorists the sanctuary they seek in failed States is becoming a central feature of the US counter-terrorist strategies and the administration had already declared its

[2] For instance the 1981 Israel raid on Osirak nuclear reactor under construction in Iraq.

[3] While the concept of *imminence* has no precise definition in international law, most writers define it in a narrow temporal sense.

willingness to use preventive force, against suspected terrorists inside a State that is incapable of policing itself or even to overturn 'hostile regimes' that willingly harbour and support terrorist activities within their borders.

Unlike the previously mentioned anticipatory action, the so-called preventive strikes are not about pre-empting an imminent and credible security threat, but about foiling some unspecified threats that might have occurred at some uncertain time in the future. The Bush administration made its case for military strikes against the non-conventional threats even where 'uncertainty remains as to the time and place of the enemy's attack'. It is virtually undisputed that this proposal radically departs from the existing legal regime on the use of force. States themselves are reluctant to endorse it; apart from the US, Russia and Israel, most other key actors have expressed both political and normative resentment of the idea of preventive strikes. And if I may make another policy statement, I believe that the logic of unilateral preventive strikes against hypothetic, unspecific future threats, should also in the future remain unacceptable: in my view, this doctrine is completely incompatible with the fundamental logic of the contemporary regulation of military violence in international affairs, since its implicit aim is a complete deregulation of the unilateral use of force, at least for one or a few of the most powerful States.

Obviously, power politics will always play an important role in the international system and the legal constraints on that power will probably never be completely free from uncertainties. But opening the way to military actions subject only to more or less reliable threat assessments by single States and incapable of formal legal scrutiny, could lead to an unrestricted exercise of power against some perceived threats. I simply believe that there must remain certain minimum non-political standards by which the military actions of States can be evaluated and either supported or condemned as illegitimate.

Conclusion

The current international legal framework of collective security, combined with the contemporary regime of self-defence, allows States to respond to terrorism fully, reactively or preventively, even with military force in the last resort. As a rule, military counter-terrorist operations should be taken on a multilateral basis; especially any eventual *preventive* military action should be taken *exclusively* on the basis of a multilateral decision via the Security Council. In the case of a large-scale terrorist attack, the victim State may lawfully react on its own, so long it respects the fundamental legal requirements of self-defence.

In conclusion, let me point out that the fight against terrorism should primarily be understood in a long-term perspective, which requires a careful reconsideration of the relationship between the rise of terrorism and deep social inequalities such as poverty, economic, social and cultural underdevelopment, lack of political pluralism and democracy, and so on. Looking at it through a military lens can thus be merely a short-term approach and perhaps not the most effective in strategic terms, or politically wise. That is why it is especially important for military force to be used only in the last resort and strictly within the limits of international law, so as not to collide with the generally accepted principles of the international system. After all, international law on the use of force has been one of the greatest achievements of the international community in the

20th century and States must strive to respect it to prevent the anarchy so eagerly pursued by terrorists themselves.

Legal Aspects of Combating Terrorism
Centre of Excellence Defence Against Terrorism, Ankara, Turkey (Ed.)
IOS Press, 2008

doi:10.3233/978-1-58603-930-1-141

The Future of Legal Aspects of Combating Terrorism

Prof. Robert CRYER
Professor of International and Criminal Law, University of Birmingham, UK

Abstract. This paper will not speculate directly about exactly what will happen to the law in the future. There are far too many variables at issue for any such prediction. The discussion will limit itself to identifying trends that are likely to have an impact on the law in this area. The first part of this paper will argue that the rhetoric adopted by many after the 11 September attacks was of a "war on terrorism" as a legal paradigm. However, the concept of a separate, non-territorial armed conflict on terrorism has begun to fall from favour. Rather, there is a move towards improving the existing law on the basis that the relevant law is criminal law. This is the approach that has been taken by various organs of the United Nations. This second part of this paper outlines the development of the law on terrorism: the UN Global Counter-Terrorism Strategy, and developments on the issue of human rights and terrorism. While not compromising with the terrorists, there is an increased recognition of the social conditions which have facilitated the spread of terrorism.

Keywords. Legal aspects of terrorism, future trends in legal aspects of terrorism, war on terror, International Humanitarian Law, criminal law, UN Global Counter-Terrorism Strategy.

Introduction

We have, in this decade, lived through a time of much uncertainty, in which the legal regime relating to terrorism has been put under considerable pressure. However the purpose of this discussion is to look a little at the future of the law relating to terrorism. It is not the time to engage in clear, direct speculation about exactly what will happen to the law in the future. There are far too many variables at issue for any such prediction to be anything more than a hostage to fortune. Therefore this discussion will limit itself to identifying trends in international society that are likely to have an impact on the law in the area. Even to fulfil this modest aim, however, it is necessary to look to the (recent) past.

War and Crime

In the immediate aftermath of the September the 11th terrorist attacks on the US, the rhetoric adopted by many was of a "war on terrorism" as a legal paradigm implying that there is an armed conflict against (the abstract noun) terrorism, and a conflict which is global, in the sense in which it is not territorially bounded. Perhaps the most vocal of the non-governmental voices supporting such a view was Professor Ruth Wedgwood of John Hopkins University. Soon after the attacks she averred that:

> The great debate at the moment poses a paradigm choice—under what regime of law should we think about and act against al-Qaeda? Should we think of the network in criminal justice terms, as we have throughout the 90s, or in war and armed conflict terms? Lawyers have a vested interest, some might suppose, in choosing criminal justice. But the law speaks as loudly in armed conflict as it does in criminal justice. The scope of the damage caused on September 11th makes the language of war seem apropos.[1]

This paradigm of a global war against terror was taken up, particularly in the United States, with the acronym GWAT (Global War Against Terror) being a staple of debate. One of its first outings was in George Bush's speech to a Joint Session of Congress on 20 September 2001:

> The enemy of America is not our many Muslim friends; it is not our many Arab friends. Our enemy is a radical network of terrorists, and every government that supports them … Our war on terror begins with al-Qaeda, but it does not end there. It will not end until every terrorist group of global reach has been found, stopped and defeated … How will we fight and win this war? We will direct every resource at our command—every means of diplomacy, every tool of intelligence, every instrument of law enforcement, every financial influence, and every necessary weapon of war—to the disruption and to the defeat of the global terror network. This war will not be like the war against Iraq a decade ago, with a decisive liberation of territory and a swift conclusion. It will not look like the air war above Kosovo two years ago, where no ground troops were used and not a single American was lost in combat.[2]

Perhaps the most notable place it can be found as a proposition of law is its acceptance in the US Supreme Court in the well-known *Hamdan* v *Rumsfeld* case, where the Court determined that Common Article 3 applied to the conflict between the United States and al-Qaeda, in distinction to the conflict with the Taleban in Afghanistan.[3]

The terminology of war has been adopted elsewhere, most particularly by Tony Blair, whose speech in Sedgefield in 2004 made the point clearly and forcefully:

> September 11th was for me a revelation. What had seemed inchoate came together. The point about September 11th was not its detailed planning; not its devilish execution; not even, simply, that it happened in America, on the streets of New York. All of this made it an astonishing, terrible and wicked tragedy, a barbaric murder of innocent people. But what galvanised me was that it was a declaration of war by religious fanatics who were prepared to wage that war without limit … It means getting the UN to understand that faced with the threats we have, we should do all we can to spread the values of freedom, democracy, the rule of law, religious tolerance and justice for the oppressed, however painful for some nations that may be; but that at the same time, we wage war relentlessly on those who would exploit racial and religious division to bring catastrophe to the world

---

[1] Ruth Wedgwood, 'After September 11th' (2001-2002) 36 *New England Law Review* 725, p. 727.
[2] Available at http://www.whitehouse.gov/news/releases/2001/09/20010920-8.html.
[3] 548 US __ (2006) pp. 67-9.

> … But in the meantime, the threat is there and demands our attention. That is the struggle which engages us. It is a new type of war.[4]

However, for most the phrase was considered to contain a more metaphorical use of the term war than a literal one,[5] rather like that in the term "war on drugs" or "war on want". There was less support for the specific legal argument that there is a non-territorially-based armed conflict in the legal sense between the United States (and its allies) and al-Qaeda, separate from the specific conflicts, e.g. in Afghanistan.

The new British Prime Minister, Gordon Brown, for example, has been careful to avoid the terminology of war, speaking, for example after the failed attacks on London and Glasgow in 2006, pointedly of the 'struggle' against terrorism. During his visit to the United States in 2007 he was careful to avoid the terminology of war.[6] The reasons for this appear to be a concern that the language of war was considered to have too many costs. It is also the case that the British courts have been unsympathetic to ideas of a global war/armed conflict—in the legal sense—against terrorism.[7] The concept of a separate, non-territorial armed conflict on terrorism has thus begun to fall from favour as a matter of legal argumentation. As such, claims that the law of armed conflict is insufficiently equipped to deal with this asserted new type of war have become less urgent, and strident.

This is not to say that there is not terrorism within armed conflicts. Far from it. However, the law of armed conflict (or, in the terminology preferred by the ICRC, international humanitarian law) already has structured into itself mechanisms for dealing with terrorism in armed conflicts. It has express prohibitions on such conduct, and has provisions relating to terrorism, security and the rights of civilians.[8] With the current move away from the terminology of armed conflict as being the relevant paradigm, the general approach to the suppression of terrorism is not one of war, and of changing humanitarian law, but of improving the law on the basis that the relevant law is criminal law.

In many ways this reflects the understanding that terrorism is multifaceted. Where it occurs as part of an armed conflict (as more traditionally understood), then humanitarian law provides the legal tools for dealing with it. Where it does not, however, it is better to look into methods that adopt a different starting point from humanitarian law. This is the approach that has been taken by various organs of the United Nations, and, as the suppression of global terrorism requires global solutions, it is the approach of this universal international organisation that it is appropriate to concentrate on when we seek to speculate about the future development on the law against terrorism.

---

[4] Speech, Sedgfield, available at http://politics.guardian.co.uk/iraq/story/0,12956,1162991,00.html

[5] Although at least one American Presidential hopeful has also taken that view, see 'A Strong Military for a New Country' speech at the Council of Foreign Relations, 27 May 2007, available at: http://www.johnedwards.com/news/speeches/20070523-cfr/. Others, however, have not, Rudolph Guliani, 'Towards a Realistic Peace' (2007) 86 (September/October) *Foreign Affairs* 2.

[6] 'Sending the Right Signal', *The Guardian* 31 July 2007.

[7] *A* v *Secretary of State for the Home Department* [2004] UKHL 69 Para 69.

[8] See, e.g. Hans-Peter Gasser, 'Acts of Terror, 'Terrorism' and International Humanitarian Law' (2004) 847 *International Review of the Red Cross* 547.

The Development of the Law on Terrorism

As we have seen, a large number of the acts that can be considered to be terrorism have already been the subject of multilateral treaties requiring States to prosecute, or co-operate in the prosecution of, those acts. Indeed regulation now extends (rightly) to provisions that require States to prevent and punish financing of terrorism.[9] Still, since 2001, it has been increasingly realised that the counter-terrorism effort requires a holistic, integrated and co-ordinated approach at the international level. This is evidenced by the UN Global Counter-Terrorism Strategy.

1. The United Nations Global Counter-Terrorism Strategy

One of the largest developments in the area, with considerable implications for the future, is the United Nations Global Counter-Terrorism Strategy. This was adopted by consensus by the General Assembly on 8 September 2006. Of course, as a General Assembly Resolution it is not in and of itself legally binding.[10] However, it has considerable moral authority, and is clear evidence of various trends in the international fight against terrorism. The strategy begins as follows:

> We, the States Members of the United Nations, resolve:
> 1. To consistently, unequivocally and strongly condemn terrorism in all its forms and manifestations, committed by whomever, wherever and for whatever purposes, as it constitutes one of the most serious threats to international peace and security;
> 2. To take urgent action to prevent and combat terrorism in all its forms and manifestations and, in particular:
> (a) To consider becoming parties without delay to the existing international conventions and protocols against terrorism, and implementing them, and to make every effort to reach an agreement on and conclude a comprehensive convention on international terrorism;
> (b) To implement all General Assembly resolutions on measures to eliminate international terrorism and relevant General Assembly resolutions on the protection of human rights and fundamental freedoms while countering terrorism;
> (c) To implement all Security Council resolutions related to international terrorism and to cooperate fully with the counter-terrorism subsidiary bodies of the Security Council in the fulfilment of their tasks, recognizing that many States continue to require assistance in implementing these resolutions;
> 3. To recognize that international cooperation and any measures that we undertake to prevent and combat terrorism must comply with our obligations under international law, including the Charter of the United Nations and relevant international conventions and protocols, in particular human rights law, refugee law and international humanitarian law.

As might be expected on a matter of such importance and controversy, as the President of the General Assembly noted "the text is carefully crafted, and every word has been scrutinized. There is no delegation in this Hall which got all it wanted."[11] Each of the paragraphs has something that assists understanding the trends that are likely to be influential in the future of the law on terrorism.

---

[9] See my lecture earlier in this book, fn. 24f.

[10] *Advisory Opinion on the Legality of the Threat or Use of Nuclear Weapons* [1996] ICJ Rep. 4, pp. 254-5, para 70.

[11] A/60/PV.99. p. 4.

To take the first paragraph, there is an purportedly unequivocal condemnation of terrorism "in all its forms and manifestations, committed by whomever". This seems clear, and it might be thought that this, alongside the frequent use of the phrase in other General Assembly and Security Council Resolutions meant that the old debate on whether State terrorism comes under the definition and the question of whether actions by self-determination units fell under the definition had finally been transcended. Unfortunately, however, the statements made by a number of States at the adoption of the Resolution make clear that underneath the consensus on the text, there remain divisions about both issues. For example Syria stated that:

> It is our understanding that the implementation of the Global Strategy laid out in the draft resolution will not prejudice the right of peoples to self-determination and to fight for their own independence ... We continue to believe that the proposal that Syria has advocated since the 1980s to convene an international conference to define terrorism and to distinguish between it and the right of peoples to self-determination should be given due attention as soon as possible ...[12]

A number of delegations also criticised the fact that there was no definition of terrorism in the strategy,[13] or that it did not deal sufficiently with State terrorism.[14] It is true that not all of the States expressing their concerns are considered good international citizens, but the concerns do reflect the still considerable divisions that exist in the area.

These divisions, which are usually metonyms for disagreements about the Middle East, are also the fundamental stumbling block that is still preventing the creation of a generalised treaty on terrorism. The proposed treaty is that which is mentioned in paragraph 2 of the Strategy, however, for some considerable time the negotiations on a comprehensive treaty have been hampered by the self-determination issue, and although it is dangerous to make confident predictions about the future, unless and until there is a settlement of the Middle East crisis, the comprehensive definition of terrorism, and thus the comprehensive treaty, will remain some way off.[15] It thus seems likely that the call for increased ratification of the sectoral treaties by the General Assembly will have more of a practical outcome than the call for the comprehensive treaty. Indeed, it may be that more sectoral treaties are the best way forward, although it must be said that most forms of international terrorism are covered by the various treaties already. There are, nonetheless, some areas, such as inciting terrorism, that are not completely covered.

Which leads us to the Security Council's role, which the Strategy makes clear is supported by the General Assembly. The Council, beginning in 2001, moved from dealing with specific acts of terrorism to dealing with terrorism more in the abstract, and in a pro-active, rather than reactive manner. This was first seen in Resolution 1373, which set up a comprehensive anti terrorist financing regime, a precedent that was built on in Resolution 1540, which imposed non-proliferation obligations on States. However, later resolutions, responding to fears that the Security Council was imposing long lasting obligations on all States that would better be dealt with through treaty negotiations, have been a little more circumspect. So Resolution 1624, which deals with the exceptionally important issue of incitement of terrorism, which is a pressing

---

[12] A/60/PV/ 99, p. 5, see also p. 7 (Cuba), p. 7 (South Africa), 13 (Libya)
[13] *Ibid.*, pp. 6 (Cuba), 11 (Sudan).
[14] *Ibid.*, pp. 5 (Syria), 10 (Iran), 11 (Sudan), 13 (Libya), although see p. 9 (Pakistan).
[15] For the disagreements see UN Doc A/C.6/62/SR4 and A/C.6/62/SR5.

matter in the internet age, when terrorists use the internet to promote their activities and seek to gain new recruits, calls upon States to criminalise incitement of terrorism, but does not do so under Chapter VII of the Charter, hence is hortatory, rather than mandatory. The issue is one, however, which could usefully be the subject of a treaty regime.

2. Human Rights and Terrorism

Resolution 1624 also raises another issue that is likely to have an impact on the future law in the area, the importance of ensuring that the fight against terrorism pays due regard to human rights law. Resolution 1624 expressly recalls the provisions of the Universal Declaration of Human Rights and the International Covenant on Civil and Political Rights that protect freedom of expression, and, like the Global Counter-Terrorism strategy, stressed that:

> States must ensure that any measures taken to combat terrorism comply with all their obligations under international law, and should adopt measures in accordance with international law, in particular international human rights law, refugee law and humanitarian law.

This is becoming a standard paragraph in Security Council Resolutions, and other documents emanating from the United Nations dealing with terrorism. This comes from fears that early aspects of the post-September 11 response to terrorism paid insufficient regard to human rights law, and that, in addition to that being a problem in itself, they created pretexts for terrorists, and in some cases led to sympathy for terrorist groups who used human rights concerns propagandistically. This returning focus on human rights is particularly important, and is likely to maintain an influence on the developing law in the area.

Conclusion: Tough on Terrorism, Tough on the Causes of Terrorism

So, it is necessary to conclude this short run through of the developing trends in the law relating to terrorism. The law has developed hugely in the last near-decade, but the one major document that has been sought, the comprehensive treaty, has remained out of reach. At one level though, we must remember that the law alone cannot bring terrorism to an end, any more than the law of murder can bring a complete end to terrorism. A more holistic approach to the question needs to be taken. To paraphrase the British government of a few years ago, the necessity is to be tough on terrorism and tough on the causes of terrorism.[16] This is something that lies close to the heart of the Global Counter Terrorism Strategy, whose first substantive section deals with issues arising from "conditions conducive to the spread of terrorism". In a startling example of the developing holistic approach to ensuring the suppression of terrorism the Strategy states that:

> We resolve to undertake the following measures aimed at addressing the conditions conducive to the spread of terrorism, including but not limited to prolonged unresolved conflicts, dehumanization of victims of terrorism in all its forms and manifestations, lack

[16] E.g. Speech by Tony Blair, 18 September 2002, available at: http://www.pm.gov.uk/output/Page1726.asp

> of the rule of law and violations of human rights, ethnic, national and religious discrimination, political exclusion, socio-economic marginalization and lack of good governance, while recognizing that none of these conditions can excuse or justify acts of terrorism.

To recognise this is not to compromise with terrorists, but rather to accept that where there are injustices in the world they may lead to continued problems from terrorism, and to prevent terrorism the conditions that cause it must be engaged with. We could do worse than adopt international law as the framework for resolving such injustices.

Author Index